T0335117

The Eighth Wonder of the World

The Eighth Wonder of the World

THE LIFE OF HOUSTON'S ICONIC ASTRODOME

Robert C. Trumpbour and Kenneth Womack
Foreword by Mickey Herskowitz

UNIVERSITY OF NEBRASKA PRESS
LINCOLN AND LONDON

Library of Congress Cataloging-in-Publication Data
Names: Trumpbour, Robert C., author. |
Womack, Kenneth, author.
Title: The eighth wonder of the world: the life of
Houston's iconic Astrodome / Robert C. Trumpbour and
Kenneth Womack; foreword by Mickey Herskowitz.
Description: Lincoln: University of Nebraska Press, [2016]
| Includes bibliographical references and index.
Identifiers: LCCN 2015043763
ISBN 9780803255456 (cloth: alk. paper)
ISBN 9780803295704 (epub)
ISBN 9780803295711 (mobi)
ISBN 9780803295728 (pdf)
Subjects: LCSH: Astrodome (Houston, Tex.)—History.
Classification: LCC GV417.A77 T78 2016 | DDC
725/.82709764141—dc23 LC record available at
https://lccn.loc.gov/2015043763

Set in Scala OT by M. Scheer.

For Kenneth E. Zimmerman and Narendra K. Gosain,
Keepers of the Dome

Contents

Foreword

The Dome Was So Nice They Opened It Twice

MICKEY HERSKOWITZ

This is what God would do if he had the money.
—One writer's reaction after his first view of
the Harris County Domed Stadium

The fans dressed as if they were attending an opera. The president of the United States, Lyndon Johnson, was there, a guest in the private box and lavish apartment of Judge Roy Hofheinz, hidden behind the fence high above right field. The Reverend Billy Graham and the original seven Mercury astronauts were there, along with every local politician and personality physically able to appear in public.

The governor of Texas, John Connally, threw out the first pitch. This was April 9, 1965, the first of two opening nights for the Astrodome, the world's first indoor, air-conditioned, all-weather sports stadium. Yes, the Dome was so nice they opened it twice.

The official league unveiling would come three days later, with the Phillies winning, 2–0. But the opponents that night were the New York Yankees, whose immortal Mickey Mantle struck the first indoor home run. Still, the Astros won in twelve innings on a pinch single by Nellie Fox, a player-coach and future Hall of Famer. His primary job at the time was to groom a young second baseman named Joe Morgan, another future Hall of Famer.

All of the exploits and all of the famous faces were overshadowed, of course, by the object of everyone's curiosity: the big bubble that loomed eighteen stories above the playing field.

As the debate continued in 2015 over the fate of what became known as the "Eighth Wonder of the World," it seems only fitting to revisit that starry, starry night. We tend to forget that even as the fans streamed through the turnstiles, many skeptics doubted that baseball could be played under a roof. At least one Houston pitcher, Hal Woodeshick, had his wife and kids stay home, just in case the ceiling collapsed.

The closest disaster that came was in the problem outfielders had catching fly balls. In the daytime, the glare would be blinding when the sun shone through the web of spidery Lucite panels. Eventually they painted the roof and the grass died, leading to an invention called AstroTurf.

What greeted the fans on opening night was an explosion of color. For the first time, baseball fans were able to enjoy the comforts of a fine theater, sitting in cushioned seats with armrests, with each level painted a different color—royal blue, gold, purple, black, tangerine, and crimson. All the tickets were color coded to match your seat location. And none of the tickets provided a stub for rainouts.

The ground crew wore flight suits, and flashbulbs went off like so many strings of Chinese firecrackers. Yet one of my favorite personal memories is spotting Jim Owens, a relief pitcher, sleeping off a hangover on a bench in the bullpen area down the right-field line. Turk Farrell, his closest friend and one of the team's early stars, gave him a shove and yelled, "Wake up! Where the hell do you think you are, in a canoe?"

No one had seen the likes of the luxury boxes or the Skydome Club or the exploding scoreboard that celebrated those rare Houston home runs. On the huge video screen, bulls snorted, six-guns exploded, a cowboy whirled a lariat, stars danced across the cosmos, and the Texas flag unfurled in tribute. Pitchers who had just been abused invariably turned and soaked in the show.

The Astrodome was the last great bargain of the age of reconstruction. The price tag for the building, including the innovations, came in at $31.5 million, not much more than what a family of four would pay today for season tickets to NFL games. With all the amenities, Judge Hofheinz enjoyed boasting that women could finally attend a baseball or football game and not worry about having their hairdos mussed.

If you craned your neck to see the very top of the roof, you realized that the space was so enormous it didn't give the impression of what it was actually offering—sports in a gigantic climate-controlled room. You could forget the statistics that had been fed to an awed world: the eight trillion tons of air conditioning, the scoreboard longer than a football field, the center-field door big enough to admit an aircraft carrier, and so forth. The great thing about the Astrodome was simply that it was a unique place just to be inside, just to watch whatever was going on. "If they had a maternity ward and a cemetery," marveled Bob Hope, "you'd never have to leave."

Today, with stadium cities springing up here and there, and more to come, bigger and fancier and boasting of their billion-dollar price tags, some may tend to slight the excitement and grandeur of the Astrodome.

When you recall a few of the acts that played on that stage—Muhammad Ali, Earl Campbell, Nolan Ryan, Bum Phillips, Judy Garland, Evel Knievel, Billie Jean King and Bobby Riggs, Elvin Hayes and Lew Alcindor—you know it really was a magical carpet ride.

And always there was the joy of discovery and controversy. Baseball faced the most serious threat in its history, the possibility that a game might have to be called on account of sunshine. The problems caused by daylight and high flies seemed funny for a time, and even the home team enjoyed the jokes. Then in July, Jimmy Wynn moved under a high fly to center, pounded his glove, and then froze in horror as the ball disappeared in a cloud of skylights. Jim Ray Hart circled the bases for a three-run, inside-the-park homer and a 5–2 San Francisco victory. The next day, squads of workers with paint guns scrambled across the roof, eliminating the glare and the need for players to wear helmets in the outfield.

But plastic, mortar, steel, concrete, and gold-plated toilet fixtures never really defined the Big Blister. People and events did. Memories of the Dome bounce through our minds like the little ball over the musical notes in movie sing-alongs of yesteryear.

Randomly, we recall the high- and lowlights, the art and spectacles that are embedded in those walls:

The first time he led his amazing New York Mets against the

Astros in their new playpen, Casey Stengel created a stir at home plate during the pregame huddle with the umpires over ground rules. Casey wanted to know about the "air" rules. Lindsey Nelson, the Mets' broadcaster, planned to describe that night's game from inside the gondola suspended from the roof.

The gondola, which resembled the basket of a hot air balloon, would be used as a photo deck for overhead shots of certain events. It had to be lowered during a pause in the infield drills and Lindsey, with an engineer, clambered aboard. Then the cables hoisted them back toward the ceiling, high above second base, as the early arriving crowd cheered their ascent. It was like a scene from *Around the World in 80 Days.*

Stengel turned to the umpiring crew and the Houston manager and said, "All right, what about my man up there?"

"What man?" asked Tom Gorman, the chief umpire.

"My man Lindsey, up there," he said, pointing, "in that cage under the roof."

All eyes were raised, as if expecting rain. Tom Gorman scratched his head and decided that, since any ball hitting the top of the dome was in play, any ball hitting Lindsey Nelson should also be in play.

Casey was pleased. "Well," he said, beaming, "my man is a ground rule. That's the first time my man was ever a ground rule."

In January 1968 the largest crowd ever to watch a college basketball game—52,693 fans—witnessed the game that changed the sport forever: Houston versus UCLA, Elvin Hayes versus Lew Alcindor (later Kareem Abdul-Jabbar.) It was the night basketball came of age in the oil and cactus belt.

That same night, the annual boat show was being held in Exposition Hall across the street. One customer wandered into the Astrodome, noticed very tall people in short pants warming up on a hardwood floor, and demanded of an usher, "Where are the boats?"

"You're in the wrong place," he was informed. "This is the Houston-UCLA basketball game."

He turned on his heel and stalked out. "I didn't come here to see some stupid basketball game."

Too bad about him. Two years earlier, the Cougars had played in a high school gymnasium that seated twenty-five hundred fans. The irony was clear: the Cougars would be drawing in one night what they recently had drawn in a year. Now the record for basketball attendance, pro or amateur, would be broken in the first match of national importance in a state where football was king.

Every seat in the building had been sold out ten days before the game. What drew them was a matchup between the first- and second-ranked teams in the land. In Houston, the buildup to the game had begun six months earlier. Students and fans could talk of little else. Some confessed that the game was too big for them, but they hoped to grow into it.

The challenge for the number-two Cougars was as clear as lacquer. The question was not whether UCLA had the best basketball team in the country but whether UCLA had the best basketball team of all time. The Bruins had not lost in two seasons, not in forty-seven games, a streak that included a victory over Houston in the NCAA semifinals the previous spring. If the Bruins of Coach John Wooden were not invincible, they were doing a dandy imitation of a team that was.

The Cougars had not lost since the teams had last met, winning their first sixteen games in 1968. To add an odd twist to the story, UCLA would in one respect own the home court advantage. Since basketball had never been played inside the Astrodome, a portable floor had to be borrowed, not an easy task in the shank of a season. The one they found belonged to the Los Angeles Sports Arena, where the Lakers had played before their move to the Forum in Inglewood. The one-ton surface was trucked to Houston in two days. The Bruins had played three games on it, the Cougars none.

So the teams would collide in a stadium built for football and baseball—on a floor shipped from California. The permanent seats were so far from the court that many of the fans in the upper decks brought binoculars or opera glasses.

Of course, the phantom of this opera was Alcindor, soon to convert to Islam and change his name to Abdul-Jabbar. From the moment he appeared on the floor, the seven-foot-two center was the focal point of the crowd. Curious Texans gawked and followed his every move. They seemed surprised to find that he had two arms, two legs, and lived out of water.

A series of medical bulletins had preceded his arrival, the result of a scratched eyeball suffered a week earlier. To protect his eye, he wore goggles.

With Hayes hitting the turnaround jumper that would become his signature move in the NBA, Houston led at the half, 37–28. In the Lew Alcindor era, UCLA had never before trailed by as many as nine points. Gibraltar was crumbling.

The score was tied at 69 with twenty-eight seconds left. Hayes was fouled by Jim Nielsen and buried them both. Houston led by two and UCLA would not get off another shot. Lucius Allen's pass for Mike Warren was tipped by a teammate and sailed out of bounds. Here came Hayes dribbling across midcourt, a little one-upmanship aimed at those who had been gushing about Alcindor's dexterity.

College basketball would move to another level—of bigger arenas and bigger coverage, and a pageant called March Madness. And the image would linger, even fifty years later, of a packed Astrodome, Elvin Hayes hitting the jumper, and the scoreboard lights frozen forever at 72–69.

Just eleven months later, the University of Houston football team outscored the school's hoop stars and left another indelible Dome memory. The Cougars defeated hapless Tulsa, 100–6. Coach Bill Yeoman tried sincerely to hold down the score without actually leaving the field, but it was raining touchdowns. He played defensive backs on offense in the fourth quarter. One of them, a senior named Larry Gatlin, who with his brothers would go on to fame as a country singer, caught a pass for the game's next to last score.

In a manufactured event that virtually symbolized the 1970s, the Astrodome was transformed into the world's gaudiest tennis court for one night.

Does anyone remember the '70s? Perhaps these clues will help: *Roots*. Digital watches. The Fonz. Patty Hearst. The Pet Rock. *Rocky*. The whole enchilada. Petrodollars. Racing stripes. Pong. Live via satellite. Ten-four. Macho. Watching Johnny Carson's hair turn white. And Billie Jean King challenging Bobby Riggs in what was labeled "The Battle of the Sexes."

More than a symbol of the '70s, like it or not—and she never said she didn't like it—Billie Jean became a symbol of the Women's Lib Movement. Part tennis, part social liberation. In September 1973, before a glittering crowd of forty thousand, Ms. King wiped out a fifty-five-year-old hustler and removed from the sport the last major element of chauvinist piggery.

The match was no contest. She woman-handled him, winning in straight sets in one of the truly bizarre moments in sports biz. It was the classic confrontation, a geezer approaching his dotage playing junk shots against a girl who wore glasses, and in thirty-six countries millions tuned in via satellite TV.

The scene seemed primed for a clash between the Christians and the lions, a cross between the grandeur of Rome and Disneyland. All of which meant that the setting was ideal because the idea for the Astrodome had been inspired by the Roman Colosseum during a business trip Judge Hofheinz had taken to Italy.

King's entry into the arena set the tone. Eight helmeted centurions carried her on an Egyptian sedan chair with plumes and fans. She did a lot of waving and throwing of kisses, although she seemed vaguely embarrassed by the whole parody.

Riggs arrived by rickshaw, with the band playing the soundtrack from some epic film like *Quo Vadis* or *Lawrence of Arabia*. He was wearing a warm-up jacket with the words "Sugar Daddy" emblazoned on the back, and he presented his opponent with a giant caramel candy on a stick. The gesture, he told the press, was meant to emphasize that "she will be a sucker for my lobs." He and Billie Jean split $20,000 from the candy manufacturer.

In return, Billie Jean presented Riggs with a live baby pig. Bobby had hustled relentlessly to build interest, and the box office, for this event. His training regimen included a cocktail of twenty-six daily vitamins and herbal pills. But when the match began, the action turned serious, partly because the winning purse was reportedly $200,000, with the loser's share being half as much.

Riggs had his hair styled and colored for the occasion, with enough spray that his hair didn't move until the sixth game of the first set. Billie Jean was the aggressor from the start. Bobby tried to play his predictable soft, tantalizing game, returning every shot with lobs and cuts, trying to force her into errors. But his teasing shots were chased down and blistered by his twenty-nine-year-old foe. As the upset wore on, Bobby frequently shrugged in resignation.

The women's pro tour, her thirty-five major titles, including six at Wimbledon, would be Billie Jean's legacy, not this carnival stunt. "It may have been a gimmick," she said years later, "but it was a gimmick that worked. Eighty million people saw that match. In 1973, tennis was still a small sport. . . . It helped put us on the map. What I didn't expect was how it helped women in general to gain a little courage. Their self-esteem went up a little bit."

A lot of men felt that civilization as we knew it ended that autumn night in the Astrodome. Bobby Riggs did everything but wear a sandwich board onto the court. But it was Billie Jean King who emerged as the queen of mixed singles in tennis.

Between the late 1960s and the mid-1970s, the Houston Oilers drew sellout crowds with mostly losing teams. There were great times coming—Earl Campbell, Bum Phillips, the joyous noise of the "Luv Ya Blue" years, "The House of Pain" and the run-n-shoot offense. But the Oilers won only one game in 1972 (and again in 1973) and provided *Monday Night Football* with one of its most unforgettable moments.

They were getting blown out by the Oakland Raiders, 34–0, when an ABC camera zoomed in on a fan who appeared to be asleep. Sensing the camera, the fan opened an eye and without moving his head gave a one-fingered salute to the viewing audience.

In the broadcasting booth, an alert Don Meredith turned to the sensitive Howard Cosell and assured him, "It's all right, Howard. He's just saying 'We're Number One.'"

By the end of the decade, the Oilers almost were. Twice they lost in the AFC championship game to the Pittsburgh Steelers—the Terry Bradshaw, Lynn Swann, Mean Joe Greene dynasty. The Steelers won the Super Bowl both years. But the Oilers had reason to hope, and his name was Earl Campbell, voted both Rookie and Player of the Year in 1978. On a Monday night in November, the Tyler Rose rushed for 199 yards and four touchdowns as the Oilers whipped Miami, 35–30, to keep their playoff hopes alive.

On his twenty-eighth carry, Earl turned the corner, saw nothing but open space, and sailed 81 yards to the game-clinching score. This was the game Frank Gifford called the most exciting *Monday Night* telecast of them all.

The Oilers and the Astros created their own folklore, but for pure weirdness nothing that was offered at the Dome could top an event that was shown on closed-circuit television.

A standing-room crowd of over forty-seven thousand turned out for a hybrid fight that was being held across the Pacific Ocean. The United States and Japan had been at peace for thirty years at the time, and nothing about this performance would disturb the peace.

Muhammad Ali, the boxer, and Antonio Inoki, the wrestler, met in Tokyo to decide the Bossling championship of the world. After fifteen rounds of exquisite boredom, the referee declared the match a draw. Saving face is a fine old Japanese custom.

The dispute proved nothing about boxing or wrestling or sports. It only proved that Inoki's legs were longer than Ali's arms. As the night wore on, the greatest fear was that Inoki would develop a cyst on his tailbone. He would slam himself to the floor, then chase Ali around the ring, scooting along on his rump. You had the feeling that Inoki was confused. This time it wasn't his face that needed to be saved.

His strategy was to lash out at Ali with his feet, lunging wicked karate kicks, while Ali walked around him as though he were a swamp. On occasion, Ali kicked back, short, impatient jolts to the ankle, a fair imitation of a fight between two angry five-year-olds.

When Inoki entered the ring, as tall and strong and as handsome as his storied American opponent, what caught your eye was his chin. He had a gorgeous chin, the size of an average person's forehead, and the saddest part of the night was that not once did Ali make contact with it.

What a waste. One good right hand to that chin and it would have sounded like a waiter dropping a tray of glasses on a tile floor. To miss that chin was like visiting northern Arizona and missing the Grand Canyon.

Yet, incredibly, in fifteen rounds, Ali threw only two punches, both light left jabs. The fact was that Ali, aware of the danger in Inoki's kicks—it was a great way to get a kneecap broken—stayed out of range. That tended to reduce the threat, but also made the chances of landing a solid punch almost impossible.

Still, the fact that so many curious fans showed up to watch this drama unfold was stunning. "This is a travesty," decided one witness, "and there are 40,000 travesties watching it."

The Astrodome was the scene of several nationally televised boxing matches and at least one that was close to historic. In November 1982, Larry Holmes, the heavyweight champion, won a unanimous decision in fifteen rounds over a stubborn but inferior Randall (Tex) Cobb. By chance, I sat behind Howard Cosell at ringside, as Howard called the blow-by-blow. He also implored the referee to stop the fight as Holmes turned Cobb's face into something resembling hamburger meat.

Cobb wouldn't quit, but Cosell did, unable to tolerate what he had observed. When Howard announced that he would never broadcast another fight, Tex Cobb called it the highlight of his boxing career.

In the end, the Astrodome was designed for baseball, and picking out one or two memories is like asking which noodle was your favorite in a spaghetti dinner.

But there was hardly a more dramatic, or meaningful, game than Mike Scott's no-hitter to clinch the division pennant in 1986—the first time that had happened. In all modesty, I predicted that he would no-hit the San Francisco Giants way back in the third inning. I turned to the sports editor of the *Houston Post*, Clark Nealon, my boss, and said, "Clark, Scott's going to get a no-hitter."

He smiled, humoring me, and said, "It's only the third inning."

"Yes," I agreed, "but I have never seen big league hitters missing pitches by as much as the Giants are." I also noticed that they were dragging their bats back to the dugout, like shovels, not hoisting them on their shoulders.

The no-hitter, the pennant, the tension in the stands, all came together in one shining moment. The Astrodome was the only sports stadium in the world with padded, cushioned theater seats with cups in the armrests—because there was no fear of rain. But from the third inning, few people were sitting in them.

One could go on and on. The pity is that after 1999, the Astrodome did not.

Prologue

A Noble Idea for the Oil Patch

In the late 1950s, Houston was growing rapidly, but its reputation was far from positive on the national, much less international, stage. People thought of it as a backwater town that attracted an odd mix of roughneck oil workers and gun-toting, redneck cowboy types. Almost no one looked at Houston as a "Major League" city with a high-culture reputation.

Yet its population had jumped significantly, and a mix of local power brokers and enthusiastic civic boosters had grand visions of turning Houston into a respected big league city. Some of these people would be happy just to get a Major League Baseball team, but Judge Roy Hofheinz had much bigger plans. He wanted Houston to be a world-class Major League city that rivaled all others. His commitment to building a giant domed stadium was the first volley in that overarching plan.

At the time, no one had ever built a gigantic indoor sports complex, let alone one that would have premium luxury suites, climate-controlled, air-conditioned comfort, and plush theater-style seating. Pittsburgh's Civic Arena was the first modern circular indoor sports arena, but it seated fewer than twenty thousand people. That project broke ground in 1958. It was designed with a retractable roof that seemed visionary, but no one had ever tried to build an air-conditioned indoor sports facility that would entertain more than fifty thousand people. Besides, Pittsburgh's retractable roof was poorly designed, so the retractable feature was rarely used.

Five decades ago, as construction of the famed Dome unfolded, Roy Hofheinz contemplated this project as something that would distinguish Houston on an international scale. The hard-charging, cigar-chomping judge faced big challenges in getting the Astrodome built, but getting a baseball team to come to Houston had to come first. Houston's summers are oppressively hot, so selling baseball to Houstonians, even at the Major League level, would not be easy. Hofheinz had a role in bringing a Major League team to Houston, but George Kirksey and Craig Cullinan did most of the heavy lifting, and oilmen such as Bob Smith provided much of the capital that was needed to step up to the Majors.

Before committing to the Astrodome, Hofheinz was working on a plan to build a domed shopping mall. He was captivated by Buckminster Fuller's commitment to the geodesic dome. When another developer edged him out in attracting the high-end retail commitments that he would need to launch a successful Houston-based mall, Hofheinz stepped away from this project and immersed himself in plans to construct the Astrodome. He transferred his enthusiasm for a domed shopping mall to his ballpark design, convinced that Houston could be the first city to finance such an ambitious project.

Buckminster Fuller boasted to Hofheinz that a dome could be built over a structure of virtually any size as long as enough funds were available to obtain the resources to finish the job.[1] Years earlier, Fuller had tried to sell his ideas to Brooklyn Dodgers owner Walter O'Malley, but political friction between O'Malley and the legendary power broker and urban planner Robert Moses prevented that project from moving beyond the dream stage.[2]

To get the Astrodome built, Judge Hofheinz had to be part huckster, part fundraiser, and part visionary. He had to convince the big-money forces and the less affluent taxpayers of southern Texas to do something that had never been tried before. Yet Hofheinz was never one to back away from a challenge. At the age of nineteen he passed the Texas Bar exam, and by age twenty-two he was elected to the Texas legislature. Two years later, he was a judge. He was a millionaire by his thirties and by the time he was forty he was elected to serve as Houston's mayor. He was well connected politically, successfully leading Lyndon Johnson's first campaign for the U.S. Senate.

Getting the Astrodome built may have seemed like a big deal to just about anyone in Houston. But for Hofheinz, it was just another challenge to be conquered. His vision for Houston was to have a sports enclosure that was so big and so luxurious it would change how people perceived the city. He wanted something so unique and so grand that people would come from miles around to see it, even when the local sports teams were not in town.

A tinge of Texas pride motivated Hofheinz. On the eve of the ballpark's opening, he bragged, "Nobody can ever see this and go back to Kalamazoo, Chicago, New York, you name it, and still think this town is bush league."[3] Before the Astrodome, much of Houston's citizenry regarded their sprawling metropolis as hardly a cutting-edge city, and its leaders sometimes unintentionally contributed to these stereotypes.

At the groundbreaking for the ballpark, instead of performing the ritual with bright metallic shovels, as is common, the dignitaries bizarrely chose to fire ceremonial wax bullets into the ground. This was followed by the launching of forty-five aerial bombs from the spot where home plate was to be located.[4] City officials broke the ground, Texas style, but the move likely fed the "yee-hah" cowboy stereotypes that northeastern and midwestern citizens might have held about Houston's perceived redneck culture.

This book is, first and foremost, an attempt to capture what unfolded as the Astrodome was planned and built, with specific focus on the larger-than-life personalities who were instrumental in bringing the project to fruition. Roy Hofheinz, Bob Smith, George Kirksey, Craig Cullinan, Kenneth Zimmerman, and many others worked tirelessly to bring Houston to the "Major Leagues." Their stories offer a fascinating look into what Houston was and what it has become. The Astrodome was a reflection of the creativity and vision of these strong-willed individuals, so the publicity it initially received was overwhelmingly positive. Houston rapidly moved away from its image as a cattle town with a vibrant oil industry to become a space-age city that was on the cutting edge of new technology. The National Aeronautics and Space Administration helped Houston to transition away from the old stereotypes, but the Astrodome served as a more visceral example of Houston's commitment to modernity.

New York Times reporter Leonard Koppett called the new ballpark "the most spectacular one of all" in an article summarizing baseball's Opening Day matchups.[5] His colleague Arthur Daley said that the Astrodome "stuns the eye with such dazzling splendor that even the natives find themselves groping for words" to describe it. Daley further asserted that "the only sight this wandering reporter ever saw that surpasses it is the exquisite Taj Mahal at Agra in India." He concluded, "Superlatives can't do justice to the Astrodome, a fantasy that defies description."[6] Magazine articles appeared in *Time, Look, Newsweek, Sports Illustrated,* the *Sporting News,* and many other venues. It was dubbed the "Eighth Wonder of the World," a term that became a general catchphrase to describe the Astrodome.

However, early praise for the Astrodome was tainted by worries that ballplayers would lose sight of fly balls during day games under the clear Lucite ceiling panels that covered the Dome. Until the issue was resolved, some outfielders wore batting helmets and tests were undertaken with baseballs of various colors, while the general public was solicited for ideas. Over one thousand telegrams with an array of possible solutions flowed in, with some of the suggestions bordering on the bizarre. As an example, one person suggested releasing thousands of helium-filled balloons before every home game to block the sun's rays.

Eventually, the clear panels were painted with a white acrylic paint, solving one problem but causing another. The paint fixed the fly ball issue, but the lack of sunlight killed the natural grass. The team was forced to play on green-painted dead turf until the 1966 season, when a synthetic product called AstroTurf was installed.

New York Times sportswriter Robert Lipsyte, a baseball purist, was among the most vocal critics of the new Dome. He used the pop fly problem as a springboard to criticize the new facility. His articles tended to isolate remarks from people who were not impressed with the Dome, even if he did balance them with observations that put the facility in a good light. His page-one article on the first game in the building contained a number of positive elements but also included a quote from an anonymous young woman stating, "I think it's rather sterile. No warmth, no real humanity here."[7] In another article, he provided a forum for Houstonians with negative things to say about the Astrodome.

Lipsyte compared the new facility to Dodger Stadium, indicating that "someone said that the Astrodome is like Chavez Ravine with a silly hat." He called the Astrodome a "gleaming bubble in a city of contrasts," then launched into a variety of negative descriptions of Houston. He asserted that the city was "considered 'dead' by the travelling man," while explaining that "men walk by with open shotguns and one can buy a good automatic pistol for less than $50." If that was not enough, he described much of Houston's architecture as "cheesebox modern, some of it allegedly shoddy."[8]

Lipsyte's negativity was the exception, not the rule, as the Astrodome brought a flurry of positive publicity to Houston during its first decade of operation. Still, as time unfolded, criticism of the Astrodome emerged from other baseball traditionalists. The respected stadium scholar Philip Lowry, in his book *Green Cathedrals*, called the Astrodome a "plague" that would "infest" other cities.[9]

Nevertheless, the Astrodome was the most recognized indoor facility for its first decade of operation. High-tech innovations could be found everywhere. The world's largest electronic scoreboard, 474 feet wide, was so intricate that it required seven people to operate. As Astros legend Larry Dierker recalled, the scoreboard's "home run display made Bill Veeck's Comiskey Park look like bottle rockets."[10] The air-conditioning system was so complex that a 260-page promotional booklet dedicated six pages to describing its design.[11] Opulent touches such as custom-designed skyboxes that were wired for closed-circuit television added further to the high-tech image of the Astrodome. Private clubs and public restaurants moved Houstonians away from the basic fare that other ballparks offered at the time. Other features, too numerous to mention, made the Astrodome look like the pinnacle of technological achievement.

Criticism for the AstroTurf playing surface eventually became widespread, but as the stadium opened, the public generally bought into the many opulent touches that were woven into the Astrodome's design. The padded, theater-style seating, the luxury skyboxes, the hugely expansive high-tech scoreboard, the lavish press facilities, and the wide range of unique eateries installed around the stadium generated excitement from a curious public. In its first year alone, four hundred thousand people paid a dollar each to tour the Astrodome at times when events were not scheduled.[12]

The city may not have shed its backwater reputation entirely, but over time, both the Astrodome and the strong presence of NASA helped to better position Houston as a city that was perceived to be capable of high-tech innovation.

For better or worse, the Astrodome changed the way people viewed sports. It shifted the emphasis of sports from a focus on rabid team fans to a marketing strategy that would bring in casual fans whose goal was to have a good time, irrespective of the game on the field.

As the Astrodome opened, the Astros were not even close to a winning ball club, struggling in their first few years to stay out of last place. Yet the Astrodome attracted strong attendance, surpassing the 2.1 million mark in its first season alone.[13] The Los Angeles Dodgers, a highly successful team in their own right, were the only club to outdraw the next-to-last-place Astros. The success of the Astrodome had other owners eying similar strategies to lure casual fans.

If the current focus on skyboxes and opulent stadium clubs irritates many sports fans, they can look to the Astrodome with contempt. However, many fans appear to enjoy the luxury, even if the cost is high, paying robust amounts for entry to lavish club seats and skyboxes. Team owners and those who profit from an amazing new generation of sports palaces in New York, Dallas, Indianapolis, and elsewhere can look to the Astrodome as a facility that inspired a new business model in sports infrastructure. It revolutionized how fans watched sports, introducing unbridled luxury to the spectator experience.

For better or worse, the Astrodome changed the sports landscape in a profound way. The story of how the Astrodome was built is an incredible one, with many odd twists and turns. Although a distant memory for many, the Astrodome is a project that had far-reaching implications for Houston and beyond.

The Eighth Wonder of the World

COW TOWN

1

Roy Hofheinz
Houston's Grand Huckster

Somewhat fittingly, it all began at the circus.

With carnival music filling up the big top, young Roy Hofheinz peered up at the drab canvas ceiling above him. As a massive drum pounded away, he stared downward at the action, bouncing up and down with giddy enthusiasm on his hard wooden seat. As the music reverberated and a kitschy assortment of circus performers moved about the arena, Hofheinz marveled at the spectacle that was unfolding below him. But he was equally awed that all of this live entertainment was happening, of all places, indoors. Nothing this impressive ever took place indoors, he thought to himself.

The whole spectacle, the large fabric roof included, amazed Hofheinz. If stormy weather moved in, he thought, the circus calliope would play on and the frivolity brought on by the slapstick comedy of the clowns would continue unabated. He was tucked into a corner with a general admission ticket stub resting in his pocket. The youngster could fully see only one of the three rings of the famed Ringling Bros. Circus. His seat was an uncomfortable wooden plank rather than the plush, padded chair of a movie theater.

Yet the young boy was too excited about the great show unfolding below to worry about luxury seating. He was immensely grateful merely for the opportunity to see such an amazing spectacle. Days earlier, when Hofheinz learned that the circus was coming to Beaumont, Texas, his early boyhood home, he pleaded with his parents to allow him to attend this grand extravaganza.

Unable to afford the three tickets that would allow the entire family to enter, his parents patiently waited outside as their only son enjoyed the entire show inside. The sacrifices made by Fritz and Nonie Hofheinz would fuel the curiosity and passions of their extremely bright son. Such selfless investments would indirectly contribute to the reshaping of one of the nation's largest metropolitan areas while changing the nature of sports spectatorship globally. At the time, however, the two parents were simply trying to please their young son.

Although of limited means and raised in austere, rugged working-class neighborhoods, Nonie Hofheinz protectively encouraged her young son to focus on his interests and passions as she challenged him to excel in education. She set high standards that would shape a thirst for success throughout his life. Despite maintaining a modest lifestyle, his mother had a desire for luxury. It was a preference that was quickly absorbed by young Roy, too, and carried through to adulthood.

The precocious Hofheinz had many interests as a youngster, but for him nothing was more exciting than the circus. Despite his gratitude for his parents' selfless sacrifice during their trip to the big top, many years later he recalled uncomfortably sitting "on a damned narrow board" as exotic animals, clowns, and acrobats performed under a massive tent.[1]

His father, Fritz Hofheinz, often worked two or more jobs just to make ends meet. In his limited time off, he brought his young son to Beaumont's shipyards, railroads, sawmills, and city landmarks, meticulously explaining their subtle inner workings. After moving to fast-growing Houston, Roy Hofheinz saw his family struggle to maintain a modest big city clothing laundering business.

He pitched in, often working twelve-hour days, helping by washing clothes and making deliveries with his father in an old, worn-down truck. The work gave him an intricate knowledge of city streets and general urban infrastructure. It also helped him to learn how to interact with customers. This early work was something that his biographer, Edgar Ray, suggested "would enable him to later analyze the city's needs and to understand its people."[2] Fritz Hofheinz struggled to keep the family business afloat and, after a year in Houston, opted instead to drive a delivery truck for a rival laundry company.

Fritz Hofheinz's career change would allow young Roy the freedom to pursue a wide array of unique business opportunities

4

that would hone his skills as a promoter and salesman. From that environment, he would develop book smarts, street smarts, and an enthusiastic passion for urban culture. Unknowingly, Hofheinz was building a skill set that would enable him to build the first massive climate-controlled stadium.

After establishing a career path that was highly impressive by any measure, Hofheinz would take the lead in creating an edifice that would change the face of spectatorship, not just in Texas, but on a vast and global scale. Houston's Astrodome was Roy Hofheinz's brainchild. Although he was not an architect, an engineer, or a construction worker, without Hofheinz's vision, determination, and persistence, this luxurious facility would not have been built.

Hofheinz was, in part, inspired to build a domed stadium after a visit to Rome's famed Colosseum in 1955, long after his professional and political career had unfolded. The bread and circuses of Rome made for an apt symbol of what Hofheinz hoped to achieve for Houston. Roman leaders regarded the entertainment that was taking place inside the Colosseum as a way to showcase the vast greatness of the Roman Empire to its many citizens. In a similar manner, Hofheinz hoped that the profound luxury of the new indoor sports facility would build pride in a fast-growing Houston, while demonstrating to the entire world that this Texas locale had emerged as a genuinely Major League city.

Before the Astrodome was built, Houston was defined by livestock and oil. It was the largest city in Texas, with a rapidly growing population. In 1940 Houston's population was 384,514. By 1960 it had swelled to more than one million.[3] By that time, it was the largest U.S. metropolitan area not to have a Major League team. It also had abundant wealth. However, the city's image may have been the single biggest factor working against achieving Major League stature. Until NASA and the Astrodome were entrenched in the city's culture, outsiders did not regard Houston as cutting-edge or forward thinking.

The path to the construction of the Astrodome took several decades to unfold. However, it was not the first sports facility to attempt to weave in opulence. In the nineteenth century, sports entrepreneur Albert Spalding oversaw construction of a ballpark in Chicago that featured eighteen private luxury boxes that allowed a small number of well-heeled patrons to watch a ballgame from padded chairs. At approximately the same time, New York's famed Polo Grounds featured a full bar while hawking cigars and establishing Harry M. Stevens as an innovative concessionaire who would offer patrons a creative assortment of food options.

As the twentieth century unfolded, more modern concrete and steel ballparks were built, with greater levels of luxury than in generations prior. In 1958 Pittsburgh had begun construction on its Civic Arena, the first retractable domed sports facility to be built in North America. While the facility in the Steel City was unique and, in its own right, revolutionary, its capacity was fewer than twenty thousand and its amenities paled in comparison to what was installed in the Astrodome. As such, Roy Hofheinz took the lead in creating a structure that was truly a game changer for sports fans.

Hofheinz's meandering career path allowed him to gain stature, build unique relationships, and learn about key aspects of architecture that would put him in a position to mastermind the Astrodome's highly complex construction. His life was so remarkable that if his biography were to be rewritten as fiction, readers would likely conclude that parts of the story were implausible and wildly exaggerated. Yet, from very humble beginnings, Roy Hofheinz was able to do what most people would consider impossible. As he entered his teen years, he embarked on a wild ride that started slowly and innocently but that, over time, allowed him to earn an impressive professional reputation and learn enough about how the real world functioned to achieve goals that seemed beyond human comprehension.

Hofheinz gained media experience working in the radio industry at an extremely young age. He organized dances, too, booking the best talent possible. Young Roy Hofheinz was not intimidated by such challenges and managed to pull off successful social events that were attended by thousands of people. His wide array of talents put him in a position to meet movers and shakers while allowing him to refine and improve his negotiating and social skills in a variety of venues.

He also involved himself with political causes, managing campaigns for a fast-rising Lyndon Baines Johnson while connecting with other political luminaries. Hofheinz's friend and political ally would later wield enormous power over the U.S. Senate, rising to the rank of majority leader. By the time the Astrodome officially opened, Hofheinz was a close friend to the president of the United States.

Hofheinz was the epitome of persistence. He took on challenge after challenge, frequently doing so many years before others would have the nerve and the courage to try. At age thirteen, for example, he convinced high school officials to allow him to print football programs, something that had never before been done at his school. He assumed the cost for the venture because he was told there was no budget to print them. To defray these costs and ensure a profit, he sold advertising to local businesses. Instead of making an emotional plea to support the local school, he astutely pitched game attendance figures, an early recognition of the importance of demographics, as evidence that the advertisements would benefit the local merchants within range of his pitch.

By age fourteen, he owned an old Ford Model T that he used to move forward on more impressive projects. He took advantage of his outstanding public-speaking skills to gain employment at a local radio station after receiving awards and widespread recognition for his role in school-based oratory competitions. He also organized dances for local teens by convincing owners of the largest dance halls in Houston to rent their spaces to him despite his youth. He was rebuffed at first, but he cleverly and persistently worked with the hall owners to win them over. He agreed that he would pay his rental fee in advance, keep alcohol away entirely, and let the owners keep all of the concession revenues. He further agreed to leave the places clean after all of the festivities were concluded, and he worked long hours to ensure that he kept up his end of each deal.

To make these events a success, Hofheinz advertised on the radio, at local businesses, and even on his car as it traveled along Houston's busy streets. He was particularly creative at times, too. Friends often noticed the youngster suspiciously stuck at the busiest city intersections, repairing what seemed to be a flat tire in locations where the advertising displays on his car would be most effective. On dance nights, he acted as host and emcee. He policed the facility to keep alcohol away, and he took his agreement to clean up afterward very seriously, pushing a broom and collecting trash into the wee hours of the morning if necessary.

For each dance, he booked two orchestras, one black, one white, with the black orchestra playing late into the night, long after the white orchestra had left. With a keen eye for talent, when possible, Hofheinz booked a young Louis "Satchmo" Armstrong for the festivities before the musician had rightfully earned his legendary status. The entrepreneurial talent of Hofheinz and the musical excellence of Armstrong were a powerful combination that attracted a wide following.

Even when Armstrong was unable to perform, which occurred quite often as his fame increased, Hofheinz provided unique creative touches that attracted a crowd. He acted as talent scout and recruiter for a newly formed band, the Birmingham Blues Blowers, an assortment of local jazz talent that he tapped to fill the void when Armstrong was unavailable. Thousands of people flocked to these dances, allowing young Roy to connect and interact with a highly diverse clientele.

His mother, despite struggling to make ends meet, had exceedingly high expectations for Hofheinz. After bringing in $1,500 for one dance, a figure that would approach $20,000 in today's dollars, he asked, "Aren't you proud of me?" Instead, he was confronted with a humbling and direct "No, I expected it of you" from his mother.[4] Such lukewarm reactions to his success kept young Roy on his toes and propelled him to achieve greater things later.

His first foray into the political realm was an endorsement of Walter Embree Monteith, a Texas judge for more than a decade and a former Houston mayor. As a teenager, Hofheinz impressed local leaders, who had yet to see a teen speak so eloquently without relying on notes or a script. The experience at rallies and community events activated his desire to attend law school since such legal training was the most common path for success in the political arena.

Hofheinz graduated from high school just two months after turning sixteen, earning high honors for his academics. He was accepted into the University of Texas at Austin, receiving a merit-based scholarship, but chose, instead, to attend the Rice Institute, now Rice University, in part because it would grant him free tuition and keep him closer to his ongoing activities in Houston. A year later he transferred to Houston Junior College because this option consisted primarily of night classes. The change would free up his work schedule so that he could promote various business opportunities during weekdays. At Rice he was able to continue his dances and radio work, but at the junior college he had a chance to do even more, which led to greater income.

Before attending college, Hofheinz planned to more fully immerse himself in the political realm because Houston was hosting the Democratic National Convention in July 1928. It was the first major party political convention in a southern state since the end of the Civil War. With New York governor Al Smith likely to get the nomination that year, Hofheinz cleverly coaxed the New York delegation to hire him as a page, making the case that his local knowledge would be of benefit to the visitors from the north. Hofheinz never spoke directly with Smith, but despite that disappointment, he gained unique inspiration elsewhere. He saw an energetic Franklin Roosevelt fighting through his paralysis to organize the New York delegation on behalf of Smith. Hofheinz was able to watch Roosevelt nominate Smith to be the Democratic presidential candidate and, despite Smith's subsequent loss to Herbert Hoover, later observed that, in spite of his physical ailments, Roosevelt emerged through hard work and persistence to become the governor of the Empire State.

The spectacle and the unfolding drama at the Democratic National Convention captivated a young Hofheinz, but his work at the convention took him beyond the New York delegation's drama. Hofheinz was able to connect with a twenty-year old Lyndon Baines Johnson, and the two became extremely close, lifelong friends. Johnson had hoped to cover the convention as a reporter for his college newspaper, and once inside the venue, he focused on the Texas delegation. When possible, Hofheinz was able to spend time with the Texas delegation, too. His periodic visits allowed him to solidify his relationship with young Lyndon Johnson while connecting with another future vice president, John Nance Garner, a legendary congressman and House Speaker in Sam Rayburn, and a future U.S. senator, Tom Connally.

Less than two months after the convention, and about a month before Roy was scheduled to begin college, the Hofheinz family was rocked by tragedy. Roy's father was killed in a traffic accident while working, propelling young Hofheinz into the role of breadwinner for the family before he spent a single day in a college classroom. With this pressure, he worked tirelessly to both earn money and finish school.

After his father's death, Hofheinz pushed himself with even greater tenacity to achieve lofty goals. Two years after entering college, he was enrolled in the Houston Law School, gaining a full scholarship as a result of his strong oratory skills and considerable potential. By age nineteen, he had successfully passed the bar exam and was practicing law with an office of his own, even though he had not yet graduated from law school. His office was a block from the county courthouse and jail, allowing him to save time as he worked in the courthouse and in his office with clients. He took on criminal cases, defending a broad variety of clients. However, he stepped away from the practice after learning that he was responsible for the acquittal of a guilty man. Though he had no idea that the man was guilty when the acquittal was rendered, the subsequent revelation left Hofheinz feeling deep remorse.

He graduated from law school in 1933, just weeks after turning twenty-one, and married Dene Cafcalas, a law school colleague who, like Roy, graduated with high honors. Dene took detailed notes and shared them with Roy anytime he missed class, which occurred from time to time as a result of his law practice. Her kindness caused a sort of frustration that Dene joked about later in life. Hofheinz's biographer, Edgar Ray, asserted that "after Roy's photographic mind had studied her notes, he got better grades than she did."[5]

With the law practice behind him, Hofheinz set his sights on political office, getting elected to the Texas state legislature at just twenty-two, the youngest legislator ever to be elected in the state. His experience at the Democratic National Convention just six years earlier and a desire to confront the economic ravages of the Great Depression propelled his wish to serve. His hard work and oratory skills earned him the informal title of the "boy wonder of the legislature."[6]

While in the legislature he befriended John Connally, then a student at the University of Texas. Connally lived within walking distance of the capitol building and would visit periodically in an attempt to learn the inner workings of the Texas political system. As an observer, Connally was impressed with the way Hofheinz carried himself, asserting that he "showed great courage in tackling the problems of the state."[7] Connally would later rise through the political ranks to be elected governor as the Astrodome was being built. The friendship was a political connection that would serve Houston well, though at the time, Hofheinz had no way of knowing that.

After serving two years in the legislature, Hofheinz hoped to move back to Houston. He took on a new challenge. He became Harris County judge in 1936, the youngest person in the nation to ever be elected to such a position. To do so, he had to defeat an experienced incumbent. His outstanding oratory, his ability to use radio effectively, and missteps from his more experienced opponent helped him overcome long odds and initial skepticism from power brokers and area newspapers. Despite an inability to get the *Houston Chronicle*'s endorsement, Hofheinz defeated his opponent by a dramatic 44,195 to 18,726 votes.

A year later, Hofheinz encouraged his young friend, Lyndon Johnson, to run for a U.S. congressional seat after J. P. Buchanan, the Tenth Congressional District incumbent, died of a heart attack. With eight candidates running, Johnson managed to win in a highly splintered field despite getting only 27 percent of the total vote. Johnson hired their mutual friend John Connally to be his aide, giving Hofheinz connections in the nation's capital that he did not previously have.

Johnson was so impressed with Hofheinz and his political savvy that he selected him to manage twenty-six southeastern

Texas counties during his first U.S. Senate campaign in 1941. Hofheinz undertook this challenge while serving as Harris County judge. Although Johnson was hospitalized and in ill health during the campaign, Dene and Roy worked tirelessly to bring in voters. Hofheinz stepped in to speak at events where the candidate was previously scheduled to appear, while Dene worked with Johnson's wife, Lady Bird, to organize and coordinate activities, too. Johnson finished a very close second among a field of four candidates, carrying every single county under Hofheinz's supervision. Some speculated that the vote count was suspicious, with Johnson losing votes during a postelection recount.[8]

Johnson knew that Hofheinz had done a solid job despite the campaign loss and appreciated his hard work. He tapped him again and again for insight and assistance as he rose through the ranks of the House and Senate to his eventual service in the White House. The Johnson-Hofheinz relationship was more nuanced than that of a campaign manager and candidate, however, and it was built on more than political calculus. The two had cultivated a strong friendship and abiding respect for each other years before either one had emerged as a recognizable national figure. They developed and refined their ideological outlooks together at a formative time for both of them. Before Johnson entered into his first election campaign, he invited Hofheinz to serve as a guest speaker at Sam Houston High School, where Johnson had secured a teaching job in 1930. Hofheinz assisted him in teaching high school students how to hone their oratory skills. After teaching their classes, they would engage in conversation, periodically walking the streets of Houston.

Both men contemplated the challenges brought upon by the Great Depression as they passed soup kitchens and watched the unemployed struggle to survive. For Johnson, the experience likely contributed to his tenacious focus on antipoverty programs. For Hofheinz, it likely further inspired him to focus on juvenile rehabilitation while a judge, then later propelled him to introduce luxuries typically unavailable to the general public so that all Houstonians could experience brief moments of opulence, with the Astrodome as his crowning achievement in that regard.

The two were such close friends that on the day President John F. Kennedy was assassinated, Hofheinz and Johnson spoke twice, with Hofheinz consoling and advising Johnson.

As Hofheinz closed in on his eighth year as judge, he explored the option of moving back into the radio business, with a goal of achieving financial security by age forty. He famously asserted, "I'm not going into politics again until after I am a millionaire."[9] Although he never complained about his salary as a public servant, it would not be sufficient for Hofheinz to enjoy the level of luxury that he coveted throughout his life. In addition, he understood the temptations that led politicians to sell out to special interests and did not want to reenter the political realm until he felt sufficiently insulated from the financial pressures faced by public servants. He knew the radio industry well and was in a position to earn strong profits as a station owner, but he would not rely on one venture or one industry to reach his goals. When Hofheinz tendered his resignation in October 1944, the county did not accept it, instead requesting that he continue his service until January 1, 1945. Hofheinz abided by the county's wishes, staying on the job until his term was fully completed. When he finally stepped down, three people had to be drafted to serve in order to account for his wide range of duties.

To get back into broadcasting, he applied for a station license. Before doing so, he carefully worked to stockpile the necessary equipment. His rationale for doing so was simple and well reasoned. With America's entry into World War II, the Federal Communications Commission (FCC) placed a freeze on new broadcast licenses unless an individual could fully demonstrate that he or she already owned the requisite equipment to operate a radio station. Adding further complexity to the application process, Hofheinz was required to file a report that thoroughly detailed the programming of other stations in the Houston market. Understanding that the application decision would be made by Washington DC administrators—some of whom might not be on his side—he wisely did all in his power to ensure full compliance with every aspect of the FCC application.

Nevertheless, he faced stiff tailwinds at FCC headquarters, where

Chairman James Fly, a Dallas native, pointedly told a colleague that Hofheinz "was not going to get a station."[10] The opposition was so palpable that after the first day of hearings, an emotional Hofheinz called home to explain that his trip would be a failure. His wife, Dene, consoled him, supportively stating, "Don't worry, honey, we started out with nothing, so when you get home, we can start all over again."[11] Before the next day, his well-heeled financial partner Dick Hooper, a 25 percent partner in the station, admonished Hofheinz for his negativity and indicated a willingness to back an expensive court appeal if necessary. Despite a barrage of tough questions from the FCC chairman, Hofheinz pushed forward and was able to convince the full FCC board to grant him a license. He applied for the call letters KTHT, which he proudly asserted stood for "keep talking, Houston, Texas."

As with his other pursuits, Hofheinz was determined to leave his mark on broadcasting. He pioneered the use of recorders in news reporting, he was an early leader in FM broadcasting, and he worked hard to put his station on solid financial footing. His hard-charging management style prompted his staff to jokingly present him with a bullwhip at the 1945 KTHT Christmas party.

However, his indomitable professional zeal could hardly be limited to broadcasting. To further supplement his income, he maintained a law practice, though in that venture he was more of a supervisor than a day-to-day practitioner. He also teamed up with George Mattison, a Birmingham entrepreneur, to create the Houston Slag Materials Company. The firm took waste content from Houston-area steel mills, a major industrial byproduct during World War II, and converted it to useful materials such as railroad-bed foundation and a binding agent for concrete and asphalt paving projects. As with many Hofheinz initiatives, he had done the investigative work and had established the necessary partnerships to put the slag business in place during 1943, over a year before he tendered his resignation as judge.

Despite his heavy plate of commitments, Hofheinz kept his hand in in the political arena. When Lyndon Johnson decided to run for the U.S. Senate once again in 1948, he was particularly impressed with Hofheinz's skill and expertise with radio;

LBJ benefited from that expertise now that radio was in virtually every Texas household. When Johnson successfully campaigned against former Texas governor Coke Stevenson in 1948, his biographer, Robert Caro, has argued, Johnson "wanted key supporters, Judge Roy Hofheinz of Houston, for example—on the air frequently and also over statewide networks."[12] Now that Hofheinz was unencumbered by the constraints of being a county judge, he was able to work more diligently to mobilize radio resources for his close friend. Once again, allegations of impropriety and ballot miscounts unfolded as Johnson sought the Senate seat, but this time Johnson was the victor.

Hofheinz now had a powerful friend and ally in the U.S. Senate. Two years later he achieved a major financial milestone, too. By 1950, at just thirty-seven years of age, Hofheinz was a millionaire. He had AM and FM radio stations and a slag business and had immersed himself in real estate ventures. Despite his many personal victories, he charged into new frontiers, taking dramatic steps to avoid complacency.

He ran and won the race to be Houston's mayor in 1952, a job that tried his patience, possibly more than any other challenge he had undertaken. Nevertheless, his experience as mayor taught him much about the inner workings of day-to-day government operations and the many constraints to progress, lessons that would later assist him in overcoming the challenges of getting the Astrodome constructed. As mayor, he was a highly polarizing figure, but he worked hard to serve the people. He learned much about high-volume purchase and acquisition, saving the city considerable sums of money by insisting on competitive bidding rather than the deal making among cronies that was often tolerated in the past. He dealt with issues that other mayors may have ignored but, in the process, managed to anger members of the city council to a point at which impeachment was threatened and cooperation came to a standstill. Despite the acrimony, Hofheinz was able to get freeways installed in places where two-lane roads had previously slowed traffic to a crawl. He saw to it that school playgrounds were renovated and neighborhood swimming pools were installed, and he even confronted the ongoing problem of stray dogs and cats.

He also gained insights as mayor that spurred his interest in building a large indoor facility. In 1955 Hofheinz journeyed to Rome as Houston's representative at the World Council of Mayors annual conference. While visiting the ancient city, he learned that the famed Colosseum had been protected by a temporary cover on occasion. It was believed to have been made of papyrus and moved into place by slaves. Describing the discovery, Hofheinz later joked, "I guess they didn't want to spoil the lion's appetite with too much heat." Subsequently, he more soberly observed that "the emperor and the bigwigs all sat at the top of the Colosseum. Standing there looking back on those ancient days, I figured that a round facility with a cover was what we needed in the United States, and Houston would be the perfect spot for it because of its rainy, humid weather."[13]

The trip to Rome was a brief respite from the ongoing tensions that he faced as Houston's mayor. The acrimony between the city council and Hofheinz caught up with him during his second term. While in Rome, his opponent, Oscar Holcombe, the man who had preceded Hofheinz as mayor, organized a campaign to oust the mayor. Hofheinz lost an acrimonious election to Holcombe by a vote of 38,818 to 21,153. It was a campaign that left him angry. In his view, the voters had "thrown out the warden and turned the city over to the inmates."[14]

Despite the deep disappointment of losing the mayoral race handily, Hofheinz remained resilient. With just three days left in his tenure as mayor, he announced that he would head a four-person law firm that would specialize in municipal and administrative law. Hofheinz, Sears, James, and Burns began practice on January 2, 1956. But the law firm was not enough to keep him fully satisfied. In true Hofheinz fashion, long before his second term as mayor expired, he had worked to gain ownership of a television station. He secured the legal services of Red James, lined up financing partnerships, and put a management team in place in order to avoid distractions while carrying out his commitments as mayor. In order to comply with FCC requirements, he was required to divest himself of the majority of his radio interests and fully walk away from all station management duties. While serving as mayor, he turned administration of his radio stations over to his close friend Bill Bennett. After all of the necessary arrangements were in place, he obtained a television license, learning of this success on July 7, 1954. Willard Wallbridge, a television executive from Lansing, Michigan, was brought in to get KTRK-TV up and running and to supervise day-to-day operations. Walbridge asserted that "the brilliance of young Mayor Roy Hofheinz was one of the things which lured me to Houston."[15]

With a television station and law practice in place, Hofheinz looked for new challenges. He intensified his focus on real estate, with an eye on doing something unique and revolutionary for Houston. Before contemplating the Astrodome, he considered the possibility of bringing a large indoor shopping mall to Houston. It was an idea that had been successfully implemented in Minnesota and New Jersey but was never tried in Texas. Hofheinz felt strongly that the emergence of an automotive culture in the 1950s and Houston's hot and oppressive summers would make such a concept popular and profitable.

While researching the project and its feasibility, Hofheinz brought in and worked closely with the visionary architect Buckminster Fuller. Fuller was an early advocate of sustainable design and conservation, believing that with proper use of resources, humanity could maximize the quality of life on planet Earth. Like Hofheinz, he was a charmer and a compelling personality, a sort of pied piper of unique designs. He was best known for popularizing the geodesic dome. Fuller was a salesman with a poetic impulse and a visionary desire. His iconoclastic dedication to innovation and his willingness to look beyond conventional wisdom appealed to Hofheinz's unbridled desire for creative and pragmatic problem solving.

Fuller persuaded Hofheinz that his geodesic dome design was a practical concept that might be efficiently woven into Hofheinz's shopping mall plans. Efficiency was a strong argument for adopting the dome concept, according to Fuller, although Hofheinz likely saw the potential for cost savings that might make the dome feasible on a massive and unprecedented scale. The geodesic dome "encloses more space with far less material than any other form of structure known to man," asserted Fuller's biographer Alden Hatch in summarizing the practicality of Fuller's ideas.[16]

Hofheinz's larger-than-life ambition had him dreaming of an exceedingly large dome as he contemplated drawing up plans for the shopping mall. Fuller, sensing Hofheinz's desire for the grandiose, did not disappoint in his role as a consultant. His influence on the potential design for this project was profound. According to Hofheinz, "Buckminster Fuller convinced me that it was possible to cover any size space if you did not run out of money."[17]

Hofheinz's vision for a shopping mall never came to fruition. Although he had done substantial homework and had purchased land that would make such a project feasible, Frank Sharp, a competing developer, beat him to the punch in the mall-construction sweepstakes. As 1960 approached, Hofheinz was thoroughly convinced that only one large indoor mall project could succeed in Houston. When Sharp managed to corral a commitment from a major retail tenant, Foley's department store, Hofheinz quickly dropped his shopping mall plans and moved on. While the dome idea may have created a more futuristic mall than the competing Sharpstown Center, Sharp's project cleverly lured in a retailing giant with the promise of ten acres of land, an enticement too attractive for Hofheinz to counter. As a result, Hofheinz divided the land that he had acquired for mall development into smaller parcels, primarily for home development. He then sold it off in pieces and allocated much of the proceeds to paying off the loans he had secured in order to buy that land.

Instead of sulking in defeat, Hofheinz continued to explore new opportunities. With the mall project now off of his desk, he was ready to put his vast knowledge and energy to work with the express desire of bringing his beloved city into national prominence. Not too long after he abandoned the shopping mall project, he became determined to bring to fruition the holy grail of all Houston area development, the Astrodome, as his crowning achievement.

The historian Jason Chrystal offers substantial evidence that Roy Hofheinz was not the first individual in Houston to conceptualize a multipurpose stadium, despite his leading role in making such a project possible. Chrystal points to Houston city council-man Matt Wilson, oilman Glenn McCarthy, and a five-member parks commission, all approved by Harris County as advocates for the concept at a time when Hofheinz was still focusing his energies on possible mall construction. All of them believed that Houston, which by 1957 was the United States' eighth most pop-ulous city, deserved to be recognized as a Major League city, with Wilson recommending a $5 million bond issue to finance a pub-licly constructed stadium.[18] In addition, McCarthy had advocated for an enclosed structure, one with a roof that might be retracted instead of one of fixed design.[19]

Outside of Houston, New York City power broker Robert Moses had envisioned building a municipally controlled, all-purpose sta-dium in Flushing Meadows, Queens, for Walter O'Malley's Brook-lyn Dodgers during the 1950s. It was eventually built as Shea Stadium, but after much acrimony between the two men, Moses was unable to convince O'Malley to work with him. O'Malley coun-tered the Moses concept with a proposal for a domed ballpark in Brooklyn. He first worked with the famed industrial designer Nor-man Bel Geddes, whose designs included heated seats and hot dog vending machines, but after estimated costs began to rise, O'Malley shifted his preferences to the more efficient designs inspired by Buckminster Fuller. Before any construction could unfold in New York, lingering distrust between Moses and O'Malley prompted the team owner's move to Los Angeles after the 1957 season. While this put Fuller's visionary concept on hold, the departure of two teams, the Giants and the Dodgers, from America's most populous city raised some hope that Houston might get a ball club via similar means.[20]

As it happens, William Kirkland, Craig Cullinan, George Kirk-sey, and civic leaders affiliated with the Houston Fat Stock Show and Livestock Exhibition had worked behind the scenes within the Houston Sports Association to attract a ball club long before Hofheinz was brought into the picture. Kirkland was a promi-nent Houston banker, Cullinan was heir to the Texaco petroleum empire, and Kirksey was a national sportswriter turned public relations executive whose true passion was to bring Major League

Baseball to Houston. In 1958 and 1959, a county-level Parks Commission board, with Kirkland at the helm, worked to gain funding and acreage for a new ballpark as a way to attract a team.

These men laid the groundwork for what was projected to be an all-purpose outdoor stadium that would be connected to an arena, gaining the necessary approvals from voters to fund $20 million in taxpayer bonds for the project. The measure was approved by Harris County voters by more than a three-to-one margin on July 26, 1958. The leaders of the board visited other cities while exploring site options. By early 1960, after hitting turbulence in the site selection process, these leaders were frustrated and deeply concerned that plans to attract a Major League Baseball team might fall through.

As a baseball fan and Houston civic booster, Hofheinz remained aware of the plans as they unfolded, but with the mall project on his plate, he generally remained in the background. In early 1960 Bob Smith, a wealthy oil tycoon and real estate magnate, was brought in for advice when Kirksey and Cullinan felt they had hit a brick wall. Smith indicated that to secure his further involvement, the two men would have to meet with Hofheinz.

Smith had served as a leader in various capacities while Hofheinz was mayor. Shortly after Hofheinz became mayor, he appointed Smith to head up civil defense for the city, and Smith agreed to do the task for a salary of one dollar per year. Cold War sensibilities ensured that this was a high-profile position, but Hofheinz felt Smith's insights and talent might be of greater service to Houston. He tapped Smith to head up a committee to explore the fast-growing city's future. They had collaborated on various real estate deals over the years, and in the process the two had developed an abiding trust and respect for each other.

When contacted about the stadium project, Hofheinz was thrilled to step up and assist the effort, moving away from any work related to a shopping center immediately. Hofheinz had an abundance of insights as to how a large sports and entertainment complex might be configured.

In his view, constructing an outdoor stadium as anything more than a temporary measure would be a mistake and would jeopardize the profitability of any incoming Major League team. Fan comfort propelled Hofheinz's recommendation. "I knew with our heat, humidity, and rain, that the best chance for success was a weather-proofed, all-purpose stadium," he asserted. Recognizing that constituencies such as the Houston Fat Stock Show would be partners in the effort, he further asserted that "we had to have a stadium that would be a spectator's paradise, but also one that could be used for events other than sports."[21]

However, fan comfort could not be the sole driver of construction. Because Houston had not yet secured a team, player comfort and the ability to impress old-guard Major League owners were also considerations. Baseball expert Roger Kahn noted that in the brief time before the Astrodome was completed, "visiting ballplayers complained about mosquitoes as big as vampires." Dodgers pitcher Sandy Koufax noted that the mosquitoes were so large that "some of the bugs are twin engine jobs."[22]

Understanding that getting Major League owners in other cities on board was a prerequisite to obtaining a Major League team, Smith and Hofheinz rolled up their sleeves and went to work. At a September 8, 1960, meeting of the Houston Sports Association (HSA), Smith took over as chairman of the board, with Cullinan assuming the role of president. Kirksey was made executive vice president, serving as a public relations front man and liaison with the many baseball people he had known from his time as a sportswriter. Hofheinz and Bud Adams, an influential oil executive, were appointed vice presidents. At the urging of fellow oilman Lamar Hunt, Adams invested in a football franchise in the newly formed American Football League, a competitor of the long-established National Football League. The HSA was committed to having a football presence in the new facility as a way to bring in additional revenue to fund construction debt.

Smith and Hofheinz insisted on maintaining a controlling interest in HSA stock, putting up $330,000 worth of capital to do so. Smith's real estate prowess and financial resources would ensure that the land issue would be sufficiently confronted, while Hofheinz would act as a visionary workhorse capable of bringing the stadium project to fruition. Fresh off his dome-based research with Buckminster Fuller, he was more than ready to plunge into the challenge.

Rumors swirled that Hofheinz might contemplate running for a U.S. Senate seat or perhaps for Texas governor, particularly since his close friend Senator Lyndon Johnson had been tapped to run for vice president in 1960. He put those rumors to rest and did everything in his power to ensure that the stadium project would move forward. After facing the harsh sting of mayoral defeat, Hofheinz never ran for elective office again. However, that experience had prepared him for the challenges ahead. He was better positioned to cajole others into buying into his vision for Houston after facing the barbs of political foes and resistance from antagonistic media professionals. He better understood when to work in the limelight and when to work under the radar, although he still preferred to bask in the limelight whenever possible. In addition, he knew the inner workings of government on many levels and had the energy and drive to get things done. Equally important, he held a deep passion for Houston and its people.

With a meeting involving Major League owners scheduled for October 17, Hofheinz attacked his new project with vigor and flair. Ben McGuire, a financial adviser, indicated that Hofheinz immersed himself in everything he could find on Major League Baseball, reading voraciously and around the clock "so that when he went to see National League owners about a franchise, he could speak their language."[23] He initially believed that private financing for the project was possible and might afford better flexibility during construction, but when advised by various financial experts that tax-supported bonds would assure much lower interest rates, he thoughtfully agreed.

Hofheinz worked closely with Pennsylvania native Stuart Young, an expert carpenter and fabricator who had settled in Houston, creating an impressive $35,000 scale model of a sports dome that displayed the many futuristic amenities envisioned by Hofheinz. When the Houston contingent met with Major League team owners on October 17, Hofheinz delivered an emotional sales pitch. Years of careful preparation by Kirksey, Cullinan, and Kirkland were required to make this meeting possible, but the scale model and Hofheinz's compelling pitch made it difficult for National League owners to react with negativity. Before the meeting was over, Houston was approved for an expansion franchise that was slated to begin play in 1962.

The team's initial name, the Colt .45s, after a popular Old West handgun, reflected long-held Houston stereotypes, yet the proposed futuristic ballpark achieved quite the opposite effect, one that was more in line with Hofheinz's grand vision. After the meeting, National League president Warren Giles posed with a five-foot-wide drawing of the proposed stadium as Kirksey and Hofheinz beamed in victory.

A project as intricate and as revolutionary as the first-ever indoor, air-conditioned ballpark could not be completed in the short timeframe allotted before the team's inaugural season. This meant that Houston would have to either expand Busch Stadium, home of the Minor League Buffs, or quickly build a new, temporary ballpark to meet the Major League deadline. Hofheinz pushed for a temporary ballpark, even though it meant that he would be simultaneously supervising the construction of two venues.

Hofheinz's passion was clearly for the Dome, yet with the bulk of his energies devoted to that project, he still put much vigor and time into getting a temporary ballpark ready for opening day. Colt Stadium was projected to cost $800,000 to build, but by the time all of Hofheinz's touches were installed, the price tag had ballooned to $2 million.

Before plans for a temporary ballpark unfolded, a new public vote was put in place to reconfigure the financing for the Astrodome. At that time, slim hope persisted that the Dome could be constructed in time for the 1962 season. According to county judge Bill Elliott, the newly structured bonds would save Harris County $414,000 per year on what was proposed as an $18 million bond issue. The $20 million worth of bonds that were authorized in 1958 as revenue bonds carried an interest rate of 6 percent, while the proposed tax bonds would be set at a much lower rate of 3.7 percent.[24]

At first Hofheinz and Elliott had hoped to circumvent the electoral process, but uneasy county legislators refused to ratify a measure that would send the plan to the Texas legislature for approval, forcing a public vote on the measure. After much public debate and wrangling, a vote was set for January 31, 1961. Of the $18 million requested, $3 million was estimated for site acquisition, with the $15 million balance to fund construction. Folded into the referendum was a vote on $4 million in road and infrastructure funding, an allocation that would substantially expand roadway capacity surrounding the stadium site. The bond enjoyed highly publicized backing from the *Houston Chronicle* and the *Houston Press*. Writing for the *Chronicle*, Dick Peebles proclaimed that if the bond issue failed, it would "set back sports in Houston at least 10 and probably 20 years" and it would cement the city's reputation as a "hick town" incapable of rewriting its destiny.[25] Meanwhile, Bob Rule of the *Houston Press* lauded the city for being on the verge of building a world-class "showpiece" that would "prove to a doubting United States that Houston really can build the world's first domed stadium."[26] The bond was not without its detractors, including George W. Eddy, whose late January editorial in the *Houston Post* described the bond issue as the most "shameful" event he had observed since his arrival in Houston in 1927, adding that there should be "a pox on the newspapers for supporting this scheme."[27] Writing in the *Post*'s Sound-Off column, Phillip M. Blair charged the HSA and county officials with hastening the bond election for political gain: "What's the hurry?" he wrote. "Are they afraid that if they give us a little more time we'll start thinking of all of the roads and schools that this money would buy?"[28]

While the editorials in the *Houston Chronicle* and *Houston Press* proved to be valuable in securing the bond, the city's African American vote likely made the difference. Hofheinz and Smith sought support from Quentin R. Mease, an influential African American businessman and World War II veteran. Mease and other local leaders championed the bond issue, provided that the Astrodome be opened as an integrated facility, complete with fully integrated drinking fountains and restrooms. Such an initiative would serve as a significant and progressive move in the very early stages of the civil rights era, given that Houston's lunch counters had only been integrated since 1960.[29] In the end, 61,568 voted in favor of the bond and 54,127 voted against the measure.[30]

Hofheinz excitedly worked to begin construction at a 240-acre South Main site that was primarily owned by Bob Smith, with part of the acreage controlled by Hilton Hotels. Permissions were hastily obtained, and excavation began on February 2. Land negotiations still needed to be hammered out, construction issues had to be settled, and the bonds had not yet been sold, creating a strange situation in which the HSA would have to fully finance the excavation work and any other costs in order to continue. Beyond that, architectural plans had yet to be finalized.

Further complicating matters, the HSA was prevented from moving forward, even if it chose to tap HSA funds, because a lawsuit filed by Ned Gill, a printing executive, challenged the constitutionality of the election. The legal challenge went forward mere hours after excavation began.[31] Although the suit was eventually dismissed, a subsequent appeal held up progress further. In April the county agreed to two terms demanded by Gill—first, inclusion of language that the bonds would be fully paid for by stadium revenues, and second, that the $20 million in bonds approved in 1958 would be invalidated.[32] However, that did not mean Hofheinz could resume construction.

Judge Elliott, though typically supportive of the project, asserted that contracts for stadium construction could not be issued until a formal agreement was reached between the HSA and the county and until the bonds were actually sold. The bonds were slated to be put up for sale on August 1, with construction set to unfold on November 1. With these delays, *Houston Post* reporter Marshall Verniaud reported concerns about the potential loss of a Major League franchise while explaining that the prospects of ballpark completion in time for the 1962 season opener were fast evaporating.[33] To forestall such a scenario, state approval was obtained to build a thirty-three-thousand-seat temporary stadium on the 240-acre site.[34] It would be built on the same acreage that was approved for the Dome, allowing Hofheinz to showcase progress on the Dome project every time a fan steered into the parking lot of the temporary ballpark.

Instead of being satisfied with a run-of-the-mill ballpark with traditional features, Hofheinz did his best to make the temporary setting a unique experience for the fans. He steered clear of the traditional drab-green color for the ballpark, blending burnt orange, the team color for Texas's flagship university, with turquoise, flamingo red, and chartreuse. He installed bright umbrellas in a picnic area adjacent to the outfield and contrasted the bright colors with vivid signage and banners. As a harbinger of the Astrodome, he designed expansive seventy-five-foot-long dugouts and installed a club-style restaurant named the Fast Draw Club in the ballpark. With mahogany and brass features, the club featured a western theme that borrowed heavily from the saloon on the popular c b s television program *Gunsmoke.* Membership was available only to season ticket holders at a cost of $150 per season.

Mosquitoes and oppressively high temperatures were commonplace, so concession stands sold repellent as well as cool beverages. The fan experience was shaped by color-coordinated employee uniforms, another Hofheinz idea that was a precursor to what would unfold in the Astrodome. A Dixie-style band was hired to offer cheerful music as fans entered the ballpark, and a corps of 150 female ushers called the Triggerettes wore western-themed outfits while politely escorting fans to their seats. Other employees, from the concession workers to the grounds crew, wore carefully tailored uniforms, too. A *Los Angeles Times* reporter, overwhelmed by the color explosion, suggested that the atmosphere in Houston put many other ballparks to shame.[35] A New York reporter called the ballpark's ambiance "a blend of Disneyland and the old wild west." He further suggested that the new ballpark was "the talk of the majors," an indication that Hofheinz had achieved success.[36]

Hofheinz had done a masterful job in constructing a nontraditional temporary stadium, even collaborating with workers to get parking lot slag delivered and spread just one day before opening day, but the themes and motifs adopted by the Colt .45s did little to recalibrate people's image of Houston as an old-style southwestern city dominated by cattle and oil interests. Although positive national attention helped reaffirm that Houston had achieved Major League status, a transformation of Houston's image, at least on a national scale, would not occur until the Dome project was completed and the world was exposed to the most futuristic ballpark ever built.

Given the complexity of this project, Hofheinz knew that design flaws could undermine the success of the effort and prove exceedingly costly. To avoid such flaws, three architectural and design firms were tapped for their expertise. Praeger, Kavanagh, and Warterbury, a New York–based firm, was brought in as consultants. The firm had successfully designed District of Columbia Stadium (later RFK Stadium), the first modern, all-purpose stadium in Washington DC, a project that was completed in 1961. Like the Astrodome, it was a circular design. In addition, they had been named architects of record for another all-purpose stadium to be built by Gotham power broker Robert Moses in Flushing Meadows, Queens.

Two Houston-based firms were hired to serve as principal architects: Wilson, Morris, Crain, and Anderson and Hermon Lloyd and W. B. Morgan. Robert Minchew led the Wilson, Morris, Crain, and Anderson team, with James P. Muller taking charge for Lloyd and Morgan. To add further technical insight, Walter P. Moore and Associates, a Houston-based firm, was brought on board as structural engineers, with Kenneth E. Zimmerman overseeing the complex engineering process necessary to make the Dome a reality.

Fearing potential technical challenges and cost overruns, Hofheinz made an attempt to corner architect S. I. Morris early in the process, indicating that he had been in contact with others who were confident the Dome project was feasible. When Morris hesitated slightly in indicating that his firm would rise to the challenge, Hofheinz bluntly asserted, "If you don't think you can do it, I'm going to hire Buckminster Fuller." Morris's firm took on the project. After looking over all possible options, including the potential for a retractable dome, Morris determined that a lamella truss system was more practical than Fuller's geodesic dome design. In keeping with his willingness to explore all options, Hofheinz was in contact with Dodgers owner Walter O'Malley in order to determine what he had learned in his failed quest to build an indoor facility for the Brooklyn Dodgers several years earlier. O'Malley offered various insights, while suggesting that his motivation was to avoid the financial loss that came with rain cancellations.[37]

With roadwork for freeways adjacent to the stadium site underway, the Harris County Commissioners Court approved a $430,311 bid for excavation on December 19, 1961, awarding the contract to Jack Kraack, Incorporated. Frank Newman, a representative of the architects, suggested that the excavation work be undertaken as general contracts were being solicited. The hope was that builders would be able to examine soil conditions and other factors as the work was underway, with the possibility that such information might allow for lower overall bids.[38] Unfortunately, as plans came together, it became increasingly apparent that the $15 million allocated for construction would be insufficient. Hofheinz tried to gain $750,000 in federal funding after receiving indications that the U.S. Department of Defense might consider allocating tax dollars for a fallout shelter, but the unsuccessful attempt to do so cost the project time, human resources, and money.

By May 1962 the architects were asserting that $15 million for construction would be woefully inadequate, but specific figures were elusive since the size and scope of the project were unprecedented.[39] The prospect of moving forward on Hofheinz's vision was challenged by an alternative construction proposal offered by Welden F. Appelt, a pipeline bridge contractor. Although Appelt had no tangible record of stadium building, the county commissioners, in an effort to break the cost-overrun logjam, met with him to determine whether his ideas had merit. He explained that he could build a retractable roof structure with a Quonset hut–type design for less than $6 million. Cost savings, he explained, could be achieved by using the hollow support tubing as air-conditioner ducts and sandwiching insulation between sheets of aluminum that would make up the exterior shell. One concern was the impact that high winds might have on the exterior, since Houston was within range for hurricane-force winds.

Hofheinz also rejected the feasibility of the idea, arguing that this alternative would not have the capacity to generate the necessary revenue to pay the construction costs because the design would place seats "so far removed from the sports arena that binoculars and transistor radios would be needed for the fan to know what was going on." After consulting with architects, the commissioners rejected the concept with the hope that bids, once solicited, would bring promising news.[40]

In the interim, the HSA and county commissioners battled over finances, with infighting swirling within the HSA membership. The unease and uncertainty on both fronts prompted some to question whether the HSA was acting as a responsible public steward. The county commissioners and the HSA met in November to resolve payment issues and long-term contractual details, eventually hammering out an agreement that would defer HSA lease payments until the new facility was completed, with $99,898 tendered as the HSA payment for 1962.[41]

HSA infighting took shape with Bud Adams leading the charge against the Smith and Hofheinz team. Adams, a 10 percent owner of HSA shares, expressed frustration with a lack of opportunities to provide input and his feelings of uncertainty about the future. He indicated that his football team, the Houston Oilers, despite losing money, would remain at Jeppesen Stadium instead of moving into the HSA-controlled Colt Stadium as anticipated.[42] He also offered to sell his team for $2.5 million but indicated that it lost him money in 1961, a confession that may have undermined any potential follow-through on his offer. With Adams's displeasure on record, the HSA had to adjust to the revenue loss that would unfold if professional football games could not be counted on in the future.

As 1962 came to a close, Bob Smith decided to double down on his investment in Roy Hofheinz as the administrative leader of the HSA. As infighting unfolded within the HSA—and with concerns swirling around spending levels related to stadium construction—Smith agreed to buy back the shares of all but four HSA stockholders at the price they initially paid. Shortly thereafter, on December 12, Bob Smith was reelected HSA chairman, with Hofheinz assuming the role of vice chair and president. Craig Cullinan, a founding investor, tendered his shares for sale, indicating that "the departure of these stockholders left Hofheinz more entrenched than ever before."[43]

As the restructuring unfolded, Hofheinz was faced with a dilemma. The architects had made it fully clear that cost overruns were inevitable. Bids from the general contractors, once submitted, confirmed that their assessments were correct. The low bid came from H. A. Lott, Inc., a Houston firm, and Minneapolis-based Johnson, Drake, and Piper. The joint bid came in at $19,440,000. With slightly more than $13 million remaining from the 1961 bond issue, that meant that even with no budgeting for other issues, construction alone would exceed $6 million more than was available to spend.[44]

Hofheinz and the county commissioners worked to identify all other reasonable costs as well as potential areas to cut so as to determine what would be required to move forward. Parking, extra land acquisition costs, and added architectural and planning fees all meant that approximately $9 million was the minimum amount needed to move forward. The county commissioners determined that a $9.6 million bond issue would cover what was needed without forcing Hofheinz to chop major items from the project. The Houston Sports Association would have to agree to fund $15 million to forestall the need for a tax hike, and yet another bond referendum was set to take place on December 22, the Saturday before Christmas.

The mood of Houston was not nearly as optimistic as it had been in 1960 and 1961, but Houston's citizens also knew that failure on this scale might subject their city to ridicule on a national stage. In contrast to prior elections, Hofheinz was less prominently involved in any up-front attempt to persuade the public, perhaps as a calculated response to public skepticism that cost overruns may have created the recent infighting among HSA stockholders. Nevertheless, the criticism launched at Hofheinz, even if indirect, was stinging. W. Gail Reeves, a former city council member and a longtime Hofheinz foe, argued that "the domed stadium has been misrepresented, mishandled, and mismanaged." He asserted that taxes would rise if the bond issue were to be approved, while strongly advocating high turnout to defeat the bond issue.[45]

Even though no legitimate number crunching could demonstrate that taxpayers would not absorb some of the construction costs, a core argument was that taxpayers would not see an increase of any kind because the county's rapid population growth would offset the need for any tax increase.[46] Labor leaders, Fat Stock Show officials, minority groups, and local newspapers lined up to support the referendum, whether as the result of a behind-the-scenes effort by Hofheinz or not.[47]

To suggest that the overruns were not out of line and wasteful, the *Houston Chronicle* compared the costs of the Dome project to those of three open-air stadiums, one under construction in New York at a projected cost of $20.5 million and two fully completed stadiums in Washington DC and Los Angeles with completed costs of $20 million and $22 million, respectively. The *Chronicle*'s editorial further suggested that Houston's plan was so superior that it would make people in the other cities "green with envy" once the Dome was completed.[48] If positive reinforcement was not sufficient to move voters, a *Houston Chronicle* article appeared in the sports section a day before the vote. It featured National League president Warren Giles ominously asserting that a negative vote might cause Houston to lose its Major League team.[49]

With the high stakes apparent, Houstonians approved the bond measure by a vote of 42,911 to 36,110. With a giant hole dug and slightly more than two years to build the most ambitious sports facility the world had ever seen, Bob Smith recognized that public trust would be undermined if they needed to seek additional funding. In response, as the election results became apparent, Smith stated that "by the time the doors open, we hope that every person who voted against the bonds today will be glad the stadium was built." After some haggling about setting the timetable for construction, the bonds were sold on January 24 to a Chicago bank, gaining an amazingly low 3.155 rate, a milestone that Judge Elliott stated "represented a tremendous trust in Harris County." The Houston and Minneapolis contractors with the low bid were brought on board and began their work in March.[50]

Hofheinz readied for a tight building schedule. He told the evangelist Billy Graham that booking a show in 1964 would not be possible. The challenge now was to get everything ready for the 1965 baseball season. Initial hopes of booking 1964 political conventions had all but evaporated, yet Hofheinz remained optimistic and hard-charging as the foundation was poured and the lamella trusses were hoisted into place.[51]

The architectural and engineering challenges confronted by Ralph Anderson, Hermon Lloyd, Robert Minchew, S. I. Morris, Kenneth Zimmerman, and countless others involved in the massive project may have been daunting, but Hofheinz interacted with each of them often, offering input and suggestions as construction neared completion. Lloyd indicated that Hofheinz "didn't have to sleep much. He just had endless energy. He was always running on our tails. He was always getting new ideas and saying, 'let's try this.' . . . He was irritating at times, but not to the point where it wasn't helpful."[52]

Once the skyboxes were in place, Hofheinz moved in furniture, began to reside in the Dome, and according to Bill Mackay, former president of the American Seating Company, "every time the Judge saw someone loafing on the job, he'd get on his radio." Mackay continued, "The Judge had to have his hand in every angle of construction of the Astrodome. The fact that it is one of the most marvelous, magnificent buildings in the world today is partly due to his attention to the smallest detail."[53]

Nevertheless, the Astrodome was not the sole project managed by Hofheinz. On February 13, 1964, the Houston Livestock Show and Rodeo's executive committee agreed to terms with the HSA to construct a massive five hundred thousand square foot building adjacent to the Dome, a facility that when combined with the Astrodome would provide Houston with more total exhibition space than any other complex in America. Hofheinz was also contemplating opening a grand entertainment complex called Astroworld, a magnificent theme park that would create a world-class entertainment district unlike anything found in any other city in the world.[54] The adjacent livestock show exhibition center would be better known as the Astrohall.

In 1964 Hofheinz and Smith faced an unexpected curveball that had the potential to undermine their project revenues. Mayor

Louis Welch, a Hofheinz adversary, pushed hard for the expansion of a downtown civic center, one that might draw convention business away from the Astrodome. As the $7.3 million public referendum neared, Hofheinz was under tighter scrutiny than ever, with some in the public suspecting that his hard work on the Dome might be driven by personal greed. His push for luxury skyboxes as a way to bring greater revenues to the project may have contributed to that image, whether fair or unfair.

The mayor cleverly turned objections from Hofheinz and Smith into political fodder, suggesting that the project he wanted to build was located in a more centralized downtown location, had the endorsement of the chamber of commerce, and was being constructed solely for the benefit of Harris County's citizens, "not for the private profit of two individuals."[55] The voters turned out and supported the bond issue, a move that put increasing pressure on Smith and Hofheinz to lure events and activities to the new Dome and its adjacent exhibition space. Although disappointed, Hofheinz indicated that he supported and respected the will of the people but cautioned that he likely would not have supported paying the county a sizeable $750,000 per year in rent if he had known at the outset that the Dome would have a major competitor for convention space.[56] Instead of sulking, Hofheinz kept his eye carefully focused on completion of the Dome as well as the various other responsibilities he had accumulated. Handling the overall management of a Major League Baseball team, supervising operations for a temporary ballpark, following through on plans for a nearby exhibition hall, and overseeing all aspects of construction of the first ever fully enclosed, air-conditioned stadium may have overwhelmed any other person, but Roy Hofheinz had grown up taking on challenge after challenge.

After friction unfolded with the Colt Firearms Company regarding the use of the Colt .45 name on fan merchandise, Hofheinz changed the team's name to the Astros, which he announced at the National League's winter meetings. He continued to push forward with negotiations involving the Houston Oilers, despite an icy relationship with team owner Bud Adams. In December Hofheinz was able to secure a ten-year agreement that, with the cooperation of the mercurial football team owner, might ensure uninterrupted tenancy in the Astrodome for a full decade.[57]

Hofheinz was not intimidated when he saw opportunities, even if his plate was already full. As his life unfolded, he developed an attitude that hard work and brainpower could overcome almost any challenge imaginable. As April 1965 approached, he made plans to unveil the greatest sports palace ever built. In true Hofheinz fashion, his plans for an opening extravaganza were as opulent and impressive as anyone could imagine. He secured a commitment from the world champion New York Yankees to play an exhibition game against the newly renamed Houston Astros. Further, he gained a commitment from his close friend President Lyndon Johnson to attend the game, indicating he would be watching the game from the posh Presidential Suite, high above the action. He also booked Texas governor John Connally and twenty-one NASA astronauts to throw out ceremonial first pitches.

The party that unfolded on April 9, 1965, garnered dramatic national attention, as Bob Smith, Roy Hofheinz, Craig Cullinan, and George Kirksey enjoyed the fruits of many years of planning, struggle, and hard work. All of the Houston newspapers featured bold, front-page stories, while newspapers elsewhere made sure to cover the event, too. In fitting fashion, the home team won 2–1 before a crowd of 47,876, though Yankee hero and Oklahoma native Mickey Mantle slugged a home run for the Yankees. *Houston Chronicle* sports editor Dick Peebles described the opening exhibition as "an artistic as well as financial and every other kind of success."[58] *Houston Post* reporter Sandra Bybee stated that the event was "a tableau of society and fashion, entertainment and prestige."[59] Even the ballplayers were impressed. Astros pitcher Larry Dierker remembered "crossing the concourse, passing through a tunnel leading to the field-box seats. The interior of the stadium was breathtakingly beautiful, like a huge flying saucer. I thought I had just walked into the next century."[60]

The new palace gained widespread attention well beyond Texas. *Montreal Star* reporter Andy O'Brien suggested that the new indoor facility would change the overall direction of sports in a dramatic manner.[61] *New York Times* music and drama expert Howard Taubman asserted that the Dome was "bigger than show biz, even Texas style."[62] Despite many accolades, lingering concerns remained that fly balls could be lost in the less predictable indoor environment, particularly during sunny day games. Baseball purists were much less likely to cozy up to the idea of indoor baseball.

The early coverage tended to focus on a long list of awe-inspiring amenities. Instead of selling just hot dogs, beer, and soft drinks, as was the custom in other ballparks, the Dome afforded every fan restaurant options generally unavailable in America's stadiums at the time. Although the luxurious skyboxes and club-style restaurants gave the wealthy a unique experience, Hofheinz offered less affluent fans a comfort level previously unheard-of in modern sports. All fans could access some of the restaurants, and every customer was afforded a padded theater-style seat and air-conditioned comfort.

The Astrodome still had a natural grass surface, one that was painstakingly developed by agricultural experts at Texas A&M University, but that would change in 1966 when a plastic substitute for grass was installed because tracking fly balls remained a complex and difficult to resolve problem. Even without the installation of artificial turf, Hofheinz had caused a seismic shift in how sports were viewed in America. His innovation brought unbridled luxury to the rich, who may have grown accustomed to such amenities, though perhaps not as part of sports spectatorship. Yet Hofheinz had raised the bar of luxury for the average citizen, too.

The construction process took many years to unfold, but Hofheinz had achieved his goal. In 1962, as plans to build the stadium were taking shape, *Sports Illustrated* writer Roy Terrell heaped praise on Hofheinz for his brilliance, suggesting with hyperbole that he "sleeps only when there is nothing else to do, and would, if charged with the U.S. space program, have John Glenn in orbit by the astronaut's third birthday."[63]

Thirty-two years later, *Sports Illustrated* celebrated its fortieth anniversary by identifying key individuals who most profoundly changed the sports environment in the twentieth century. The 1994 special issue appropriately identified Roy Hofheinz and Roone Arledge as the two people at the top who merited this unique recognition. Fittingly, both had adapted to dramatic changes in postwar America to innovate the fan experience in ways few others could have imagined at that time.

Both saw things with a similarly creative impulse, even if each of these men took an entirely different trajectory to achieve his goals. Each focused on creatively reshaping the fan experience while adapting to new and emerging technologies. Arledge, as a young television sports producer in the 1960s, sought to bring the fan experience, as it unfolded within the ballpark, to the sports fan through the television screen decades before the first large digital TVs would begin to transform American households. In an often-quoted memo to his ABC production crew, Arledge famously asserted that instead of simply covering a game competently, as was past practice, "we are going to add show business to sports!"[64]

In a similar vein, when Hofheinz was interviewed by *Newsweek* magazine, he asserted that when opening a stadium, "like it or not, you're in show business."[65] Arledge was trying to bring the fan experience into the home, while Hofheinz was trying to bring the home-based comforts of a newly emerging suburban lifestyle into the stadium. Roy Hofheinz and Roone Arledge were insightful enough to see the ways that new media technologies and broader consumer trends were recalibrating the way fans consumed sports and entertainment in general.

Noting these changes in society, Hofheinz invested vast sums to adjust the fan experience in ways other people were incapable of grasping. The Astrodome's massive $2 million, three-hundred-ton scoreboard was the first true large-screen TV ever built in America. Those who have seen it function understand that it was an experience that cannot ever be fully explained or replicated. It spanned 474 feet wide, over 100 feet longer than the length of an entire football field. While higher resolution and greater picture clarity have been achieved with digital technologies, with the Astrodome scoreboard, Hofheinz was able to create a larger-than-life fan experience that no other sports executive had envisioned being possible.

The scoreboard offered visitors thundering, over-the-top cavalry charges intended to rally the home team, unique home run celebrations that featured an animated Dome's roof exploding open, video images of various individuals, and professionally produced commercials between innings. *Sports Illustrated* writer Joe Jares explained that "the scoreboard is so much a part of the show under the dome that spectators at early season games even applauded the between-innings picture-screen commercials for clients like the Jones Apothecary and Morton's Chip-O's."[66] The ever-creative Hofheinz used this massive screen to raise revenue, selling advertising packages that ran between innings long before anyone else considered such strategies. However, Hofheinz was savvy enough to use the scoreboard primarily for entertainment, bringing a unique feature to fans that they would not be able to enjoy while in the comfort of their living rooms.

Additionally, the posh environment he created attracted a new generation of fans to the sports world and prompted rival sports executives to rethink their marketing tactics to adjust to a rapidly changing, consumer-driven environment that would later have to compete against video games, pay-per-view, and streaming online technologies.

Hofheinz devoted inordinate amounts of energy to getting the Astrodome built. He assembled the best team possible and oversaw virtually every aspect of design and construction. In the process, his reputation went through some challenges, particularly as the initially projected $20 million for the project proved to be inadequate. However, once the regal splendor of the Harris County Domed Stadium, as it was officially known, was opened to the public, the awe-inspiring results ensured Hofheinz a unique place in sports history.

Yet Hofheinz was not willing to take a chance that history would look kindly on his years of hard work and sacrifice. The Houston Sports Association, under his leadership, produced a 260-page book that provided the public with "the complete story of the world's first Domed Stadium." In the first page of noncommercial content after the opening welcome, his friend Lyndon Johnson, now the president of the United States, praised the "imagination, energy, and sheer determination" of those behind the project, while asserting that "the Astrodome will stand as deserved tribute to the genius of its planners, to be welcomed by all those who respect industry and dedication."[67]

Many others were instrumental in contributing to this massive construction project. The story of the first-ever domed stadium provides a unique look at how American technology and persistence reshaped leisure patterns and the general nature of spectatorship on a global scale. Although Hofheinz's reputation may have taken some hits as the Astrodome's construction process unfolded, the arc of history has demonstrated that this bold Houstonian, with all of his quirks and eccentricities, is likely to have had more of an impact on how stadiums are planned, constructed, and designed than any other person on planet Earth.

2

Of Cows and Construction
Houston's Livestock Show and Rodeo

Before the Astrodome was built, Houston was best known for oil and livestock, probably in that order. As a result, it should not be surprising that outsiders often saw Texaco heir Craig Cullinan Jr. as the prime mover in early deliberations to bring a professional sports team to Houston. Given his family's reputation in the oil industry, such a conclusion was not out of line with conventional stereotypes. When baseball executive Gabe Paul contemplated taking over as the first general manager of the Houston franchise, he said that as he approached the opportunity, he thought Cullinan was in charge, even though well-connected Houstonians knew that Roy Hofheinz was running things and Bob Smith was the big money behind the overall operation.[1]

During the 1950s, outsiders and insiders alike regarded the oil and cattle stereotypes as valid. Political decisions and news reports from Houston did little to disprove this conventional wisdom. Houston's oil industry was an industrial giant that fueled the American economy in numerous ways, flooding the market with technology and products that had an amazing impact worldwide. During the 1960s and 1970s, Houston emerged as a global leader in oil extraction technology, and despite a shift of oil production to numerous foreign locales from the 1960s onward, Houston still impressively produced two-thirds of all petroleum industry tools during the 1980s.[2]

The Houston Ship Channel, an engineering marvel that solidified Houston's role as a commercial and industrial force, was made possible through the leadership and vision of Joseph S. Cullinan, a petroleum industry legend and Craig Cullinan Jr.'s grandfather. During his tenure as president of the Houston Chamber of Commerce from 1913 to 1919, Joseph Cullinan testified frequently in

Washington DC in an effort to improve Houston's position as a commercial center. He pushed tirelessly to gain extensive federal funds for the Houston Ship Channel project and to advocate for local funding of measures that would deepen and widen the channel, moves that allowed a city fifty miles inland from the Gulf of Mexico to emerge as a major industrial port.[3] World War II and the postwar economy intensified the need for oil and petroleum-based products, as well as other war-related goods, raising Houston's stature and significance in the process.

The ship channel did much to advance the oil industry. However, the channel was used by manufacturers, importers, and agricultural entrepreneurs, too, making Houston a major commercial hub. Houston's role as a port city made it a natural distribution point for agricultural goods and livestock. Despite the power of the oil industry over the entire region, the cattle trade still served as a commercial and cultural force within the community and beyond. As a result, Houston historian Jason Chrystal has observed that men involved with the Houston Livestock Show and Rodeo were "some of the wealthiest, most powerful, and politically connected in Houston history."[4]

As such, it should be no surprise that the Houston Livestock Show and Rodeo was a major force whose leadership was sought to get the Astrodome built. Roy Hofheinz, Bob Smith, Craig Cullinan Jr. and George Kirksey needed the backing of various power brokers within what was then called the Houston Fat Stock Show and Rodeo organization in order to move Astrodome construction forward. Without their involvement, the case for construction would be weakened considerably, and public support to fund the project might have failed.

As Houston evolved from a medium-sized city to a major metropolitan area, its cow town image lingered, in part as a result of stereotypes but also as a result of the enormous success of the Houston Livestock Show and Rodeo. From somewhat modest origins in 1932, the Houston Fat Stock Show, as it was originally named, has expanded from a week of activities into an impressive three-week-long extravaganza that features an extraordinary slate of world-class entertainers. Its fame is sufficiently impressive that *American Cowboy* magazine has described it as thriving "on the theory that bigger is better and biggest is best." In many ways, it is the city's premiere annual event—and one for which "no detail is spared in the production of the astronomical extravaganza." Each year the rodeo requires the energy and commitment of more than twelve thousand volunteers, and its annual attendance regularly exceeds two million spectators.[5]

Luminaries such as Elvis Presley, Bob Dylan, Garth Brooks, Selena, Michael Jackson, and Taylor Swift have been featured, and in 2014 alone the Houston Livestock Show and Rodeo featured twenty major musical acts, including Luke Bryan, Maroon 5, Brad Paisley, Robin Thicke, and Keith Urban. In that same year, more than 2.5 million people attended the events coordinated by this powerful organization.[6] This attendance milestone is far better than the annual draw of many top-tier professional sports teams.

The Houston Livestock Show and Rodeo is a cultural behemoth that is supported by the entire region, not just the affluent and well-connected. Linda Alonzo Saenz asserts that "my parents did not have a lot of money [when I was young], but they would save so we could go." She currently serves as senior vice chair of the three-hundred-person Go Tejano Committee, a unit charged with marketing many of the show's events. She states that throughout her life, the show formed a big part of her "identity as a Houstonian."[7]

Longtime Livestock Show and Rodeo president Leroy Shafer is proud that the event attracts youngsters from agricultural families throughout Texas, who proudly display livestock, indicating "This is the big time, but they have been to county fairs." The extent of its "big-time" stature can be seen in the amount paid for show-related items. Bidders pay as much as $250,000 for grand champion–ranked livestock, student-produced art can fetch as much as $200,000, and enthusiastic families treat winners as celebrities, maintaining contact with these youngsters for many years after their victories. Even a lowly goat, if a prizewinner at the show, can fetch in excess of $150,000 at auction as part of the show's activities.[8]

The Houston Livestock Show and Rodeo is an opportunity for

the entire state to place its considerable agricultural muscle on display. Shafer proudly calls it "the world's largest rodeo and largest fair in North America." In 2012 alone, rodeo-related activities donated $18.8 million to scholarships, grants, and other educational opportunities, all benefiting youngsters devoted to agricultural improvement throughout the state.[9]

Like many Houston institutions, its roots were humble. Before moving to the Astrodome, the show took place in much smaller downtown facilities. The first show was spearheaded and promoted by James W. Sartewell, a take-charge Houston businessman who was president of the local stockyards. He was convinced that an annual livestock showcase had the capacity to improve breeding and cattle-raising practices, so he organized the first show in 1932. That first Houston Fat Stock Show lost $2,800.[10] It was held in Sam Houston Hall, the same cavernous but spartan twenty-five-thousand-seat capacity, wooden facility that connected Roy Hofheinz and Lyndon Baines Johnson during Houston's hosting of the 1928 Democratic National Convention.

Six years after it began, in 1938, the Houston Fat Stock Show was moved into the brand new Sam Houston Hall, with 1937 as the only year in which the show did not take place. During that off year, in anticipation of the move to a much more modern facility, a parade and rodeo were held and were subsequently woven into the annual event. The more modern facility served the show well, but over time a desire emerged to further expand the event.

When the show's attendance slumped in the early 1950s, Fat Stock Show executives met at Houston's famed Shamrock Hotel and convinced local media to cover a seventy-five-mile cattle drive from Brenham to Houston. E. H. Marks, a lifelong cattle rancher, invited newspaper and radio reporters to join the drive, and its arrival in Houston was met with curiosity and fanfare that were replicated with increased enthusiasm in future years. The publicity stunt was responsible for the creation of the Salt Grass Trail Association, an organization that continues the cattle drive to this day. More importantly, however, the high-profile cattle drive was credited with reviving the Fat Stock Show, as it attracted imitators elsewhere who helped to further expand the Houston event.[11]

After the Salt Grass Trail Ride gained prominence and spurred imitation, rural communities were more viscerally embedded into the fabric of the Fat Stock Show. This prompted an expansion during the 1950s that made the construction of new facilities much more important to the organization's ongoing success. The show's evolution from a regional agricultural showcase in the 1930s to a multimillion-dollar annual extravaganza required a transition into a larger, first-rate facility. Once built, the Astrodome would permit the Fat Stock Show and Rodeo to grow into the vast and diverse program that it is today.

An energetic and ambitious Archer Romero took over as president of the Houston Fat Stock Show in 1954, serving until 1957. He had been elected vice president in 1951 and was instrumental in supporting some of the early 1950s publicity efforts that ensured the show's growth, including the initial Salt Grass Trail Association's annual cattle drive. He was among the influential voices who worked from the Shamrock Hotel and elsewhere to lay the foundation for the organization's substantial growth during the 1950s and 1960s.

Before Romero's tenure as president began, live musical performances were added to the slate of events, as was the rodeo. Musical acts began with popular regional talent such as local honky-tonk bands, then moved to big-time stars. The show booked the internationally known cowboy, Texas native, and celebrity entertainer Gene Autry in 1942 as its first nationally recognized musical act. Autry made five additional appearances after this first performance, and other major acts followed.

However, Romero had a broader vision for the multiday event, unwilling to focus on just entertainment and exhibition. He worked with colleagues to develop plans that would turn the show into an even more prominent Texas-based extravaganza that was much more viscerally intertwined with the culture of the entire state. In 1954 he formed and chaired the Go Texan Committee. Romero and his committee colleagues created and introduced Go Texan Day, a highly popular preshow day of activity that encouraged participants to wear Texan-style clothing while prompting the entire community to buy event tickets, distribute posters, and display publicity materials.[12]

As Go Texan Day increased the popularity of the Houston Fat Stock Show and Rodeo, Romero introduced the first major scholarship award, presenting $2,000 to student Ben Dickerson in 1957, a sum that would exceed $16,000 in today's dollars. The scholarship program was positively received, with livestock show historian and journalist Jim Saye calling this community service concept something that officials soon recognized as "an area with the potential for future growth." Saye has asserted that, over time, the scholarship program evolved into a "centerpiece" of the entire event.[13] The vast allocation of resources to student-based scholarships in subsequent years provided incentives and motivation for youth to invest their time, effort, and brainpower into endeavors that would improve agricultural productivity throughout the state. As such, the vast expansion of scholarship programs in the decades after 1957 had a positive impact that was far-reaching and profound.

Romero's success as Houston Fat Stock Show and Rodeo president propelled him to serve on a commission formed by the Harris County Commissioners Court in February 1958. The commission's primary purpose was to explore various options and strategies to achieve the goal of stadium construction. The move was preceded by the Texas State Legislature's passage of Senate Bill 23 on October 10, 1957. This legislation gave Harris County the ability to issue bonds to build a new stadium. The legislation's passage triggered the formation of the Harris County Board of Parks Commissioners. The seven-member commission was assembled to move stadium financing, construction strategies, and land acquisition plans forward so that Houston could inch closer to achieving Major League status.

In addition to Romero, the composition of the commission was heavily weighted toward banking and oil interests. It was chaired by William Kirkland, one of Houston's most influential bankers. The Princeton University alumnus with a law degree from the University of Texas served as board chairman of the powerful First City National Bank. Romero was second in command. Also serving were Herbert Allen, Eddie Dyer, E. B. Mansfield, Corbin J. Robertson, and Wilton Roper.

The commission made plans to visit and gather information from various cities. The fact-finding extended to more than a dozen cities, with a goal of sorting out what worked well and what might be improved upon so that Houston could enter the stadium-building process with advantages previously unavailable to projects elsewhere.[14] They visited Baltimore and Milwaukee as well as California, where plans for ballpark construction were underway in Los Angeles and San Francisco. Commission members investigated California's impressive livestock shows during the fact-finding process, with Archer Romero spearheading a trip to the California State Fair Exhibition grounds. Exploring what transpired at San Francisco's Cow Palace and at fairgrounds in Oklahoma was also part of the commission's itinerary, suggesting that any stadium construction plans undertaken were likely to fully consider the needs of the Houston Fat Stock Show and Rodeo, not just the needs of professional sports teams.[15]

The fact-finding process steered the commission in the direction of a multipurpose stadium, something that had not been built yet in other cities, although Washington DC and New York had plans underway to achieve a similar goal. The commission felt that such a building strategy would give Houston an advantage over other cities, and a multipurpose design would ensure a degree of cost savings in the process. *Houston Chronicle* sports editor Dick Peebles explained that the commission believed that "the modern design eliminates the necessity of duplicating plumbing, wiring, restrooms, concession stands, and numerous other facilities."[16]

The commission further expressed a desire to construct a facility that could host more than just football and baseball games, identifying in particular livestock exhibitions, conventions, and trade shows. The initially proposed multipurpose design would include a rounded, open-air stadium with moveable lower-level seats that could be flexibly reconfigured for a variety of purposes as needed, and the commission indicated that the complex should have abundant parking.

Beyond that, if the vision of the commission unfolded as recommended, the stadium would have an added feature not yet planned in any other city. The stadium itself would be physically connected to a large, air-conditioned coliseum. This area could be used to host trade shows, conventions, musical entertainment, several activities related to the Fat Stock Show, and a multitude of other regional and national events. Although the livestock exhibition was not central to the construction plans, the adjacent facility, potentially unique to North American sports construction, was prompted, in part, by a desire to ensure that Romero and his Houston Fat Stock Show colleagues would be fully and comfortably in support of the new facility plans.

The commission presented a formal report to the Harris County Commissioners Court on June 20, 1958, recommending that voters be asked to authorize a $20 million bond sale "involving, of course, no taxes . . . for the purpose of the development of stadium and related facilities." The report's recommended date was July 26, 1958, a day already set aside for a primary election. The commission emphasized that Houston was the largest city without a Major League Baseball team in the nation, while indicating that "the people of the Gulf Coast already look to Houston for much of their sports, recreation, and amusements, and if big league baseball and professional football were offered, they would be attracted more than ever to our city." The most important uses for the facility, as specifically outlined in the report, were: "1) Major League Baseball, 2) Football, professional and college, 3) The Fat Stock Show, [and], 4) various other outdoor and indoor events such as music festivals, religious meetings, industrial exhibits, horse shows, ice shows, boxing, and youth activities." The report showed Houston's population base exceeding five million people within 250 miles of the city, a range that suggested the citizens of Dallas, San Antonio, and New Orleans might be tapped as potential visitors. The graphic further showed that at least one million people were located within an hour's drive of the city.

The commission was emphatic in its emphasis that the project could be undertaken and fully funded without taxpayer subsidy. Despite indications that taxpayer backing of the bond issue was necessary to move forward, the commission projected gross annual revenues of $693,994, an amount sufficient to fully underwrite the cost of the bonds. The report's final sentence offered a tone of advocacy, asserting that "the spirit of progress that has played such a vital role in making Houston the dominant city of the South should be harnessed to this worthwhile project."[17]

The measure was quickly placed on the ballot after gaining the approval of Harris County's Democratic executive board. Because the county primary was an open one, Republicans and Democrats alike were able to vote in this election, but the stadium issue had to compete with a school tax increase and calls for hospital funding.[18]

Nevertheless, a variety of factors made the stadium issue a prominent one as the vote neared. As an example, heavy coverage of a lightweight boxing championship match at the Sam Houston Coliseum four days before the vote raised awareness of the inadequacies of Houston's sports infrastructure. *Houston Post* sports editor Clark Nealon, in particular, brought attention to the inadequate parking and seating capacity that caused chaos and meant thousands of boxing fans were denied access to the bout despite making an effort to attend. Nealon's opinion piece, featured just one day before the election, offered sports fans a powerful rationale to support new construction.[19]

However, voters were primed to support the measure by much more than a single boxing fiasco. On June 24 the Houston Fat Stock Show's executive committee, frustrated at the inadequacies of the Sam Houston Coliseum, announced plans to donate 230 acres of land if the project moved forward as the organization desired. According to the terms, the land, located near the city's South Main area, could be used or sold, with gas and oil rights included in any deal that was brokered, as long as the Fat Stock Show leadership approved of the site selection and project plans. Archer Romero, a strong advocate of the donation, asserted that the land would be given to the county "if the provisions as set forth are met."[20] The offer provided tangible evidence that the Fat Stock Show leadership was fully behind the project and, if the right location were to be chosen, they would enthusiastically move the show's operations to a newly constructed facility. It also guaranteed that the Fat Stock Show hierarchy would play a major role in any deliberations that followed.

Although not as sizzling as the land donation announcement, the Harris County Commissioners Court lent its support to the project, establishing a three-member Citizens' Committee, interestingly described as "non-partisan," to publicly seek support for the project. Among the appointees were L. F. McCollum, president of the Continental Oil Company, Robert E. Smith, a wealthy oilman and real estate entrepreneur, and Gus Wortham, president of American General Insurance Company.[21] These three heavy hitters in turn formulated grassroots committees to build momentum for the stadium initiative at the neighborhood level. They gained the support of the chamber of commerce and several former Major League ballplayers.[22]

While the court-appointed committee and its supporters pushed for the project's success, the Houston Sports Association, then headed by Craig Cullinan Jr. and George Kirksey, worked behind the scenes to ensure that the public would frame the project as an engine for economic development. Ten days before the vote, the HSA brought in Ray Weisbrod, executive vice president of Milwaukee's chamber of commerce, to tout the economic benefits that a professional baseball team brought to his city. Weisbrod asserted that the presence of a Major League team had provided a seven to eight million dollar boost to the region's economy since the team's arrival, while providing the community with positive, family-oriented entertainment.[23]

The flurry of support from leaders, local media, and grassroots sports enthusiasts, along with repeated assurances that stadium revenues would fully fund the project, led to a massive victory on election day, July 26, 1958, with support outpacing negative votes by more than a three-to-one margin. When the votes were fully tallied, the vote was 81,403 in favor of underwriting $20 million in bonds for the project to 24,395 against. In gaining victory, the Fat Stock Show leadership had positioned itself to be a major force in how stadium plans would unfold, though plans at this point were for an open-air stadium connected to a large, air-conditioned auditorium, not a massive dome.

Armed with authorization to move forward on the project, the Harris County Parks Commissioners now focused on securing a location. The promise of Fat Stock Show land offered one pos-sibility, but to guarantee twenty thousand parking spots, more land might be required. Beyond that, they would have to consider whether other sites might be superior to the Fat Stock Show's prof-fered location, so all options were on the table. Land acquisition costs were a factor because these expenses would be bundled into the total cost of construction, making undeveloped and less cen-tral locations potentially more attractive. The 230-acre Fat Stock Show donation gave the organization considerable influence over the decision, yet proposals came in for various locations.

Officials from the North Harris County Chamber of Commerce proposed using acreage that was slated for new airport construc-tion as one option, arguing that the northern option had distinct advantages other sites could not match. Among the most compel-ling arguments were close proximity to a vast network of inter-state highways, the ability to avoid highly congested downtown traffic to get in and out of game events, lower overall land costs, and easier access for visitors from cities north of Houston.[24]

To the south, James Lain, the president of the Galveston Cham-ber of Commerce, lobbied to have the facility built on the other side of the county, suggesting that close proximity to the Gulf Freeway and Galveston County would create synergies between the two counties, particularly with two million tourists visiting the Galveston area each year.[25]

Other ideas came in, with one in particular raising a good amount of attention. The possibility of a stadium on the Memo-rial Park site, land that was sold to Houston at its original cost by the influential Hogg family to be used as parkland, seemed attrac-tive in that it was near downtown, but the site was not locked in and as congested as a downtown location. Nevertheless, when the real estate deal was made, the family had negotiated with then mayor Oscar Holcombe to ensure that any use other than as city parkland would have to be approved by the family.

The Harris County Board of Parks Commissioners evaluated fourteen different sites and determined that the park site was the best. Unfortunately, public outcry over the potential loss of park-land and an eventual veto from Ima Hogg, the family matriarch, moved that option off the table.[26] The Houston Sports Association did not want to begin the construction process with public opposition tainting early planning, so once political leaders indicated a desire to step away from the initially favored site, they pushed no further.

The Memorial Park controversy suggested that the site selection issue would face a difficult political future. That reality was reinforced when Houston mayor Lewis Cutrer backed away from weighing in, quickly pledging neutrality while arguing that site selection was in the hands of the county.[27] The site selection process took over a year to unfold, setting back construction plans accordingly but allowing time to modify the project to fit Roy Hofheinz's vision.

The delay also allowed the sports issue to sort itself out, putting more intense pressure on county officials to resolve the site location issue. Instead of reaching a firm resolution, the site location issue took a circuitous and confusing path. Yet for a brief period, the sports issue seemed to be on a path to resolution.

After numerous delays by Major League Baseball's hierarchy, the process of getting a Major League team to play in Houston seemed to be going nowhere. However, the Houston Sports Association, through the leadership of Craig Cullinan Jr. and George Kirksey, agreed to join the Continental League in 1959. The new baseball league had an uncertain future, but it was being organized by Branch Rickey, a legendary baseball executive with a track record of success.

In football, oil magnate Bud Adams joined with fellow oil baron Lamar Hunt to start a top-tier professional league, too. With their sizeable wealth, Hunt formed the new American Football League and acquired a team, while Adams agreed to step up as one of the league's original owners. Hunt initially located his team in Dallas, while Adams's team would anchor the Houston market. Despite the uncertain future of both the baseball and football ventures, Houston officials believed they would need to resolve the stadium issue quickly to satisfy the needs of both teams.

The baseball issue may have seemed clear-cut early, but as time passed, it became ever more obvious that luring a Major League team would mire the Houston Sports Association in a battle over territorial rights. To gain access to those rights, the HSA would have to negotiate with the local Minor League team, the Houston Buffs, who were demanding a massive amount of money to relinquish their legal claim on the Houston market.

Buffs co-owner Marty Marion, a former Major League star, offered a rent guarantee, suggesting that revenues from his team might allow for the new facility to get started. The move, he asserted, would help the Fat Stock Show. In reality, the offer was less than helpful and served to undermine the Continental League's progress. It sent a clear signal to all involved that the Buffs maintained territorial rights to the Houston market. Speaking for the Board of Parks Commissioners, Kirkland and Romero politely indicated a willingness to work with Marion and the Buffs, but in reality, they wanted no part of housing a Minor League team in the new facility.[28]

Because his football team would play during the cooler fall and winter months, Bud Adams could rent a college facility in a pinch, although he admitted that was not a favored option. The Fat Stock Show hierarchy looked at the uncertainty of the sports issue and contemplated moving in a different direction.

Mayor Cutrer added to the uncertainty by stepping away from his previous pledge of neutrality. He recommended the construction of a new downtown convention center, arguing that Houston could lose revenue if more was not done to shore up the downtown. He argued that an expanded downtown convention center would bring new revenues to downtown hotels and would be close to other services as well. With less than forty acres available for such development, construction of a new facility would require buying higher-priced land on the open market or it would be clearly inadequate to include a stadium as well. The goal of vast parking capacity was also less likely with a downtown site, even if a costly parking garage or underground facility were to be added.

While other cities were locating sports facilities in less central locations to provide abundant parking and easier highway access, a feud was underway about doing the opposite in Houston. Doug Marshall, the president of the Fat Stock Show, appeared to be more willing than Romero to contemplate a downtown location for the organization's future home.[29] While suggesting that federal monies might be sought for such a project, Mayor Cutrer asserted that convention centers were being located downtown in other major cities, and doing so in Houston would ensure "a strong central city."[30]

As was expected, the Board of Parks Commissioners announced that the South Main site was best suited for the construction of a new multipurpose facility that, unlike the downtown proposal, would include space for sports teams.[31] Even though the plan received a prompt and enthusiastic endorsement from Harris County judge Bill Elliott—and it was formulated after careful negotiations with hotel magnate Conrad Hilton and real estate entrepreneur Bob Smith—the mayor's focus on downtown construction created a political divide that unleashed further chaos.

The lack of decisiveness from Fat Stock Show leadership did not help matters, but their goal was to do what was best for that organization, not to set public policy. Unfortunately, their leadership was anything but certain as to what outcome might best achieve their goals for their organization. Cutrer continued his advocacy for a downtown convention center, with the Fat Stock Show's decision likely to determine its fate.[32]

Cutrer suggested that two facilities might eventually coexist but that at the time a downtown coliseum could be completed faster and was more feasible given existing resources. However, before a clear-cut decision between either of these two alternatives could be made, the Board of Parks Commissioners was challenged to consider yet another site, this one north of Houston. A petition signed by more than fourteen thousand citizens was submitted in hopes of reopening the site location issue.[33] It was presented by Roy Hohl, an automotive dealer who was located north of Houston.

Hohl firmly believed that the location would best serve Harris County, citing convenient highway access and a more central location within the county itself as key advantages. He created the Sports Center North Committee to formalize the case for a northern location. Kirkland tried to explain that his board had moved too far along with the South Main site to consider alternatives, but Hohl and his followers tried to offer free land in an attempt to reopen the issue.[34] Commission members were far from unified regarding what might be best and, as a result, stadium advocates became increasingly pessimistic.

The uncertainty and chaos were spinning in a direction that might result in no new construction whatsoever. More likely, if something did not break the logjam, dramatic delays could negatively affect the Fat Stock Show and the prospects of hosting a Major League team. As a result, Judge Elliott called for a special meeting that would bring various stakeholders to the table.

On March 22, with Judge Elliott at the helm, the Harris County Commissioners met with the mayor, members of the Board of Parks Commissioners, the Fat Stock Show, the Sports Center North organization, and the Urban Renewal Commission in an attempt to resolve the issue. County commissioner E. A. "Squatty" Lyons expressed anger that the mayor had not revealed his downtown plan in 1958, as the Board of Parks Commissioners was weighing all the options. The mayor skirted that issue, instead asserting that his convention center idea was best for the city, particularly for the hotels and retailers located downtown. He further argued that if another forty acres were obtained, the site could serve as home to the stadium, too. The mayor's proposal lost some of its luster when John Andrew of the Urban Renewal Commission asserted that if the mayor's plan was developed as proposed, it would create severe traffic bottlenecks. Although no firm conclusions were made, Board of Parks Commissioners chair Kirkland indicated that without Fat Stock Show support, the stadium project would not be successful.[35]

The Board of Parks Commissioners did not move off its preference for the South Main site, but without Fat Stock Show support, its ability to successfully move forward on stadium construction was tenuous at best. Kirkland and Romero awaited input from the Fat Stock Show leadership. In June the Fat Stock Show's Leopold Meyer, head of the organization's Buildings and Grounds Committee, announced that the organization favored the South Main site.[36] No deal was set, but the informal endorsement was a major boost for the South Main site's viability.

Cutrer refused to surrender, hoping that he could somehow cajole the Fat Stock Show and Rodeo hierarchy to support his vision for downtown. He recommended inviting independent consultants from New York to assess the situation, suggesting that Houston would lose opportunities if it did not act quickly. He further proposed erecting a less expensive permanent building for the Fat Stock Show that might be connected to the larger and more elaborate convention center. He tried to explain that this new option might better serve their ongoing needs, while continuing to beat the drum that downtown construction was best for Houston.

Kirkland tried to steer clear of the mayor's meddling, working to solidify financing resources instead. With his top assistant, Archer Romero, in support of the South Main site, Kirkland had a degree of confidence that the Fat Stock Show leadership would stay with their plan. After all, Romero had led the Fat Stock Show's recent success and was respected by the organization's top insiders. However, Kirkland fretted that a lack of definitive action could undermine the ability of Houston to get a baseball team, and that loss, in the process, would eliminate what might be the largest guaranteed revenue stream, which was needed to fund the stadium's ongoing operating costs. As a banker whose investment inclinations were highly conservative, he wanted assurances that the baseball issue would work itself out. As a long-time baseball supporter, his emotions were pinned on the hopes of luring a big league team as well, but in August 1960 no such assurances were in place.

Dallas, in particular, was cited as a rival that could edge out Houston if a difficult choice had to be made. Dallas announced plans for a domed "all-weather" facility that would include a "supper club" overlooking the playing field. The Dallas contingent indicated that such construction could be undertaken on budget and within tight timelines by using prefabricated materials as part of the construction process.[37] Fortunately, by this time, Roy Hofheinz had abandoned his mall project and was heavily involved in supervising dome construction plans in Houston.

Even though Houston had no ironclad guarantees from Major

League officials in place, Craig Cullinan, as president of the Houston Sports Association, indicated a willingness to sign a thirty-year stadium lease.[38] Cullinan recognized that getting the stadium funding on track was the best way to ensure that a Major League team would be installed in Houston, and the conventional wisdom of the time put New York and Houston as the top sites for Major League success. Cullinan also knew that the domed stadium plan led by Roy Hofheinz was a futuristic enticement that would be hard for the lords of baseball to bypass.

Confident that the elements were in place to make a deal work, on August 21, 1960, the Harris County Commissioners Court and the Harris County Board of Parks Commissioners met to jointly announce approval to move forward with the stadium proposal. The construction would take place on the South Main location that was partly Fat Stock Show property but largely adjacent land owned by Bob Smith and Roy Hofheinz. To assure the Fat Stock Show executives that the plan would not overlook any of their concerns, one day later, Kirkland asserted that "our first job is to satisfy the Fat Stock people."[39]

Although backroom assurances were made that Houston was a front-runner to obtain a new big league baseball team, the Houston Sports Association still had to negotiate territorial rights with the Buffs, and the two parties had been playing hardball for months with no resolution in sight. Beyond that, not one shovel of dirt had been moved. The Major League executives had a meeting scheduled with the proposed owners of Continental League teams, and reports were swirling that instead of joining a new league, Houston would be chosen to host an expansion franchise in one of the existing leagues.

Baseball's owners had stonewalled expansion for years, however. No teams had been added to the Major Leagues in more than half a century, and baseball's reigning leadership had done their level best to sabotage Branch Rickey's efforts to form a new league. In addition, the stadium bonds needed to be sold, and market forces, not charismatic personal appeals, would determine whether typically conservative financial institutions could be enticed to buy them. As such, Kirkland and his colleagues had an uneasy feeling about where things might be headed. The future looked bright, but enough uncertainty lingered to prompt discomfort.

In June 1958 William Kirkland, Archer Romero, and the Board of Parks Commissioners prepared a twenty-five-page report that offered a comprehensive overview of Houston's sports-related needs. The report advised the Harris County Commissioners Court to "develop an aggressive program, backed by the enthusiastic support of citizens of all walks of life, designed to bring Major League Baseball to Houston. The next city to get both sports [football and baseball] might well be decided by the simple question of: 'who wants it most!'"[40] In moving forward to finance the first fully enclosed air-conditioned sports facility large enough to host a Major League team, Houston's city leaders had demonstrated that they were willing to step up with resources and labor in order to achieve Major League status.

The Houston Fat Stock Show's power brokers had put the pieces in place to attain their long-term goals, too. What they did not know then was that the decision they made in 1960 to support the Harris County Domed Stadium project, as it was then called, would contribute to substantial growth of their organization in the decades ahead. A year after supporting a move to the new facility, the organization changed its name to the more broadly recognizable Houston Livestock Show and Rodeo. Once it made the Astrodome complex its home, the organization was able to routinely surpass the one million mark for attendance. It was a milestone not approached in previous facilities.

The addition of the Astrohall, a massive though less dramatic structure that was built adjacent to the Astrodome, gave the Livestock Show and Rodeo a permanent outpost and an ongoing presence that continued to influence the Astrodome. That influence carried into the twenty-first century, with the Astrodome hosting the multiweek event through 2002. However, as decisions were being made in 1960, the Houston Fat Stock Show alone could not dictate the future of Houston's entertainment infrastructure. Although the organization's support was essential to get construction underway, it was just one piece of a much larger puzzle.

Luring Major League Baseball to Houston and convincing a professional football team to move into the new facility were the next big challenges for Houston's civic leaders. The Bayou City's hot, humid, and oppressive weather provided an obstacle that would have to be confronted. The reluctance of professional sports executives to expand beyond the comfort of their traditional northeastern and midwestern locales created an ongoing barrier that Houston would have to confront.

In reflecting on the battle to bring Houston into the Major Leagues, George Kirksey asserted that "big league baseball was a citadel and . . . we would have to take it by storm."[41] Nevertheless, Houston had wealth, power, and a unique energy. That combination of assets would put it in a position to win such a battle.

3

Going Pro

George Kirksey, Craig Cullinan, and the Major League Dream

Roy Hofheinz was a human dynamo whose energy level far surpassed normal standards. Even before the Astrodome was built, he had confidence that he could move mountains in ways that would benefit Houston. However, without the presence of a Major League sports team, he could not muster the degree of public support necessary to build a unique multipurpose facility. Without a team, Hofheinz would be challenged to obtain even rather limited seed money to mobilize the general public to back his vision.

Hofheinz was considerably wealthier than the typical Houstonian, but he was not nearly as affluent as the richest Texans, the sort of big-money people who are necessary to move mountains, and build sports stadiums. Such individuals did not accumulate their vast wealth betting on uncertainty. Mobilizing the movers and shakers and, subsequently, the general taxpayers, to fund a giant indoor stadium would require the clear commitment of a major sports league to Houston.

No Major League teams were located in the Lone Star State throughout the 1950s or at any point before. Houston had to attain Major League status for a project of the Astrodome's size and scope to gain the momentum necessary to gain widespread public support. To do so, metropolitan Houston would need someone with tangible and meaningful connections to the national sports community. Despite Roy Hofheinz's intellect, charisma, energy, and ability, as well as his vast network of impressive connections within Texas, he was not the right person to handle this particular challenge.

Houston's best opportunity to connect to the national sports world emerged through George Turner Kirksey, a Houston-area native who rose to global prominence as a sportswriter. He has been described as "flamboyant, colorful and sometimes disagreeable." He exuded a Texas-sized level of self-confidence and was published in *Colliers*, *Look*, and the *Saturday Evening Post*, all premiere publications of the era. While most sportswriters were happy to simply file their stories, Kirksey put himself in the limelight.

After a stellar career as a high-profile journalist, Kirksey stepped away from self-promotion, choosing to ply his trade as a public relations executive in Texas. In that capacity, he worked long and hard to shine a spotlight on Houston and Houston-based businesses. Yet his passion for sports was so intense that it appeared that his public relations efforts were secondary to his work to bring Houston into the world of Major League sports. Some residents seemed satisfied with Houston remaining a city with a strong Minor League Baseball team, but, much like Hofheinz, Kirksey dreamed big and regarded the status quo as entirely unacceptable.

Both Hofheinz and Kirksey knew that to secure funding and begin construction of a giant indoor sports facility they would need a vast array of resources and widespread community support. They further understood that for success to unfold, they would require the kind of enthusiasm that comes to a city only after a Major League sports team commits to that city. The project that Hofheinz envisioned was much more ambitious than any sports-related construction project ever undertaken, making both public and private support essential. This meant that Houston's Minor League team had to be replaced by a Major League team before construction of the Astrodome could unfold. To build a structure as impressive and as luxurious as the Astrodome to house a Minor League team, no matter how good that team might be, would be sheer and utter folly.

The Houston Buffs were as close to Major League as Houston could get in the 1950s. They were a highly respected Texas League franchise that began play as an independent team in 1888. From 1921 onward they served as the Triple A affiliate of the St. Louis Cardinals. The Buffs were just one tier away from the coveted Major League designation and were a talent pipeline for a franchise that had earned World Series crowns in 1926, 1931, 1934, 1942, 1944, and 1946. They were so successful in the years immediately following World War II that the team's gate revenue was sufficient to fund the Cardinals' entire Minor League system. They had also outdrawn a few Major League teams at the turnstiles.[1]

In Kirksey's mind, however, Houston was too important, too infused with big money, and too full of vast potential to be classified as a "Minor League" town. Until Houston had a Major League team, Kirksey would not be satisfied. For Kirksey, success required bringing Houston into the exclusive fraternity of Major League cities. However, getting a team installed as far south as Houston would require extraordinary creativity and hard work. Until the Dodgers relocated to Los Angeles in time for the 1958 season, St. Louis was as far south as any Major League team went.

Houston's population had grown to be Major League in size, but in the 1950s the leadership of the highly insular professional sports hierarchy was geographically wedded to the old-money Northeast and the industrial cities of the Midwest. Because twentieth-century sport was predicated on tradition, with the Midwest and Northeast largely controlling the professional sports landscape, obtaining a Major League team south of the Mason-Dixon line was an uphill battle for any city, not just Houston. The shift of two Major League teams to California at the start of the 1958 season was a dramatic change to the geographic power structure at a time when sports owners generally resisted any type of change. Even minor change was resisted, rendering the goal of a seismic shift in the geography of Major League sports problematic and unlikely.

The emergence of air travel would allow for play beyond the Northeast and Midwest, but Major League team owners were less than enthusiastic about taking on the cost of airline travel and, with it, the prospect of allowing new team owners into the tent, with all the unforeseen issues that expansion might bring. Although adding teams was discussed on occasion, baseball's hierarchy would have to agree to share future revenue streams with a new crop of team owners for expansion to unfold. The thought of splitting the financial pie into even more pieces dampened that possibility. Professional football had yet to surpass baseball in overall popularity, so baseball's team owners were generally satisfied to maintain the status quo.

To make matters more difficult for cities hoping to get a Major League team, baseball was exempted from antitrust laws as a result of a 1922 Supreme Court ruling rendered by Oliver Wendell Holmes. Although some legal experts argue that this decision may have been flawed, the result is that baseball was ruled to not be interstate commerce and, as such, Congress had no jurisdiction to regulate the sport. The decision meant that baseball officials had jurisdiction over franchise relocation and could control or inhibit league expansion and territorial rights as desired.

The 1922 ruling was challenged in 1953 in *Toolson v. New York Yankees* and again in 1972 in *Flood v. Kuhn*, but in both cases the high court upheld baseball's special status. Nevertheless, the 1972 ruling did open the door to congressional oversight of the sport. However, Congress was and still is reluctant to step in to challenge the antitrust exemption. Baseball's ability to control its own affairs is sufficiently powerful that as recently as 2013 Adam Liptak of the *New York Times* suggested "baseball is intellectual kryptonite for lawyers."[2] In that year, San Jose tried to challenge the antitrust exemption in an effort to move the Oakland Athletics less than fifty miles and achieved no success whatsoever. Although the collective bargaining aspects of baseball's antitrust exemption have been eroded more recently, team owners still have abundant control over franchise relocation and team ownership issues.

With legal advantages unavailable to any other business entity, baseball owners protected their turf aggressively in post–World War II America. They limited who could be in their ranks and who might be excluded. The Major Leagues had a total of sixteen teams in 1905, when the nation's population was less than 90 million. By 1955, with a national population of over 160 million people, professional baseball still had just sixteen teams. The lords of baseball had no incentive to add teams, and as a result, they worked behind the scenes to maintain the status quo. To make matters even more difficult, the last team move took place after the 1902 season, meaning at least fifty years elapsed between any team moves whatsoever. With baseball's top brass highly comfortable with the existing rivalries and traditions, the legal landscape, among other factors, made Kirksey's goals immensely elusive.

Nevertheless, Kirksey was not intimidated by baseball's hierarchy. He was an energetic and secretive man who was comfortable operating in corridors of power. Born in Hillsboro, Texas, he was tall, slender, and powerful, with piercing eyes and an enigmatic smile. Kirksey's biographer, Campbell Titchener, asserts that "figuring out what made the man tick was anything but an easy task."[3] He was a chronic saver of newspaper clippings, yet he struggled to stay organized, often losing that daily battle. He could display an enthusiastic and friendly demeanor, but he was often abrasive and intensely direct. He appeared to both infuriate and delight the people who knew him best. When he left one opportunity for another, he did not look back, and he did not often stay in touch with previous acquaintances unless some professional benefit made such reconnections fruitful.

At a time when operating in a big-city atmosphere appeared to require a degree of buttoned-down formality, Kirksey could play the part, but he preferred to dress as an iconoclast, often wearing casual loafers with no socks, and doing so long before the emergence of "casual Fridays." Kirksey's rebellious attire did not appear to hinder his career, likely because of his desire to avoid becoming the target of media attention once he transitioned to a career in public relations.

In stark contrast to Hofheinz, who seemed naturally comfortable in the limelight, Kirksey, once done with his career as a reporter, preferred to operate in the shadows, enjoying behind-the-scenes manipulation more than working in the open. Although Kirksey reveled in the publicity he frequently received as a national and international correspondent for a major global wire service, he was insightful enough to understand that highly effective public relations practitioners often functioned in the shadows. His knowledge of public relations served Kirksey well as he teamed up with Hofheinz and many other influential Houston area power brokers to engage in activities that would eventually reshape the city.

As with Hofheinz, Kirksey's upbringing and career path uniquely prepared him to achieve success for Houston. He studied journalism at the University of Texas at Austin. While doing so, Kirksey wrote articles for local newspapers. He was not content to simply learn about reporting strategies while sitting in the classroom. In 1927, by age twenty-three, he was working for United Press International (UPI), one of the premiere news organizations of that era. Before television took hold, with the exception of a handful of nationally prominent radio reporters such as Lowell Thomas and Edward R. Murrow—whose emergence in the 1930s had challenged the traditional power structure— national-level newspaper reporters were at the top of the newsgathering pecking order.

Kirksey was considered by many to be a premiere sports reporter during a period that is often regarded as the golden age of sports. The 1920s and 1930s were heady times for a young sportswriter. Luminaries such as Babe Ruth, Jack Dempsey, and Red Grange inspired banner headlines and elevated sports to the level of a coveted national obsession. While sports had a popular following for many decades, as the twentieth century unfolded, gleaming new ballparks were built in Philadelphia, Detroit, Pittsburgh, Boston, Chicago, and New York. From 1909 onward, fans flocked to see these unique structures. Though they were spartan by twenty-first-century standards, they were state of the art at the time.

These facilities contributed to a rise in the cultural capital of sports as a part of American life. Key changes in American culture gave workers more leisure time, as textile mills and auto manufacturers shifted away from a six-day work week. This move intensified momentum for a burgeoning consumer culture while creating increased demand for leisure activities such as sports. New heroes emerged as mass media flourished, with newspapers enjoying record circulation levels and a new medium, radio, offering untold possibilities for the future.

Sportswriting itself underwent changes that made reporters more prominently known to the public. Sports figures and writers alike even became major celebrities. Legendary sportswriters such as Damon Runyon and Grantland Rice emerged as familiar personalities, and their writing departed from the drab inverted pyramid to exhibit personality-driven styles that often contained a unique literary flair. The rapid adoption of radio in American households further immersed the public into the world of sports, bringing live coverage of major events right into the households of millions of excited listeners. The result, suggests sports historian Benjamin Rader, was that by the 1920s and 1930s "those standing on the assembly lines and . . . sitting at their desks in the bureaucracies increasingly found their greatest satisfaction in the athletic hero. . . . Small wonder, perhaps, that boys now dreamed of becoming athletic heroes rather than captains of industry."[4]

Kirksey had committed to a career in sportswriting when the profession was gaining credibility. Further, as the cultural capital of sports was rising, Kirksey was well positioned as a leader in the field. Simply put, he was in the right place at the right time, and his talents were dedicated to covering major events that captivated Americans in ways that previous generations might not have fully understood. While at UPI, he was assigned to report on twelve World Series, three national golf championships, and six Rose Bowls and six Sugar Bowls. According to his biographer, Campbell Titchener, Kirksey covered "just about any other kind of competition that found its way onto the nation's sports pages."[5]

He traveled widely, wrote hundreds of articles, and rubbed elbows with an impressive array of sports figures. In 1933 UPI sent him to Europe, Asia, and Africa, where he wrote on varied topics unrelated to sports, including travel. Such experience gave him a global education that would allow him to connect with high-octane power brokers, while providing Kirksey with a unique cultural cachet that was not typically held by his media colleagues. Kirksey would never have the deep financial resources required to build a stadium or own a professional sports team. Nevertheless, his ability to develop cultural depth would help him to more easily connect and interact with those of high stature who were in a position to assist him in achieving his lofty dreams.

However, during the 1930s Kirksey was not quite ready to push Houston into the Major Leagues, and the nation was not quite ready to recognize Houston in such a manner, either. Upon returning to the States, he moved back into covering top-tier sporting events, plying his trade in the nation's largest and most powerful city. While in New York he wrote about Babe Ruth, Lou Gehrig, and Joe DiMaggio, and these assignments intensified his affinity for baseball. His articles were published from coast to coast in a wide range of newspapers. He met many movers and shakers of the professional sports world, and the vast distribution of newspaper stories containing his byline made him a familiar name to power brokers he hadn't met.

When World War II unfolded, Kirksey joined the U.S. Air Force. While in the armed services, he put his writing skills to good use. He began his tenure as a first lieutenant and gradually advanced to the rank of colonel. Kirksey served as executive news editor of the Ninth Air Force under Lieutenant General Lewis Brereton, the only general to actively serve in both the Atlantic and Pacific Theaters during World War II. Despite not participating in direct combat activity, Kirksey's commitment and hard work earned him a Bronze Star, eight battle citations, and numerous other forms of special recognition. He later worked under Colonel Ed Nolan, a Houstonian who was close friends with Craig Cullinan Sr., the son of Joseph S. Cullinan.

The elder Cullinan was Texaco's founder and a legendary pioneer in the petroleum industry. The Cullinan patriarch was a native of Sharon, Pennsylvania, and knew more about the technical aspects of the oil industry than most of his southern contemporaries. He was one of the few oil pioneers in Texas with tangible experience in Pennsylvania's oil fields, where the petroleum industry first flourished and the rudimentary technology of energy extraction took shape. Furthermore, Cullinan was able to tap his eastern connections to bring investment capital to Texas at a time when the oil industry was not sufficiently developed to thrive on local investments alone.

Cullinan was instrumental in shifting the oil industry from Beaumont, Texas, to Houston, a move that he achieved in 1905. He later played a central role in getting federal and local support lined up to create the famed Houston Ship Channel. This landmark engineering project did much more than simply make money for Cullinan's petroleum interests. The ship channel paved the way for Houston to become a major commercial center. The ability to bring in large ships helped to attract industrial resources and allowed Houston to emerge not only as the central hub for the nation's petrochemical industry but, in part as a result of Cullinan's vision and determination, as a major commerce center for grain, livestock, and a broad array of consumer products.

As an important follow-up to the ship channel's completion, in the 1920s Joseph S. Cullinan led the effort to bring the North Side Belt Railway to Houston, solidifying the heavy-duty transportation infrastructure needed to allow Houston to thrive for the generations that followed. Beyond that, his contacts included former presidents, and he was recognized nationally for leading the effort to get Mount Rushmore built.[6]

Clearly, the Cullinan family was instrumental to the growth and vitality of metropolitan Houston and the entire region. As a result, Nolan's friendship with Craig Cullinan Sr. had the capacity to open significant opportunities for Kirksey, even if the youthful Kirksey appeared to be oblivious to that potential. While Kirksey was in the military, Colonel Nolan cautioned the hard-charging writer to reign in his heavy drinking, suggesting that if he could do so successfully, Nolan would actively work to put him on a positive path in Houston once the war was over.

Nolan even tried to connect Kirksey and Craig Cullinan Jr., a young, aspiring sportswriter and Joseph S. Cullinan's grandson, but Kirksey did not meet with him immediately, clearly not recognizing the benefits that a connection with the Cullinan family might bring. Surprisingly, it took ten years after Nolan's attempt to connect the two before they actually met in 1956. Despite the long delay, their subsequent collaboration was responsible for reshaping the sports landscape in Houston.

Despite his rebellious edge, Kirksey's military service helped him to recognize the value of respecting power, even if he may have been unaware of whom the movers and shakers might be. He also learned to implement and employ complex and detailed planning in a more sophisticated manner than when he was merely submitting his sports stories to UPI. Although Houston would not get a team for more than a decade after the war ended, when Kirksey moved back to Houston he was well prepared to lay the groundwork for bringing a Major League Baseball team to Texas. Nevertheless, he would have to endure rejection at numerous points along his journey.

Kirksey may not have recognized the stature of the Cullinan family when he met Craig Jr. in 1956, but once Kirksey found out that Cullinan had money and a passionate interest in luring a baseball team to Houston, the two quickly became partners. Kirksey admitted that two things attracted him to Cullinan: he "had more interest [in baseball] and more money than anybody I had talked with before."[7] In spite of the blunt candor of Kirksey's observation, the two worked extraordinarily well together, and each brought unique qualities to the relationship. Kirksey provided sports knowhow, an abundance of connections, and boundless enthusiasm. Cullinan brought credibility, resources, and a more authoritative public speaking voice to the table.

At their initial meeting, Kirksey also met with William A. Kirkland, chairman of First City National Bank, at that time Houston's largest financial institution. This informal meeting connected three individuals who were highly passionate about baseball. At least one Houston baseball historian, Robert Reed, suggests that this 1956 meeting, despite its informal nature, marked the start of Major League Baseball in Houston.[8]

Kirkland's commitment to baseball ran deep. Years earlier, he was both a player and manager in the Houston Bank League, and later he became president of the Houston Baseball Federation, an organization that supported amateur baseball while working to make baseball fields available and affordable to Houstonians. Kirkland was a highly respected community leader who could open doors and connect Kirksey with powerful and wealthy Houstonians. He was instrumental in working with Kirksey to get public funding in place as the fight to attract a Major League team got underway.

The long and frustrating daily battle to attract a Major League franchise was generally in the hands of Kirksey and Cullinan, with Kirkland as a less active ally. Kirksey needed Cullinan to succeed, and Cullinan's passion for baseball was one element that helped the relationship work. Beyond that, when meeting with powerful baseball officials, Cullinan offered a level of gravitas that Kirksey did not have. The Cullinan name and its highly impressive ties to multiple generations of oil-based wealth gave outsiders a sense that Houston could carry its weight and step up if given the opportunity to do so. If the former sportswriter turned public relations executive had been working alone, doors likely would have remained shut that otherwise had opened when the two were working as a team. Their combined talents ensured that the two could meet with team owners and cultivate relationships that would eventually get baseball into Houston.

Kirksey may have been too late to mentor Cullinan as an aspiring sportswriter, as Colonel Nolan had suggested during the 1940s, for Cullinan had moved on to other opportunities. Yet Kirksey managed to mentor other sportswriters who willingly helped the cause. One was Mickey Herskowitz, a youthful, hard-working reporter whom Kirksey guided and encouraged. Herskowitz was a fast-rising *Houston Post* sportswriter who would later move to the more prestigious *Houston Chronicle*. He beat the drum loudly to move Houston into the Major Leagues, authoring a six-part series explaining why Houston should get a team. Kirksey may not have realized it, but some of his early mentoring efforts, even if they were haphazard and uneven, put him in a position to shape local media coverage to his benefit as he pushed hard to bring a Major League team to Houston.

While Cullinan is infrequently mentioned when it comes to bringing Major League sports to Houston, his influence was profound. An introverted Yale graduate with an eastern prep school pedigree, Cullinan had the kind of cachet and credibility that Kirksey simply could not replicate. He understood the northeastern culture that for generations was central to both professional sports and the nation's deeply entrenched financial institutions. Beyond that, Cullinan was willing to bankroll major parts of the venture, allowing his office to be used as a central location for their ongoing efforts. He also funded various trips that would have depleted Kirksey's limited resources. Cullinan's ability and willingness to book airline tickets and to pay for travel as the two met with team owners and high-level baseball executives ensured that Houston was often mentioned when the subject of team relocation was being reported.

In 1951, before teaming up with Cullinan, Kirksey tried to convince the affluent oil and real estate magnate Bob Smith to buy the Philadelphia Athletics for $2.5 million during a conversation outside the Rice Hotel in downtown Houston. Smith responded, "Put me down for $250,000. Now go get nine more." Kirksey was unable to get a single other investor to step up, although this was his first recorded attempt to bring Major League Baseball to Houston.[9]

Nevertheless, with ambitions and confidence as large as the Lone Star State itself, Kirksey's next foray into the Major League sweepstakes had him working behind the scenes to bring the St. Louis Cardinals from the Gateway City to Houston. The Cardinals were not a run-of-the-mill team by any measure. From 1926 onward, the Cardinals had earned nine league crowns while winning six World Series championships. Over those years, only the well-financed, immensely powerful New York Yankees could boast a better on-field performance.

Upon learning that team owner Fred Saigh had pleaded no contest to tax evasion charges in late 1952, Kirksey took steps to pounce on the opportunity, correctly determining that Saigh would be forced to sell his team. He lined up Houston investors, made his intentions known, and then met with St. Louis's D'Arcy Advertising Company on February 3, 1953, in a strategy that was intended to put some of the final elements of financing in place for the transaction. Kirksey hoped to structure a five-year, $250,000 broadcast deal with the St. Louis–based brewer Anheuser-Busch as a way to raise $1,250,000 of the $4,250,00 that Saigh indicated would be needed to close the deal. Although Kirksey stated that the asking price was "rather stiff," he was ready to move forward until his plans were derailed by August Busch Jr.[10]

The beer baron whom Kirksey hoped to work with to finance his takeover of the Cardinals was working with local leaders and baseball executives to undermine those plans. Busch convinced Saigh, whose roots were in the St. Louis area, too, that he would be best serving St. Louis and its many fans by selling the team to the Anheuser-Busch Company for $3,750,000. It was $500,000 less than what the Houston investors would have paid, but Busch offered assurances that the team would remain in St. Louis if

Saigh worked with him. With no other deep-pocketed local buyer in the running, Saigh acquiesced, laying the groundwork for a relationship between brewer and franchise that has evolved over the years and continues to this day.

Whether a Houston deal would have gained the approval of team owners and baseball's top executives is questionable, but evidence suggests that league officials were committed to undermining any deal that would have moved the team to Houston. National League president Warren Giles flew to St. Louis and was actively engaged in meetings with banking executives as well as leaders at Anheuser-Busch, later celebrating with locals after a deal was brokered. His initial attempt to insert himself into the negotiation process without fanfare or publicity was undermined by a hotel clerk who asked, "Aren't you Mr. Giles?," immediately after he tried to anonymously register under the pseudonym "W.C. Warren."[11]

Kirksey may have been better served trying to cultivate St. Louis Browns owner Bill Veeck, who had previously attempted to undermine the Cardinals because he held an unreasonable hope that they might move. Saigh's team sale forced Veeck to eventually sell his franchise to Baltimore interests, once it became abundantly clear that his National League rival would remain controlled by America's largest brewer and St. Louis couldn't support two teams.

Two things likely made Kirksey shy away from making a move for the St. Louis Browns. First, Veeck, although eventually forced into a sale, made it clear that he wanted to maintain a controlling interest in his team, even if he intended to relocate the club. Veeck was an unpredictable, often out-of-control iconoclast whose unique marketing ideas might have worn thin with the big-money men of Houston. As an example, in a circus-like move that became legendary, Veeck allowed Eddie Gaedel, a diminutive, three-foot-seven-inch, sixty-five-pound man who had no place on any Major League roster, to bat in a 1951 game.

Second, the Browns were an awful team and for many seasons were a laughingstock within the American League for both poor attendance and on-field performance. Their attendance was sufficiently weak that strong Minor League teams, including the Houston Buffs, outdrew them in attendance periodically. For many years, the Washington Senators were the league's worst team, so, borrowing from a famed eulogy for the nation's first president, many sports-minded Washingtonians described their city as "first in war, first in peace, and last in the American League." However, by the 1950s, in a creative takeoff on that clever parody, some in St. Louis mockingly quipped that their city was "first in booze, first in shoes, and last in the American League." In 1953, the Browns' last year in St. Louis, the team lost 100 games, with the league's top team, the Yankees, 46½ games ahead of them by season's end. The Browns were on such shaky financial terrain that they could barely afford baseballs on game days, particularly as their tenure in St. Louis was ending. When the Browns finally moved to Baltimore, the new management took the unusual step of renaming the team and trading away almost the entire roster. These moves ensured that no affiliation whatsoever with the old team would remain.

During the early stages of the process of attracting a Major League team to Houston, Kirksey probably thought the city could do better than the St. Louis Browns. Nevertheless, in 1953 Kirksey watched with disappointment as Lou Perini orchestrated a move of his Boston Braves to Milwaukee. A year later, he saw the Browns relocate to Baltimore to be renamed the Orioles. Despite a desire to stay in the game, Veeck was forced to fully relinquish his ownership after being unceremoniously squeezed out by league officials and fellow owners who had tired of his offbeat, irreverent, and vaudevillian antics. In 1955 the Philadelphia Athletics moved to Kansas City in a shift that Kirksey had hoped might instead bring them to Houston.

Because baseball had legal protections well beyond other business concerns, Kirksey did not regard expansion as the best way to achieve his goal—at least not yet. He was still convinced that prompting another team to move to Houston was the wisest and easiest path to achieving Major League status. As a result, he continued his efforts to orchestrate the purchase of other teams.

After the Braves' move from Boston to Milwaukee in 1953, with an already-built, taxpayer-funded ballpark serving as a major incentive for making that move, Kirksey determined that getting a Major League–quality stadium on track would be a key advantage in moving Houston into the Major Leagues. Milwaukee's foresight in building a Major League–quality stadium before having a team in their city changed the dynamics of baseball economics. New construction in Milwaukee allowed a team owner who had been struggling in Boston to comfortably settle into a new city with the knowledge that a taxpayer-funded facility could ensure immediate profits. As Lou Perini moved his team westward, he did not have to worry about the complexities, challenges, and expenses of ballpark construction.

To overcome the ballpark obstacle when the Athletics moved from Philadelphia to Kansas City in 1954, the team acquired the local ballpark while working through the relocation process, then sold it to the city, which in turn leased it back to the team on highly favorable terms. Similarly, even without a Major League team, Minnesota's sports hierarchy was able to arrange for the construction of a new taxpayer-funded stadium that was completed in 1956, putting pressure on baseball teams to consider relocation to the Twin Cities, too.

The changing economics of stadium construction created an intractable situation for Houston's negotiators. When Kirksey and Cullinan visited other cities, any serious attempt to get team officials to relocate was met with an admonition to "get a stadium built" before serious negotiations might move forward. Yet frustratingly, when they went back to Houston, the big-money men, those with the resources and the ability to finance a team, would counter with "get us a team and then we'll build a stadium." It was a conundrum that Kirksey and Cullinan struggled to resolve and neither had the ability to fix. In addition, Houston was almost eight hundred miles away from the nearest Major League team, prompting logistical concerns among team owners.

Nevertheless, people knew that Houston had money, and the city's rapidly growing population put it in an ideal position to support Major League sports. Baseball historian Robert Reed indicates that when Kirksey visited a city, his mere presence "often touched off hot panic fires among local fans afraid that their team was about to be stolen in the dark of night by this energetic wheeler-dealer from Texas."[12] When Cullinan was involved in such visits, presumptions about his oil fortune, although not nearly as lavish as outsiders might have thought, added a further dimension of concern and fear. Among the candidates that Kirksey and Cullinan targeted were the Cincinnati Reds, the Chicago Cubs, the Chicago White Sox, and the Cleveland Indians, although none of these teams could be convinced to move.[13]

Kirksey and Cullinan worked relentlessly and diligently to lure a team to Houston. Kirksey frequently waited until late in the afternoon to swing by Cullinan's office, entering like an uncontrolled tornado. The staff jokingly called him "four o'clock Freddy" as he worked alongside Cullinan. He would ask secretaries to type up letters to baseball executives, dictating content while plotting travel and strategy. He downed coffee and puffed on thin cigarette-style cigars, although he seemed to rarely eat while in the midst of planning. At times, Cullinan would react negatively to the rejection they faced, but Kirksey would reassure him and push him to have faith in their mission.

The wild and unpredictable movement of teams in the late 1950s gave Kirksey hope that something would break in Houston's favor. After the 1957 season, the Giants and Dodgers planned moves from New York to California in one of the most heavily publicized set of franchise shifts ever. Before moving, both teams were assured that the infrastructure for new stadium deals would be in place. Walter O'Malley's Dodgers were told that the team would get a sweetheart real estate deal that would allow O'Malley to build a privately owned ballpark in Los Angeles, while Horace Stoneham's Giants were assured that they would move into a lavish taxpayer-funded ballpark in San Francisco.

The moves bode well for Houston in one sense but were problematic in yet another. On the one hand, the California market, like Houston, had enormous profit potential, but the West Coast was significantly further away from the northeastern and midwestern cities that had monopolized the Major Leagues up to this point. The two teams' California moves meant that long-distance air travel would be a future requirement for every National League team. No one could continue to argue that Houston's location made relocation impractical. After all, Houston was closer and more convenient to all current Major League cities than California teams were. However, as the Giants' and Dodgers' moves were announced, immediately after the 1957 season, Houston still had no tangible plans to build a Major League stadium.

Before Major League Baseball's move to California, Kirksey worked closely with Houstonians who could put up the money to purchase a team. His goal was to position Houston to be regarded as a consistent front-runner each time a relocation option unfolded. For the most part, Kirksey had succeeded in that regard. Houston was almost always in the conversation as team relocations were reported. However, the stadium issue remained a stumbling block. As a result, after these moves unfolded, he worked harder to get the resources in place both to buy a team and to get stadium construction on track, understanding that failure to confront the stadium issue could undo any future deals.

His effort unfolded in two ways. First, he worked with Cullinan and Kirkland to launch the Houston Sports Association, a group that began to take form in 1957, although its structure and direction would not take clear shape until 1960. Second, he worked within the political realm to get a funding mechanism in place to build a taxpayer-funded Major League stadium, as had occurred in Milwaukee and as was also undertaken in Minneapolis.

Kirksey tried to persuade Harris County judge Bob Casey to push through stadium funding in 1958. He succeeded in convincing Casey that the idea had merit, but the judge made it clear that he did not have the legal standing to act unilaterally on such funding. A voter referendum would be necessary, and it would require state-level authorization. Kirksey then met with Texas state senator Searcy Bracewell, a former client of Kirksey's public relations firm and a personal friend. To add a bit of financial muscle to the negotiation, Kirksey brought in Kirkland, too. Without delay, Bracewell pushed legislation forward that, with voter authorization, would approve the use of public funds for "public parks and entertainment venues." The legislation further created the Harris County Board of Parks Commissioners to oversee any proposed construction, with Kirkland agreeing to act as head.

After gaining state authorization, a $20 million public referendum to fund a stadium was put on the ballot, with a vote scheduled for July 26. Prior to the vote, Craig Cullinan told the media, "We're on the road to getting Houston's house in order, to attract a major league franchise or to obtain a new franchise, if and when the major leagues expand." As the referendum approached, William Kirkland emphasized that the facility would be "perhaps the finest sports center and exhibition park in the United States." He emphasized that despite taxpayer funding for the startup costs, the facility would be paid for through sports and event revenues. He further emphasized that the complex would generate larger economic opportunities for Houston.[14]

At this point, Houston's plans were to build an outdoor baseball park with an adjacent air-conditioned facility for conventions, meetings, and other events rather than a single giant indoor facility. Before the vote, baseball owners indicated that they would be meeting on July 8, during the All-Star break, with the potential for expansion as one topic that would be discussed. Houstonians overwhelmingly supported the stadium project, but not surprisingly, league officials failed to move on the expansion issue. With an approved stadium-funding package in place, Kirksey pursued two options for Houston. The first was his previous strategy of attempting to identify a baseball team to purchase for relocation. The second was to push the lords of baseball to follow through on expansion, despite ample evidence that baseball owners were approaching that issue with extreme reluctance.

When it came to the expansion issue, Houston had allies in New York City who were angered by the departure of the Dodgers and the Giants following the 1957 season. In the past, cities had lost their teams because they were struggling financially, but in this instance both the New York teams were profitable. They chose to move in attempts to make even more money in fast-growing West Coast cities. When the nation's largest city, a powerful financial center that was not used to facing defeat, lost two teams to smaller cities in California, the ramifications played out in the national media and elsewhere.

The courts offered one source of ammunition to take on base-

Fig. 1. Roy M. Hofheinz (1912–82), Texas state representative from 1934 to 1936, Harris County judge from 1936 to 1944, and mayor of the city of Houston from 1953 to 1955. Hofheinz served as the driving force behind the development of the Astrodome (née the Harris County Domed Stadium), which transformed Houston into a Major League Baseball city and redefined the growing metropolis on the international stage. Courtesy of Walter P. Moore and Associates.

FIG. 2. Colt Stadium served as the temporary home of the Houston Colt .45s—later the Houston Astros—as the Major League Baseball team awaited the completion of the nearby Astrodome. During its brief heyday, the stadium was infamous for its massive mosquitoes and exposure to the brutal Texas sun. In the 1970s it was torn down and moved to Gómez Palacio, Durango, Mexico, where it served as the home venue for a Mexican League baseball team. George Kirksey Papers, 1910–71, Courtesy of Special Collections, University of Houston Libraries.

FIG. 3. (*Opposite top*) Eschewing traditional shovels, representatives of various civic groups took their turns firing pistols loaded with blanks during the Astrodome's groundbreaking ceremony on January 3, 1962. The attendees included county commissioners (pictured here), officials from the Houston Sports Association, and African American community leaders. Darling Photography/George Kirksey Papers, 1910–71, Courtesy of Special Collections, University of Houston Libraries.

FIG. 4. (*Opposite bottom*) *Left to right*, Harris County judge William M. Elliott, his wife, Emilie Elliott, and the Houston Sports Association's R. E. Smith ponder the latest architectural model of the Harris County Domed Stadium on January 3, 1962, the day of the stadium's ceremonial groundbreaking. In the background a mockup of the Astrodome's cushioned seats is on display. Darling Photography/George Kirksey Papers, 1910–71, Courtesy of Special Collections, University of Houston Libraries.

FIG. 5. Robert J. Minchew (1920–94) pictured inside the Astrodome's framework. Minchew served as the on-site architect throughout the stadium's construction. An architect with Wilson, Morris, Crain, and Anderson, Minchew was educated at Rice University and later attained membership in the Construction Specifications Institute. Courtesy of Walter P. Moore and Associates.

FIG. 6. (*Opposite top*) Walter P. Moore Sr. (1903–83) was educated at Rice University before famously launching his structural engineering firm after selling his prized Stutz Bearcat to raise the necessary capital. In addition to its work on the Astrodome, the firm acted as engineering consultants for Rice Stadium, Jesse H. Jones Hall for the Performing Arts, the Warwick Hotel, the Bates-Freeman Building at the University of Texas M. D. Anderson Cancer Center, and the Summit sports arena. Courtesy of Walter P. Moore and Associates.

FIG. 7. (*Opposite bottom*) Kenneth E. Zimmerman (1913–2008) was educated at Texas A&M University and later served as an officer in the Army Corps of Engineers. During the Second World War, Zimmerman served under General Leslie Groves on behalf of the Manhattan Project, for which Zimmerman acted as property master in Oak Ridge, Tennessee. After the war Zimmerman rejoined Walter P. Moore and Associates and worked as the chief engineer for the Astrodome. Courtesy of Walter P. Moore and Associates.

Fig. 8. (*Opposite top*) Prior to the Astrodome's construction, Roof Structures conducted wind tunnel tests in an effort to establish the kinds of pressures that would be imposed on the building in the event of a full-scale tropical storm. The wind tunnel tests were undertaken on a 1:8 scale model of the Dome. The wind tunnel tests were carried out using the aeronautical wind tunnels housed at the McDonnell-Douglas Aircraft Corporation facilities in St. Louis, Missouri. Courtesy of Walter P. Moore and Associates.

Fig. 9. (*Opposite bottom*) The excavation of the three-hundred-acre site of the future Harris County Domed Stadium began on February 2, 1962, ultimately involving the removal of 260,000 cubic yards of dirt. Construction would be delayed until 1963, given a series of post-bond legal, financial, and political challenges, when the foundation would be laid for the Astrodome's sub–playing field level. Courtesy of Walter P. Moore and Associates.

Fig. 10. (*Above*) The future Harris County Domed Stadium's framework emerges, including several of the eventual thirty-seven falsework erection towers. Each tower was placed circumferentially at the base of the building in order to provide support for the trusses that grew to span 642 feet in diameter. The towers consisted of an inner ring of twelve 200-foot towers, an outer ring of twenty-four 160-foot towers, and a 303-foot center tower. Courtesy of Walter P. Moore and Associates.

FIG. 11. The future Harris County Domed Stadium's centroid, or geometric center, is visible atop the thirty-seventh erection tower. At a height of 303 feet, the centroid is approximately eighteen stories high. Jacks were placed at the top of each tower to make incremental adjustments as the erection of the steel progressed. Courtesy of Walter P. Moore and Associates.

FIG. 12. (*Opposite top*) The centroid, with its distinctive spiderweb design, would act as the central support mechanism for the building once the tension-ring formation was added. The Dome's structural design consists of diamond-shaped lamellas separated by ring structures, which double as the roof's trusses. Courtesy of Walter P. Moore and Associates.

FIG. 13. (*Opposite bottom*) National League president Warren C. Giles (1896–1979) inspects the construction site of the future Harris County Domed Stadium during the Colt .45s' 1963 Major League Baseball season. Three of the thirty-seven falsework erection towers are visible in the background. George Kirksey Papers, 1910–1971, Courtesy of Special Collections, University of Houston Libraries.

FIG. 14. (*Opposite top*) On February 4, 1964, the stadium's roof was liberated from the falsework erection towers completely, and the 7.5-million-pound lamella dome came to rest entirely on the stadium walls. After all of the towers had been removed, the stadium sank four inches, as predicted by the engineers, under the combined weight of the roof and the framework. Courtesy of Walter P. Moore and Associates.

FIG. 15. (*Opposite bottom*) George T. Kirksey (1904–71) and second baseman Nellie Fox (1927–75), a Hall of Famer and White Sox star who played his final two seasons with the Colt .45s. George Kirksey Papers, 1910–71, Courtesy of Special Collections, University of Houston Libraries.

FIG. 16. (*Above*) The future Astrodome's framework is nearly fully assembled, with the roof span almost complete. At this juncture, the structure encompasses ninety-four hundred tons of steel, with twenty-nine hundred tons in the roof alone. George Kirksey Papers, 1910–71, Courtesy of Special Collections, University of Houston Libraries.

Fig. 17. The Astrodome's structural design could withstand a sonic boom loading of two pounds per square foot and sustained wind velocities of 135 MPH with gusts of 165 MPH. The stadium's ability to tolerate hurricane-force winds was tested in 1983, when the Dome deflected the powerful onslaught of Hurricane Alicia. George Kirksey Papers, 1910–71, Courtesy of Special Collections, University of Houston Libraries.

Fig. 18. (*Opposite top*) The Astrodome's famous Home Run Spectacular during the final stages of installation. The scoreboard cost $2 million, weighed three hundred tons, required forty thousand lights and twelve hundred miles of wiring, and spanned nearly five hundred feet along the Dome's centerfield wall. Courtesy of Walter P. Moore and Associates.

Fig. 19. (*Opposite bottom*) With Opening Day in the offing, the Astrodome was ready to assert its place at the vanguard of contemporary stadium construction. The Dome's total building cost was computed to be $35 million, which amounts to approximately $264 million in today's dollars. George Kirksey Papers, 1910–71, Courtesy of Special Collections, University of Houston Libraries.

To Our Fans — 1965 HIGHLIGHTS OF
SPACE-AGE BASEBALL – INDOORS

THE ASTROS FIRST YEAR
IN THE ASTRODOME

Price: 50¢

Fig. 20. (*Opposite top*) The Astrodome's innovative lamella roof design in April 1965, before the opening of the Houston Astros' 1965 Major League Baseball season. The roof's Lucite panels would be painted off-white within the month in order to reduce the sun's unremitting glare, which wreaked havoc for the fielders during day games. Courtesy of Walter P. Moore and Associates.

Fig. 21. (*Opposite bottom*) A 1965 highlights brochure celebrates the era of "space-age baseball" in Space City, a reference to Houston's nickname in honor of NASA's Lyndon B. Johnson Space Center, which originally opened in September 1963. George Kirksey Papers, 1910–71, Courtesy of Special Collections, University of Houston Libraries.

Fig. 22. (*Above*) The Astrodome's infield prior to Opening Day, with the stadium's original natural grass, a carefully selected strain of Tifway 419 Bermuda, in full evidence. Later that season the painting over of the stadium's skylights in order to mitigate the sun's glare during day games spelled the end of natural grass as the indoor facility's playing surface, ushering in the age of AstroTurf. Courtesy of Walter P. Moore and Associates.

Fig. 23. On July 11, 1985, Hall of Famer Nolan Ryan struck out the New York Mets' Danny Heep in the Astrodome to become the first Major League pitcher to notch four thousand strikeouts. Kenneth Womack's private collection.

Fig. 24. (*Opposite top*) On September 25, 1986, Astros pitcher Mike Scott coaxed an infield grounder from the San Francisco Giants' Will Clark to mark the final out in his no-hit bid to clinch a playoff spot for the Houston Astros against the New York Mets. Kenneth Womack's private collection.

Fig. 25. (*Opposite bottom*) Narendra K. Gosain (1941–) joined Walter P. Moore and Associates in 1972 after earning his doctorate at Rice University. Now a senior consultant for Walter P. Moore and Associates, Gosain led the Astrodome renovation projects in the late 1980s in response to Bud Adams's design changes aimed at making the Astrodome more profitable for the Houston Oilers. Kenneth Womack's private collection.

FIG. 26. (*Opposite top*) An innovative design by Narendra K. Gosain of Walter P. Moore and Associates, the retractable upper-deck seating accommodated ten thousand additional seats in the Astrodome's centerfield rafters. The renovation project in the late 1980s involved a winch and pulley system, supplemented with a specially designed hydraulic mechanism for extending the primary balconies that would account for the majority of the new seats. Courtesy of Walter P. Moore and Associates.

FIG. 27. (*Opposite bottom*) The Astrodome's innovative lamella truss roof design as it appeared in July 2013. In January 2008 the building was denied a certificate of occupancy by the City of Houston's Fire Marshal's Office, which leveled numerous safety citations against the stadium. Kenneth Womack's private collection.

FIG. 28. (*Above*) The Astrodome's southern exterior as it appeared in July 2013. The large circular stairwell towers, complete with accessibility ramps, seen on the stadium's periphery were built in the late 1980s in order to accommodate progressive shifts in building codes since the 1960s. The towers were demolished in December 2013 after the November bond measure in support of the Astrodome's renovation was rejected by Harris County voters. Kenneth Womack's private collection.

FIG. 29. The iconic location of the Astrodome's home plate as it appeared in July 2013. The Dome's home plate figured in six no-hitters, all by Astros pitchers. Nolan Ryan's pitching gem on September 26, 1981, earned the Express his fifth no-hitter, breaking a tie with Los Angeles Dodgers legend Sandy Koufax. Kenneth Womack's private collection.

FIG. 30. Known as the Domers, avid supporters of preserving the Astrodome from the wrecking ball created T-shirts emblazoned with an iconic Texas lone star above a drawing of the Astrodome and the words "Come and Take It." The T-shirts became top sellers in the Houston area, boldly connoting the fervor of the Texas Revolution by invoking the crude flag unveiled by Anglo settlers during the October 1835 battle of Gonzales. Courtesy of James Glassman.

ball's hierarchy. *Toolson v. New York Yankees* openly challenged baseball's antitrust status in a labor issue unrelated to franchise relocation, yet the issue was of deep concern to owners nonetheless. George Toolson, convinced that he was talented enough to pitch in the Major Leagues, sued the New York franchise after facing demotion because the talent-laden Yankees' top farm team, the Newark Bears, went out of business.

Toolson lost his case in 1953, but one part of that decision had the capacity to put dramatic pressure on baseball's leadership to move forward with expansion. The Supreme Court ruled that Congress had allowed the antitrust exemption to stand for more than thirty years and asserted, "If there are evils in this field which now warrant application to it of the antitrust laws, it should be by legislation."[15] That provision overtly empowered Congress to act on baseball's antitrust clause, offering a weapon to any city that felt it was being unfairly squeezed out of the Major League's inner circle. Cities might lobby Congress for political intervention into baseball's operation, with a threat to challenge the prized antitrust exemption as a bargaining chip. But to gain momentum in this regard, team owners had to perceive the potential for tangible action as sufficiently credible.

Congressional hearings in 1951 and 1952, before the Toolson decision, had revealed that there was little will to insert Congress into labor-related issues, but the volumes of testimony at the hearing offered evidence that numerous public officials, among others, were frustrated with baseball's unwillingness to expand into new cities.[16] At the time of these hearings, a Major League team had not relocated for five decades. Nevertheless, the subsequent flurry of team relocations beginning in 1953 put the brakes on the political motivation to get involved in this issue.

By 1958, angry New Yorkers, stung by the loss of two National League teams, and frustrated Minnesotans and Texans raised the potential on several fronts to pressure baseball's owners with a threat to abolish the antitrust exemption. Such pressure, if successfully leveraged, seemed like one way to perhaps push expansion plans forward. Kirksey and others who were lobbying Major

League Baseball to expand would have to keep their fingerprints off of any such threats so as to avoid being blackballed if expansion plans were ever announced.

Baseball owners in both leagues were suggesting that expansion was possible and might happen at some time in the future, but when pushed to be specific, they danced around the issue and stalled. They created a committee to study the feasibility of expansion, appointing the long-time baseball executive Joe Cronin as head, but for Kirksey and others who would benefit from expansion, it was clear that moving forward with a tangible plan was not a priority for baseball's hierarchy. The owners were very happy with the status quo.

As Houston's stadium-funding vote neared, instead of an increase in legislative pressure to abolish or limit the antitrust exemption, quite the opposite unfolded in Washington DC. Baseball executives brazenly pushed Congress to solidify their antitrust exemption further, attempting to expand it to other sports while trying to lock in the most beneficial elements for the future. Legislation to achieve these goals was introduced by New York representative Kenneth Keating in June. It would exempt all professional sports from antitrust oversight in labor, territorial issues, and broadcasting. The exemption in the last area would allow team owners dramatic latitude to charge fees for broadcasts, something that the Dodgers had hoped to implement after relocating to Los Angeles. The measure was approved by an overwhelming voice vote in the House of Representatives on June 24.[17]

Yankees owner Dan Topping was an ally of Keating, a Harvard-educated veteran of both World Wars. Topping actively supported Keating's 1958 U.S. Senate campaign as the measure was pushed forward. For Topping, getting such legislation approved might assist him in convincing fellow owners to allow the Yankees sole territorial rights to the New York market, an outcome that would ensure the team monopoly status in the nation's largest city. Such a benefit would reap millions for this already well-financed team for generations to come. Not surprisingly, baseball officials praised the proposed legislation, and accolades poured in from NFL and NHL executives. Senate approval was the next step.[18]

The legislation died in the Senate shortly after Calvin Griffith petitioned fellow team owners for permission to move his team, the Washington Senators, with Minneapolis as his favored destination. Houston, Dallas, and Toronto were mentioned as potential suitors, too. The powerful New York representative Emmanuel Celler angrily decried the proposed move as "more evidence of money grabbing." Still angered by the Dodgers' departure, the Brooklyn-born Cellar, then chair of the powerful House Judiciary Committee, threatened to craft new legislation that would strip baseball of its antitrust exemption.

The owners understood that taking baseball out of Washington DC at this time could further agitate an already volatile political situation, so they stopped Griffith from moving forward. With Red Sox owner Tom Yawkey taking the lead, American League owners pushed Griffith back temporarily, blocking his desire to move by invoking Minor League territorial rights to Minneapolis since that city was home to the top Red Sox farm club at the time.[19]

With Major League Baseball stalling on expansion as the 1958 season concluded, Kirksey tried to arrange a purchase of the financially shaky Cleveland Indians to move them to Houston. The Indians were a respectable team on the field, but they had amassed approximately $3.5 million in debt and were struggling to stay afloat. Minnesota and Houston both pounced at this opportunity.

Minnesota tried to lure the Indians with a guarantee of one million ticket sales in 1959 if the team agreed to terms. Fewer than seven hundred thousand Clevelanders had attended Indians games in 1958, so the guarantee was an enticement that carried substantial value. The Minnesota group had successfully built a stadium in 1956, locating it in Bloomington so that it could more easily attract fans from both Minneapolis and St. Paul. The facility had a capacity of about twenty thousand, but it was designed with a footprint that could be easily enlarged as needed. Minnesota was likely Houston's biggest rival in attracting a new team. One season earlier, Minnesota had been the presumed frontrunner to obtain the New York Giants until Dodgers owner Walter O'Malley and West Coast interests enticed Giants owner Horace Stoneham to relocate to San Francisco instead.

By October, the Houston group upped the ante considerably on the Cleveland bid, understanding that without expansion, this could be the last opportunity to lure a team to Houston for some time. They agreed to absorb all team-related debt and then pay an additional $2.5 million, a commitment of $6 million. It was a deal that was far more generous than the Minnesota offer.

Nevertheless, William A. Daley, the Indians' general manager, made it clear that both the Minneapolis and Houston offers were futile, candidly asserting that "if this were a business organization whose interest was in profit, we'd have to sell," but the decision was made because "most of the directors are Clevelanders."[20] Houston's willingness to pay $6 million for the Indians when just five and a half years earlier it had put a very respectable $4.25 million offer on the table for the tradition-laden St. Louis Cardinals demonstrated the intensity of the city's commitment to achieving Major League status.

This missed opportunity stung Kirksey, although he retained an optimistic public veneer. If a team could not be convinced to move with offers that clearly exceeded what local and competing bidders were willing to pay, as had been tried since 1952, convincing baseball executives to expand seemed to be the only viable remaining option, although all past efforts to achieve that goal had gone nowhere. Once again, Commissioner Ford Frick suggested that both leagues might expand to ten teams, but after repeated stalling over many years, those pushing to obtain Major League teams were legitimately skeptical.

With no tangible progress, leaders from expansion cities that were repeatedly frozen out of the Major League process proposed the creation of a third Major League. The high-powered New York attorney William Shea worked with prominent New York officials first and then with leaders from other cities to formulate a strategy that would break the logjam.

The cities hoping to achieve Major League status collectively agreed to establish the new Continental League.[21] Among the most vociferous opponents of the new league were the powerful Yankees, who were already working behind the scenes to retain exclusive territorial rights to New York City. To get the Continental League established and on a firm administrative footing, Shea brought in Branch Rickey, a baseball insider who knew the owners well. Shea appointed him president and chief administrator of the new league.

Rickey had been a pioneer in establishing baseball's farm system, so owners understood that he had the knowhow and ability to get a new league up and running. Rickey first worked with leaders from Denver, Houston, Minneapolis–St. Paul, New York, and Toronto. Later he added Atlanta, Buffalo, and Dallas. Kirksey was appointed special assistant to Rickey, a position that solidified Houston's leadership position while signaling that Texas wealth would help to launch the new league. The eight-team league would have exactly the same number of teams as the existing leagues, so a similar schedule and similar operational decisions could be applied.

Rickey tried to work closely with baseball executives, agreeing to abide by labor and territorial rights policies as well as other terms they set as a requirement for maintaining Major League status. The owners stalled and worked diligently to undermine the new league while presenting a public veneer of cooperation. Tangible signs unfolded that such cooperation was less than sincere. Continental League owners seeking to acquire territorial rights from Minor League teams suddenly found that teams had suddenly skyrocketed in value despite general recognition that many Minor League teams were struggling to stay afloat. For Minor League teams that had been valued at $100,000, perhaps $200,000, just a few years or even months earlier, Continental League officials were being told that the cost of acquiring territorial rights would be at least double that value and could be as high as $1 million in some cities. The Houston Buffs set their price at nearly half a million dollars.

As the new league's plans moved forward, Major League team owners or league officials would suggest the possibility of expansion, offering nothing specific but nonetheless testing the unity of Continental League leadership in a clear effort to sabotage Rickey's work. When Griffith again made overtures to move his Senators to Minnesota, American League president Joe Cronin suggested that a nine-team league might be an option. It became evident that the Minneapolis group that was planning to be part of the Continental League was also soliciting the American League for inclusion, a situation that served to undermine Rickey's plans.[22]

Instead of panicking, Rickey responded rapidly, brusquely, and without apology to Major League attempts to sabotage the new league. He made it clear that he was not intimidated by the underhanded games being played by baseball insiders and cautioned the group in Minnesota that they risked being frozen out of both leagues. While doing this, he put on a charm offensive to garner public support, working to ensure that baseball fans were familiar with his league's plans. In one example, on October 23, 1960, he appeared as a mystery guest on *What's My Line?*, a popular prime-time entertainment show. While being questioned, he told a national audience that the Continental League was "as inevitable as tomorrow morning."[23]

As the public relations game unfolded, Rickey put together a well-orchestrated plan that required a major commitment from each sponsoring community. Participants were required to allocate $50,000 to the league to ensure that administrative resources were in place, while committing $2.5 million worth of capital to their team's development. That investment did not include stadium construction. To ensure a Major League atmosphere, cities were expected to provide ballparks with seating capacities of thirty-five thousand or more. Rickey also lined up Montreal as a ninth city, which was to be tapped only if another city abandoned the effort. To assure a more united front, Rickey suggested, and owners agreed, that $2.5 million in reparations be paid by any owner who abandoned the Continental League to join one of the other leagues.[24]

Rickey worked behind the scenes to make Major League insiders squirm. Getting Congress to apply pressure was one of his most effective avenues. To that end, Tennessee senator Estes Kefauver introduced legislation in February 1959 that would undermine baseball's antitrust exemption.[25] Borrowing from Keating's legislation, the Kefauver proposal cleverly extended several antitrust exemptions to other sports leagues, a move that muddied the waters in terms of behind-the-scenes lobbying and support. However, the legislation placed restrictions on how many players a sports organization could control. That provision would severely affect Major League Baseball, whose Minor League structure was woven into its operational philosophy. Senate Bill 3483 would attack baseball's ability to protect an unlimited amount of players. That provision alone would allow the Continental League to compete for top Minor League ballplayers who otherwise would be locked into restrictive Minor League contracts. Beyond that, the measure more clearly defined antitrust violations, a move that could cost baseball dearly in the future.

Baseball owners were used to dealing with Congress, but in this case, heavy lobbying and inside work caused the vote to be significantly tighter than anticipated. Lyndon Johnson, the powerful Senate majority leader who was a close friend of Roy Hofheinz, used his leverage to get the measure on the floor for a vote. In addition, Johnson twisted arms and cajoled Senate colleagues to support the measure. The measure failed, 41–45, but the closeness of the vote sent shockwaves throughout the Major League system. Owners were confident that the measure would be soundly defeated, yet just three changed votes would have ensured its passage. The legislation was sent back to committee, where it could die or be revised for a subsequent vote.[26]

Major League Baseball interests may have wanted to block expansion, but the pressure was mounting and the risks of continued stonewalling were too high for their comfort. Rickey had forced their hand. He had devised a structure that shrewdly ensured competitive teams while integrating a system for pooling scouting resources and sharing ticket and broadcast revenues. The new league would have played in newer facilities in rapidly growing cities whose demographics were increasingly favorable, and fears developed that Minor League talent might prefer the new league as a quicker route to the Majors. With all that was at stake, Branch Rickey and his Continental League executives demonstrated that the lords of baseball were no longer holding all of the cards.

If the Continental League had survived, baseball might have lost a larger slice of the pie than expansion might ever take, but losing any part of the antitrust exemption was a monumental gamble that the owners were unwilling to risk. The delays and stonewalling stopped, with baseball executives scheduling a meeting with the Continental League leadership on August 2, 1960, to determine what might come next. The anger of the baseball hierarchy was palpable. Dodgers owner Walter O'Malley asserted that "your having rocked the boat makes it hard for the major leagues to meet you halfway," while New York attorney William Shea countered that organized baseball's ongoing intransigence left them little alternative.[27]

As the smoke began to settle and emotions came under control, Milwaukee owner Lou Perini suggested an agreement to expand to ten teams in each league by 1962, with a commitment to evaluate further expansion to twelve teams at some time in the future. National League president Warren Giles had insisted that for expansion to succeed, the Continental League would have to disband. Cullinan negotiated that Continental League cities would get first consideration for future expansion, establishing Houston's spot as an early entrant. With a commitment to add eight teams to the two leagues eventually and New York and Houston firmly entrenched as front-runners, the Continental League ceased operations before a single game was ever played. Although the leagues did not grow to twelve teams until 1969, the future was set for New York and Houston. The Big Apple would presumably get a National League team, but Houston might end up in either league.

The goal of Major League Baseball was simple: if the big money brought by New York and Houston was neutralized, disbanding the new league would be an easier task to achieve.[28] To ensure that the Minnesota group was placated, the American League later permitted Calvin Griffith to move his team to Minneapolis for the 1961 season; subsequently, to satisfy politicians who might otherwise go after baseball later, expansion teams were planned for Washington DC and Los Angeles.

Although Houston was selected for expansion, the Houston Sports Association had no guarantees that they would be handed the reins of a Major League franchise despite attempts by Cullinan to achieve such a goal. Fear persisted that the ownership group of the Houston Buffs might somehow, through undetermined political machinations, move ahead of the Kirksey and Cullinan group's bid. After all, the Buffs were affiliated with the Cardinals, with Buffs part-owners Eddie Dyer and Marty Marion both maintaining strong connections with Major League officials. Further, Kirksey's proposed team takeover in 1952 may not have been forgotten by everyone within that organization. Beyond that, even if the HSA was awarded the Houston franchise, they still needed to negotiate territorial rights with the Buffs ownership group. Should Houston apply to the American League so that the HSA could distance itself from the Buffs, or would a National League application make more sense in light of prior affiliations? The Houston Sports Association solved the dilemma by applying to both leagues. Once again, Kirksey and his contingent were in the middle of several dicey political situations.

Although Houston Sports Association members had done much of the legwork to get the stadium funding in place, no documentation formally named them as the party responsible for management of the stadium issue. Still, by 1960, Roy Hofheinz was on board, and his many and varied political connections would eventually resolve that issue. Yet at the time, no one knew for sure if the Houston Sports Association or the Houston Buffs contingent would get the team.

While in Pittsburgh for the 1960 World Series, Cullinan expressed interest in committing to the National League and received an opaque, less than enthusiastic, verbal indication from Walter O'Malley that the move was "all right." Kirksey still worried that the Buffs might somehow step in front of them. With Buffs co-owner Eddie Dyer at the Series, too, Kirksey continued to torture himself as scenario after painful scenario ran through his head. When asked whether news was forthcoming, Kirksey would nervously repeat to anyone who would ask, "No champagne yet."[29]

The league set up a meeting in Chicago on October 17, inviting the Houston contingent. They were confident of approval, but Kirksey and Cullinan had worked too hard and had faced too many previous disappointments to take a single thing for granted.

With the stakes as high as they had ever been, Hofheinz asserted that he would be best positioned to deliver the final pitch. Kirksey and Cullinan had done years of heavy lifting to bring this meeting to fruition, and a case could be made for either of them to step up. Kirksey was more viscerally connected with the owners, while Cullinan's calm presence exuded the sort of Texas wealth that was likely to impress baseball's big shots.

However, Houston's attempt to get a Major League team had been undermined by struggles with the ballpark issue more than once, and Hofheinz would shine in explaining the funding already in place while showcasing the plans for a futuristic stadium that was amazingly unique. Beyond that, Hofheinz's oratory skills were outstanding. He gained acclaim as a youngster, later won over the public in elections, and even impressed Lyndon Johnson, at that time Senate majority leader, one of the most powerful positions in the nation. The choice was not difficult if emotions were set aside. Kirksey and Cullinan agreed to stay on the sidelines without a fuss, deferring to Hofheinz's charisma. As long as he didn't stumble, something that was not in his supremely confident nature, Hofheinz's role as the presumed ballpark project leader would assure the owners that Houston was their best expansion option and that the Houston Sports Association was best positioned to serve as the leader.

After Hofheinz's presentation concluded, the owners quickly approved the Houston bid, with National League president Warren Giles posing with Hofheinz, Kirksey, and Cullinan next to a huge image of the proposed domed stadium. Kirksey, Cullinan, and Hofheinz celebrated their success as they boarded a Delta jet for the trip back to Houston. As soon as they stepped off the plane, they were greeted with a second, even larger party, organized by Jack Valenti, a colorful public relations executive. Valenti later worked for Lyndon Johnson in the White House and soon after that headed to Hollywood to lead the Motion Picture Association of America for more than three decades. Valenti hired a Dixieland band to choreograph a festive greeting while well-wishers cheered, back-slapped each other, and laughed in celebration on the tarmac as the victorious Houston contingent came off the plane.

The airport party was a brief moment of fun, but now the members of the Houston Sports Association were responsible for assembling a baseball organization. Much work had to be done. So many tricky loose ends still remained, including solidifying team-related funding, identifying an appropriate site for construction, establishing a name for the team, determining the roster, developing a strategy for player development, and figuring out the front office staff.

The initial structure of the Houston Sports Association simply required that each member front $500 for a future stake in the team. At this point, the money had to be put on the table. While some initial investors backed out, for the most part, Bob Smith and Roy Hofheinz stepped up and filled the void. Smith was the big money behind the operation, while Hofheinz was the person who got things done. They were the largest shareholders. Cullinan was next in overall number of shares. Despite his enthusiasm and energy, Kirksey owned a mere 2 percent.

At the outset, the front office issues seemed to be off to a good start, as Gabe Paul, a longtime baseball executive, flew back with the Houston contingent, with intentions of stepping in as general manager. He was quickly announced as the team's first general manager, but in short order he became frustrated with Hofheinz's overbearing management style. Instead of trying to make it work, on April 27, about six months after Houston was awarded its team, Paul unexpectedly stepped aside to take over baseball operations in Cleveland, citing "personal reasons" for the decision. Much later, Paul admitted that when he signed on to Houston, "I still thought Cullinan was the big gun," but shortly after moving to Houston, "it was very obvious that Hofheinz was in the saddle—to my surprise."[30]

At the same time, the team had to settle the territorial rights issue, meaning that the same Houston Buffs owners who had hoped to lead Houston into the Major Leagues were on the other side of the negotiating table. Despite having paid about $100,000 for the team just a few years earlier, Buffs ownership set the initial asking price in the half million dollar range. Although it was a highly inflated price, on January 17 the Houston Sports Association agreed to pay $393,000 for the team. After completing the deal, Craig Cullinan expressed relief at clearing this hurdle, stating that the next major step was getting the funding on track to "give Houston the finest stadium in the world."[31]

With Gabe Paul's unexpected departure in April, for a brief moment George Kirksey, hardly a baseball personnel guru, took over as general manager as a frantic search unfolded for a qualified replacement. By September the Houston group had locked in Paul Richards, a Texas native and experienced baseball man who had guided the Orioles to a surprising second-place finish in 1960. Richards had an eye for talent and once on board with Houston was able to sign Jim Wynn, Joe Morgan, Mike Cuellar, and Rusty Staub. In Staub's case, Kirksey did the signing after travel complications from a hurricane slowed Richards's arrival. However, Kirksey proceeded with such enthusiasm that he managed to overpay Staub and offer a Minor League contract to Staub's younger brother and a scouting job to Staub's father before Richards's arrival. Despite the lack of productivity from two of the three signings, Rusty Staub evolved into a successful and charismatic contact hitter who turned out to be a fan favorite.[32]

Naming the team was yet another issue. A contest was underway to allow for public input, but this competition was more a public relations effort than an open-ended and democratic process. Kirksey liked the Colts, the name of a gun manufacturer that was part of nineteenth-century western lore, while Hofheinz preferred something that better symbolized the future. As the naming issue was being considered, television's most popular shows were Westerns, with a CBS show, *Gunsmoke*, as the nation's biggest audience draw. The gun used on this show was a Colt .45. Whether related or not, the Colt .45 was a prominent symbol of 1960s television culture, so Hofheinz, whose initial preference was the Stars, was outvoted in a rare personal defeat.

Without hesitation Hofheinz enthusiastically worked with the Colts name as the new temporary ballpark was assembled next to the future site of the Astrodome. At Kirksey's urging, the groundbreaking featured top leaders firing live ammo into the ground instead of predictably lifting shovelsful of dirt, while the outdoor stadium had a heavy western theme that reveled in old Texas culture. When it became increasingly apparent that much of the public did not connect the gun to the name, the team name was fine-tuned to become the Colt .45s. Kirksey explained that this announcement unfolded because the team wanted "to stress the fact that 'Colts' refers to guns and not to ponies."[33]

As Richards took over player-related decisions, Kirksey worked on other issues. The team also hired Bill Giles, the son of National League president Warren Giles, to serve as traveling secretary and publicist, in a move that would presumably help the Houston Sports Association in dealing with league-related issues. Kirksey worked with Giles and others to whip up publicity in both national and local media, and he organized activities intended to energize the fan base. He was involved with setting up the team's $150,000, ten-acre training facility in Apache Junction, Arizona. He also continued efforts to build enthusiasm for Houston's indoor stadium while it was under construction.[34]

Kirksey organized luncheons and community events, and he worked on outreach designed to generate excitement among women and children. Days before the start of the inaugural season, Kirksey hired Ginny Pace, a mother of five with a journalism background, to serve as a "publicist and promotions director." In covering the hire, the *Sporting News* condescendingly noted that "the ladies, bless 'em, not only will be welcomed at Colt Stadium, but they'll be given an organized program of activity under the direction of a full-time woman publicist and promotions director." Kirksey emphasized that "the success of this ball club will be in direct proportion to the promotion we generate among women and children."[35]

As the temporary outdoor stadium opened, Hofheinz reiterated that the team's marketing strategy had to "stimulate the wife and family interests." To ensure this, the ballpark was painted in bright colors and had tidy restrooms that featured kid-sized toilets with "For Future Colts Stars" signage.[36] The Colt .45s opened their season in Houston on April 10, 1962, beating the Chicago Cubs 8–2 before an enthusiastic crowd of 25,271. Surprisingly, they then proceeded to sweep the Cubs in a three-game series. Major League Baseball was finally introduced to Texas, and 924,456 fans made their way to the ballpark to see Houston's home team that season.

However, the expansion draft was not kind to the expansion teams from Houston and New York. Their rosters included less than stellar castoffs from established teams, a fact that inhibited on-field success. In their first year, the Colt .45s finished with a 64–96 record. The eighth-place finish was disappointing, but it was good enough to edge out the Chicago Cubs and the New York Mets. With identical 66–96 records in 1963 and 1964, total attendance for the Colt.45s dropped off by about two hundred thousand fans after their inaugural season. As a result, the Houston Sports Association was more than happy to change venues. To ensure a smooth transition, Roy Hofheinz took steps to remarket the team.

If Hofheinz was bothered by the testosterone-laced focus on the past during the Colt .45s' initial naming process, he did not let it show. Nevertheless, when an opportunity to shift the team name emerged, Hofheinz quickly pounced. By late 1964, when the Colt Firearms Company's legal counsel insisted that the team pay royalties for the use of the Colt .45s name on merchandise that it was selling, instead of trying to negotiate further, Hofheinz unilaterally changed the name to the more futuristic Astros. He further insisted that publications, souvenirs, and other materials be discarded to make way for the team's new name.

After three long years of baseball in the mosquito-laden and oppressive Houston sun, the newly branded team was ready to move indoors. The Harris County Domed Stadium, better known to the public as the Astrodome, opened to much fanfare, including a personal visit by President Lyndon Johnson and Texas governor John Connolly, as the newly christened Astros took on the world champion New York Yankees in an exhibition game.

One of Kirksey's jobs was to get all of NASA's original astronauts to throw out a collective ceremonial first pitch. He successfully followed through on this task with enthusiasm and gusto. The Astros won 2–1 in a twelve-inning contest that was meaningless but that received extensive national attention. Mickey Mantle hit the first home run in the Dome, and the game ended when Nellie Fox lined a walk-off single over Tony Kubek's outstretched glove to drive Jim Wynn home in the bottom of the twelfth inning. The Astros finished the 1965 season with a 65–97 record, a disappointing ninth-place outcome. Only their expansion colleagues, the New York Mets, had a weaker National League record.

The Yankees exhibition game marked the start of an amazing legacy of entertainment for the Astrodome. Kirksey reveled in the moment as the entire nation was introduced to the futuristic new facility and the Astros. But Hofheinz wanted the Astrodome to be much more than a sports facility. His goal was to make it the most amazing entertainment venue on the planet. Despite shortcomings that prompted baseball purists to attack the Dome as a suitable sports venue, for its first decade of operation it revolutionized the nature of indoor entertainment.

People excitedly made an Astrodome visit a priority when visiting south Texas, and entertainers and performers of all kinds looked at it as a premium venue that would enhance their notoriety. Celebrities such as Bob Hope, Walt Disney, and others made their way to Houston to watch events from the comfort of a luxurious Astrodome skybox. Houstonians enjoyed Astros baseball, Oilers football, the University of Houston's sports teams, and the Houston Livestock Show and Rodeo, too, but outsiders, whether famous or otherwise, were attracted to the Dome because it was unlike any other facility ever built.

Even though the Astros were not a winning team during their early years in the Dome, the Astrodome was a national venue for baseball's game of the week and, later, it hosted the 1968 and 1986 All-Star Games. As the team eventually improved, Astros fans were treated to countless memorable moments inside the Astrodome, including no-hit performances by Nolan Ryan and Mike Scott. Both pitchers also led a highly talented Astros team into the 1986 playoffs in one of the most memorable league playoff series ever to unfold. Fittingly, it matched the two 1962 expansion teams against each other, and at the time, game six was the longest postseason contest ever to be played. Although the Astros lost to the New York Mets 7–6 in that decisive game, this sixteen-inning contest has been called one of the most thrilling playoff games ever by several baseball enthusiasts.[37]

The Astrodome was the first major sports facility to offer paid, guided tours. In its first year alone more than four hundred thousand people from all over the world spent a dollar to see the facility that changed the future of sports-related construction. Athletes and coaches were also moved by the unique qualities of the Astrodome. Shortly after setting foot in the Dome, Yankees legend Mickey Mantle said that the futuristic design "reminds me what my first ride would be like in a flying saucer." Hall of Fame manager Sparky Anderson observed that "when I managed there, I always felt like I was on a stage show."

After AstroTurf was installed, Leo Durocher called it "the world's biggest pool table." That same artificial turf set off massive debates among sports purists, while forcing unexpected adjustments to ensure that baseball could be properly played. Visiting the Astrodome shortly after his retirement, second baseman Johnny Temple observed, "We were surprised by the couple behind us. They said the cheering inspired by the scoreboard reminded them of a football game." He then chuckled and asserted, "In Texas, you can't get a higher compliment than that."[38]

The Astrodome was home to some memorable football moments, too. Before Bud Adams moved his team to Tennessee, football-crazy Texans were treated to many years of exciting professional football inside the Dome. The punishing running of Earl Campbell and an extremely stout defense anchored by Elvin Bethea were exciting dimensions of NFL football played under the Dome. The Bum Philips–coached Houston Oilers made several strong runs into the playoffs. The "Luv Ya Blue" Oilers played a hard-nosed brand of football that proved to be among the toughest challenges ever faced by championship teams from Pittsburgh, Kansas City, and Oakland.

The University of Houston football team also made the Astrodome their home, treating Houstonians to memorable competitions against many nationally ranked teams. As the Astrodome opened, Bill Yeoman's exciting veer offense brought the Cougars several winning seasons, including a 1980 Cotton Bowl 17–14 upset victory over a Tom Osborn–coached Nebraska team that was ranked as high as second nationally during that season. Later, Cougar fans were entertained by quarterback David Klingler's high-flying offense, which broke several NCAA offensive records in the 1990s.

The Astrodome also hosted the event that was often dubbed the "Game of the Century." Scheduled on January 20, 1968, this college basketball game featured two powerhouse teams, the John Wooden–coached UCLA Bruins, then national champions, against the second-ranked Houston Cougars, coached by Guy Lewis. The favored UCLA squad lost 71–69 in a thrilling game that was more heavily publicized than any NCAA basketball competition before it. The Elvin Hayes–led Cougars snapped UCLA's amazing forty-seven-game winning streak. The game was featured on the cover of *Sports Illustrated* and was extensively covered elsewhere. It was the first college basketball game to attract more than fifty thousand spectators. Dick Enberg and Bob Petit hosted the national broadcast at a time when coast-to-coast coverage of a regular season college basketball game was unheard-of. The game preempted regular network programming in major cities, and many believe that this game paved the way for March Madness because it clearly demonstrated that top-quality NCAA basketball could attract, excite, and entertain a national audience.

A year after Title IX ushered in calls for gender equity in athletics, a "Battle of the Sexes" tennis match between Bobby Riggs and Billie Jean King gained immense national attention, too. Riggs was a former number-one-ranked male tennis player who had, at age fifty-five, gained notoriety for defeating top-ranked female tennis player Margaret Court several months earlier. His ongoing taunting of female tennis players in general prompted Billie Jean King to agree to play him on September 20, 1973, in a nationally televised spectacle. ABC provided network coverage of the event, with over ninety million people reportedly watching the match worldwide. King defeated Riggs in three sets inside the Astrodome. The event attracted 30,472 spectators, at the time the largest live audience to ever watch tennis.

The Astrodome was also the site of boxing matches, including a number of bouts that featured Muhammad Ali, and it hosted the 1989 NBA All-Star Game. The Houston Livestock Show and Rodeo showcased incredible athletic performances, too, including competitive bull riding, cattle roping, and steer wrestling that was often world class in quality. Mini-car racing, polo, and other, less mainstream sports-related events were booked, too, making the Astrodome one of the busiest sports venues anywhere on the planet.

Yet Hofheinz's vision for the Dome meant that Houstonians were treated to significantly more than sporting events. As the Astrodome was under construction, the evangelist Billy Graham repeatedly tried to book it. Eventually his "Crusade for Christ" event in 1965 drew huge crowds to the Dome while gaining substantial national attention. The Astrodome also hosted a variety of lower-profile conventions, trade shows, and industry-based events. As an ironic example, Texans could explore outdoor opportunities while indoors when Hofheinz booked an industry-sponsored boat show for 1965.

The Astrodome was the site of numerous concerts that featured luminaries such as Elvis Presley, Paul McCartney, Selena, and George Strait. Recalling his first dramatic indoor entertainment experience as a youth, Hofheinz also brought in the circus. He worked hard to ensure that this was a popular annual event, too. Instead of bringing in a regional or lesser-known circus, Hofheinz booked the Ringling Bros. Circus inside the Dome each year, and he eventually bought a controlling interest in that famed circus.

As the Dome aged, it was still in the running to host a Super Bowl, although it never accomplished that feat, and it eventually earned the right to host a major political convention, attracting the Republican Party to its space in 1992. In its first year, the Houston Sports Association reported that over four and a half million people entered the Astrodome, a number that strongly outpaced crowds drawn to Chicago's McCormick Place, then considered by many to be the nation's premiere all-purpose facility. Amazingly, in 1965 the Astrodome was even able to outdraw the combined tourist numbers for the Eiffel Tower, the Empire State Building, and Rome's Colosseum.[39]

The Astrodome changed the face of Houston, bringing entertainment options previously unavailable to the Bayou City while raising its stature nationally. Hofheinz's grand vision brought in new forms of entertainment while making some events that might have come anyway much bigger and more exciting. New hotels, the Astrohall, and the Astroworld theme park were all the result of the Astrodome's early success. But, unlike Kirksey and Cullinan, who regarded Major League Baseball as the prize that put Houston on the map, Hofheinz regarded baseball as a relatively small part of the Astrodome and the larger entertainment complex that would later surround it.

Hofheinz admitted to Cullinan and other insiders that, in the long run, he saw baseball as a mere 25 percent of the big picture, and that thought disturbed some of the sports enthusiasts who signed on to bring a Major League team to Houston. In 1962 Cullinan, a man who had done more to bring baseball to Houston than anyone except Kirksey, quietly approached top investor Bob Smith, asking to be taken out of the leadership mix of the Houston Sports Association. He then sold his shares and pulled out as a minority owner. Cullinan explained later that it was "one of the most painful decisions of my life," but it was predicated on clear philosophic differences with Hofheinz.

The differences extended to others who were passionate about baseball. After Gabe Paul resigned as Houston's first general manager, Hofheinz asserted, "I guess I scared the hell out of Paul. Paul had been in the business too long to have the imagination for the job we needed done here."[40] As with Paul's early withdrawal, Cullinan left even before the Astrodome was completed because Hofheinz saw sports as a limited part of a much larger entertainment empire. By contrast, Kirksey and Cullinan saw sports as the force driving the need for the facility.

Kirksey held onto his shares for longer, but in October 1965, after the Astros completed their first season inside the Astrodome, Kirksey took a trip to the Cayman Islands with plans to return in time to attend the postseason owners meetings. He found out through his secretary that his presence was not wanted, a decision clearly instigated by Hofheinz. Hofheinz had already moved

Kirksey to a smaller office after purchasing Bob Smith's stock, a move that foreshadowed what might follow.

Although Kirksey tried to stay in the good graces of both Smith and Hofheinz, his relationship with Smith was a more comfortable one, so when Hofheinz asserted his authority, Kirksey could sense that his days as a baseball man were numbered. Hofheinz had already fired Paul Richards at the close of the 1965 season, so the circle of baseball enthusiasts that Kirksey enjoyed working alongside was diminishing. Richards left Houston in such anger that when someone suggested the Hofheinz might be his own worst enemy, Richards exclaimed, "Not while I am alive."[41]

When pushed out, Kirksey was sixty-two and at a point in his life where retirement must have been in his thoughts. Instead of sulking, on May 9, 1966, Kirksey sold his Houston Sports Association shares directly to Hofheinz and made plans to move on with his life. He briefly tried to get an NFL team for Houston, one that would compete with Bud Adams's AFL squad at a time when the NFL was in a pitched competition with the upstart league. In the process, he was able to connect with Smith and Hofheinz once again as well as with numerous other Houston executives while traveling throughout the nation to meet with owners and executives. He sat down with NFL commissioner Pete Rozelle and Giants owner Wellington Mara, among others, but his passion for football was not nearly as intense as his love of baseball. As that opportunity began to unravel, Kirksey could see the writing on the wall. He stepped away, briefly dabbled in auto racing, and then began to travel around Europe, realizing that the sports-related excitement he had helped to create in Houston was no longer an option for him.

In true Kirksey fashion, he made new friends and did an uneven job of keeping in touch with his old acquaintances back home. After several divorces, he talked about marrying again but lived out the rest of his life as a bachelor, traveling throughout the world. On May 30, 1971, Memorial Day in the United States, Kirksey's extraordinarily memorable life tragically ended in an automobile accident as he drove a Porsche around the winding roads of France.

Even though Kirksey's and Cullinan's contributions to Houston's sports legacy were enormous, Hofheinz was a hard-charging bull; he was not going to let anything slow down his plans for building an empire. As Cullinan and Kirksey were quietly withdrawing from the Houston Sports Association, Hofheinz was pulling strings to build a massive entertainment empire around the Astrodome.

The presence of a Major League team loomed large as a rationale for building the Astrodome, but for Hofheinz, the baseball team was just one piece of a significantly larger puzzle. As Cullinan tried to analyze the big picture, he was troubled that the legacy of what he and Kirksey tried to achieve might be somehow squandered. As he left the Houston Sports Association, Cullinan asserted that "baseball was the life blood of the whole thing," insisting further that "without it, there was nothing—no franchise, no stadium, no hotels."[42] Whether Hofheinz wanted to recognize it or not, even if their contributions to the Astrodome were indirect, the dedication and persistence of Kirksey and Cullinan played a major role in that project's successful completion, as did the financial prowess and initial loyalty of Bob Smith.

Hofheinz was pleased to be part of the team that brought baseball to Houston, but in his mind, much more important milestones would lie ahead. He was working to engineer something that no community had ever tried. If others got in the way of his larger-than-life vision of Houston's future, Hofheinz moved onward without them, like it or not. Creating the first climate-controlled indoor sports facility required vast determination and significant expertise.

To succeed in getting the Astrodome's construction on track and completed, Hofheinz would need engineering and construction expertise not previously seen in sports construction elsewhere. As Houston's Colt .45s fought an ongoing battle to stay out of last place, Hofheinz oversaw baseball operations, but at the same time his priorities shifted to engineering a unique structure that would challenge the nature of sports spectatorship for generations to come. As fans swatted away at mosquitos and sat in the sweltering hot sun of a temporary ballpark, Hofheinz moved frantically behind the scenes to lay the foundation for the Astrodome's construction.

DOME TOWN

4

Zimmerman and the Grand Plan
Engineering a Marvel

The construction of the Astrodome was, by any measure, a tremendous undertaking. As it happens, Hofheinz and Smith's elaborate chess moves to ensure that the building had the necessary financial backing were mere prologue to the actual effort to bring the mighty structure into being. And it was a Herculean struggle, to say the least.

A host of architectural and engineering minds came together in service of the project—and, in their own ways, they represented the most influential and adept thinkers of their era. In the spirit of the finest engineering projects, the structural integrity of the proposed domed stadium would be tested and retested, time and time again, in order to ensure the highest technical quality given the available expertise. Without a doubt, the heart of the eventual building—and its most innovative feature to the present day— was the Astrodome's roof structure. In itself, the Dome's telltale roof harkened back to Hofheinz's original vision of a magisterial building that would reflect the grandeur and spectacle of the Roman Colosseum.

In early 1962, with principal architect Robert Minchew's rendering of the stadium all but complete, the responsibility for engineering the Astrodome's roof and supporting structural edifices fell upon the very able shoulders of forty-eight-year-old Kenneth E. Zimmerman, who, by the late 1950s, had already led a storied life in his own right. Born on June 18, 1913, in the tiny burg of Coleman in west central Texas, Zimmerman graduated in 1929 from Coleman High, where he was a star football player, before pursuing an architectural engineering degree from Texas A&M College. He graduated in 1934 as a commissioned officer—a second lieutenant in the army—and took a job as a draftsman in his cousin's Longview, Texas, engineering firm. By 1937 he had attained his engineering certificate, not to mention a growing family—his eldest daughter, Frances Sue, was born to Zimmerman's first wife, Weaser Rushing, in December of that year; her younger sister, Molly, followed a few years later. With his much-sought-after certification in hand, Zimmerman briefly worked for an architect in Tyler, Texas, before taking a position in Houston as an engineer with a budding firm led by Walter P. Moore Sr., a Rice University graduate. In 1931 Moore had famously established his engineering startup at the height of the Great Depression after selling his prized Stutz Bearcat. Desperate for work, Moore eked out a living designing foundations for tony River Oaks neighborhood clients at five dollars a pop. For Moore's firm, Zimmerman turned out to be the missing piece of the puzzle. As his longtime colleague Narendra K. Gosain recalls, Zimmerman was a natural. "He could look at drawings and sense if something was amiss," Gosain observes. "People trusted him [and] architects trusted his judgment."[1]

Zimmerman had scarcely worked with Moore for two years before the threat of World War II became a reality. In 1941 Zimmerman resumed his second lieutenancy and joined the Army Corps of Engineers. During the following year, he was posted to Oak Ridge, Tennessee, where he served under Major General Leslie R. Groves for the remainder of the war. Oak Ridge was the secret location selected by General Groves to carry out key aspects of the Manhattan Project before shifting the project out west. With secrecy at a premium during wartime, Groves had been afforded broad powers to oversee the development of the atomic bomb. While Groves tasked Zimmerman and others with preparing the Oak Ridge facilities throughout 1942, the general selected University of California, Berkeley, physicist J. Robert Oppenheimer to begin establishing a laboratory in Los Alamos, New Mexico.

Back in Oak Ridge, Zimmerman served as the facility's property manager, working tirelessly in the service of scientists and contractors specializing in a host of disciplines, ranging from physics and engineering to metallurgy, chemistry, and ordnance. Not surprisingly, his keen engineering mind came into play on numerous occasions.[2] At the height of its secret wartime operations, Oak Ridge's population approached seventy-five thousand people living and working on fifty-six thousand acres. The workers toiled within "The City behind the Fence" in the vaunted Y-12, K-25, and S-50 uranium plants. Zimmerman led the design and construction of lab facilities as well as all of the trappings of a workaday American town, including the installation of more than three hundred miles of road, fifty-five miles of railroad track, seven movie theaters, seventeen restaurants, and thirteen supermarkets.[3]

At Oak Ridge, Zimmerman's job was ineluctably simple and complex at the same time. As property manager, he was required to do everything possible to ensure that the Oak Ridge personnel had absolutely everything that they needed to produce and separate plutonium in order to build an atomic bomb. In one such instance in August 1942, due to the wartime shortage of copper, Zimmerman oversaw the transfer, under Groves's orders, of some six thousand tons of silver bullion, a requisite electromagnetic conductor, via train and under heavy guard from the West Point depository. In yet another unforgettable moment, Zimmerman was acting as officer of the day when Senator Harry S. Truman arrived to inspect the Oak Ridge facilities under the auspices of the Truman Committee, the watchdog group—formally known as the Senate Special Committee to Investigate the National Defense Program—that was tasked with oversight of all U.S. war production activities. As officer of the day, Zimmerman had the unenviable task of refusing entry to Senator Truman because he lacked the necessary security clearance. In an interesting irony, turning Truman away stood in sharp contrast with subsequent events. Ultimately, on August 6, 1945, it would be President Truman who ordered the dropping of the atomic bomb on Hiroshima and, a few days later, on Nagasaki in order to hasten the Japanese surrender.[4]

After the war, Zimmerman returned home to Houston to resume his work as a civilian employee of Walter P. Moore and Associates. But he didn't return alone. During his time at Oak Ridge, he became friendly with his secretary, Alma Sheffler, whom he married shortly after rejoining the firm. In the ensuing decades, Zimmerman would create structural designs for one Houston-area landmark after another, including the famed Jesse H. Jones Hall for the Performing Arts, Rice Stadium, the Warwick Hotel, the Bates-Freeman Building at the University of Texas M. D. Anderson Cancer Center, St. Vincent de Paul Catholic Church, and, later, Texas A&M's C. E. "Pat" Olsen Field, the Aggies' baseball stadium.[5]

But for Zimmerman, the Astrodome was his crowning achievement, and especially the building's roof structure, which required new and vital innovations in order to withstand seismic and weather forces—and, most importantly, the effects of time. With the bond issues having been reconciled via the election of January 31, 1961, Zimmerman and others were free to move forward with their work unabated. Indeed, the drive to bring the Astrodome to fruition in the plains on the southwest side of the city began at a furious pace. On Thursday, February 2, excavation of the site began promptly when a "huge dragline ripped dirt from a 300-acre site off S. Main."[6] Within a matter of weeks, some 260,000 cubic yards of dirt had been removed from the site in order to accommodate a mile-long drainage ditch and the building's sublevel playing field. Construction would be delayed until 1963, given a series of post-bond legal, financial, and political challenges. The new timetable meant that the Dome would be ready in time for the 1965 Major League Baseball season.[7]

In the interim, teams of engineers and architects had already begun honing and testing the final design specifications for the structure. Given their background in long-span structures, Zimmerman and Moore had been carrying out the technical analysis for the project since 1960. At one point, they considered Buckminster Fuller's famous geodesic dome designs, while also exploring the notion of wood trusses in order to support the roof structure. Ultimately, steel was selected, given its much higher tensile strength, in order to carry the massive load. A lamella roof structure, proposed by Roof Structures, Inc., headquartered in Webster Groves, Missouri, was chosen because of its spiderweb network of trusses. The lamella structure involves a double layer of steel members in order to ensure the building's engineering integrity.[8]

With Roof Structures, Inc., led by G. R. Kiewitt and Louis Bass, in tow, the project shifted to the testing phase in order to ascertain what kind of loads could be hung from and supported by the Dome's eventual roof design. The construction specifications stipulated that the roof be able to handle a live load of fifteen pounds per square foot; a sonic boom loading of two pounds per square foot; and a wind load of forty pounds per square foot, or sustained wind velocities of 135 MPH with gusts of 165 MPH.[9] Given the emergence of supersonic jet technology, being able to withstand the shockwave resulting from a sonic boom became a key issue in building construction during the late 1950s and 1960s. During the early 1960s, a load of two pounds per square foot was considered to be an acceptable limit, although Roof Structures prepared the building for an additional two pounds per square foot—or the possibility of two consecutive sonic booms—as an allowance.[10]

Perhaps even more significantly, the Dome's roof had to be able to withstand hurricane-force winds, given the building's proximity to the Gulf of Mexico and its annual assaults during the Atlantic hurricane season. For this reason, Roof Structures showed particular concern for the phenomenon of uplift in terms of high-wind-resistant construction necessitated by projects such as the Astrodome. In such cases, uplift forces must be transferred down toward the foundation in order to prevent catastrophic damage from the powerful suction associated with hurricanes. In order to properly calibrate the design, Roof Structures conducted wind-tunnel tests in an effort to establish the kinds of pressures that would be imposed on the building in the event of a full-scale tropical storm. With Moore in attendance, wind-tunnel tests were undertaken on a 1:8 scale model of the Dome. Given that such a large project had never been attempted before, a number of industry professional were on hand, including Ralph Anderson from the architectural firm of Wilson, Morris, Crain, and Anderson, along with Tom Kavanagh, a peer reviewer from New York City's Praeger, Kavanagh, and Waterbury assigned to the project.[11]

The wind-tunnel tests were carried out using the aeronautical wind tunnels housed at the McDonnell-Douglas Aircraft Corporation facilities in St. Louis, Missouri. Given that the Dome would have skylights permeating the surface of its roof, the model artificially represented these undulations via sand particles applied to the model's roof with adhesives to simulate the roughness of the skylights. In addition to outfitting the model with pressure points created by a series of pressure orifices, the team placed cotton tufts along the surface of the roof in order to visualize the wind's varying effects upon the building.[12]

After the technical data was captured from the wind-tunnel tests, the results were compiled and evaluated by Herbert Beckman, a Rice University nautical engineering professor. In his September 29, 1961, report Beckman observed that "during the tests, the model is subjected to a steady air stream while hurricane winds consist of small grain turbulence with a gust diameter of usually not more than 100 or 200 feet. These gusts will result in only partial loading of the building, and as a consequence, are less effective than a steady wind would be. The wind-tunnel data can be considered to give 'conservative' loads comparative with corresponding flow conditions in hurricanes." As it turned out, the data proved to be remarkably close to the hand calculations made by Bass in advance of the wind-tunnel tests in Missouri.[13]

Having completed this phase of the project, Roof Structures assimilated the dome roof pressure contours obtained from the wind-tunnel tests into the firm's design proposal for the lamella roof structure. Roof Structures accommodated the test results by incorporating different pressure bands across the graduated expanse of their roof design. The five bands included segments designed to accommodate twenty, twenty-five, thirty, thirty-five, and forty-five pounds of pressure per square foot, with the apex being able to withstand the highest level of pressure. Simply put, these graduated pressure bands served to contravene the suction pressure of hurricane-force winds attempting to lift the Dome away from its foundation.[14]

With Roof Structures having carried out the all-important work of testing the roof's integrity, Zimmerman's team at Walter P. Moore and Associates was left to ensure that the innovative roof structure was properly anchored to the rest of the building. This moment in the life of the Astrodome marked the design phase's most significant contribution in building the stadium to last.

Perhaps most importantly, engineering integrity of the highest order was required in order to address a multitude of safety concerns. Roof Structures, whose success with the Dome led to the firm's later work on the New Orleans Superdome, provided four drawings in support of a tension-ring design for the Astrodome. Working from Bass's drawings, Zimmerman and Moore created diamond-shaped lamellas separated by ring structures, which doubled as the roof's trusses. As a tension-ring formation, the building's dome extended across its supporting structure. Given the incredible forces and thoroughgoing tensions playing on the design, the manner in which the dome connected to the building proper was critical to its engineering.[15]

In order to accommodate the results of the wind-tunnel tests and the structural demands of Roof Structures' tension-ring design, Zimmerman devised a pair of innovations—masterworks of engineering elegance that set the Astrodome apart from any long-span structure ever conceived. Christened by Zimmerman as the "knuckle" column and the "star" column, these two deft approaches to addressing the wind-tunnel results and Roof Structures' resulting proposal were nothing short of revolutionary. The knuckle column, Gosain has observed, "was Mr. Zimmerman's brainchild." It was a "remarkable piece of engineering" that drew upon the human knuckle as a means of solving a complex problem: simply put, how do you allow for movement toward the centroid or center of the dome to account for temperature shifts, while deflecting movement of the structure caused by horizontal wind shear?[16]

To address this issue, Zimmerman devised a column that flexes, much like a person's knuckle, toward the center, while remaining outwardly fixed. The knuckle columns exist along the stadium's roofline, connecting the dome itself to the exterior superstructure. Arranged circumferentially around the interior perimeter of the dome every five degrees, the apparatus consists of four-foot-diameter steel pins at the end of each column. The lower bearing of each pin is welded to a plate support, leaving the top side of the pin to rotate freely in a close-fitted plate with a milled surface. If the top side had been welded, it would have been too rigid and in high wind conditions would have broken away from the structure, given the high tensions existing at that altitude of the building. In order to prevent uplift, anchorage was provided at the top of each column via massive U-bolts. As long as the building exists, the knuckle columns will continue doing their work, acting in concert with temperature changes while remaining rigid in the face of enormous wind shear—flexing inward, yet not flexing outward, like the human knuckle.[17] According to Gosain, when the Dome first opened, the knuckle columns at the top of the stadium were exposed, affording fans in the upper reaches of the stadium with a rare glimpse of engineering in action. Unfortunately, many visitors found the visible movement of the knuckle columns to be unsettling; hence, the joints were later concealed behind metal plates in order to prevent fan consternation at the sight of the Astrodome flexing in response to the elements.[18]

In addition to the knuckle column, Zimmerman utilized the innovation that he described as the star column, along with the concrete retaining wall at the Astrodome's base, in order to execute Roof Structures' tension-ring design. For Zimmerman, the star column and the retaining wall at the Dome's lower perimeter afforded the massive building two levels of tiebacks working in tandem with the knuckle column at the roofline. In engineering parlance, tiebacks act as anchors and stabilizing mechanisms in order to balance the heavy weight load of the roof—especially in a long-span structure such as the Astrodome—against the external forces working upon the building from horizontal and vertical vantage points. Zimmerman's design called for two levels of tiebacks, including the star columns positioned at midheight around the building's exterior, as well as the tiebacks located every five degrees at the base of the retaining wall. The lower-level tiebacks were reinforced by a series of deadman anchors, located eighty feet away from the retaining wall, in order to further support the efforts of the tension ring and preserve the building's structural integrity. The building's design criteria called for structural elements that protected the stadium against lateral wind loads and "people generated sway loads." In addition to concerns about numerous natural exterior forces, the structure had to withstand abrupt and rhythmic movements of personnel and visitors inside the building.[19]

For the most part, Zimmerman's deployment of X-braced steel bents from the top of the stadium's structure down to the foundation afforded the Astrodome with the requisite resistance to lateral wind loads working upon the building. Given the existence of expansion joints located around the stadium, each sector of the structure required its own system of lateral load-resistant frames. These midlevel tiebacks can be viewed on the building's exterior as a series of distinctive star columns, located circumferentially around the Astrodome's perimeter and positioned every five degrees. Zimmerman dubbed the features star columns in honor of the Lone Star State, Texas's distinctive nickname that refers to its former existence as an independent republic. The columns resemble giant lowercase letter *t*'s. The tieback system was completed at the Dome's lowest level with tiebacks arranged around the base of the foundation as part of the retaining wall. The concrete that formed the retaining wall required a maximum strength of three thousand pounds per square inch, with the perimeter retaining wall consisting of a counterfort system, which ties the building's slab and base together. In this instance, the counterfort system serves as a buttress in order to provide rigidity and reduce the shear forces imposed on the retaining wall by the soil. The external tiebacks beyond the retaining wall consisted of steel strands placed every 2.5 degrees around the stadium. In order to protect the strands against the corrosive effects of the soil, Zimmerman's design specified a cathodic protection system as a prophylactic measure. With such a system, the steel strands are encased in a sacrificial metal that serves as the anode of an electromechanical cell, while the steel strand that forms each tieback acts as the cathode.[20] Decades later, when unearthed for the purposes of renovation, the structural metal revealed no signs of corrosion during the intervening years, proving the original design to be highly effective.[21]

With the integrated design of redundant systems involving the knuckle columns, the star columns, the tiebacks, and the retaining wall in place, Zimmerman was able to satisfy, with great engineering elegance and innovation, the demands of Roof Structures' tension-ring specifications.

As nearly ten thousand tons of steel began to arrive at the construction site, the contractors, American Bridge, started the process of overseeing the preparations for building the concrete retaining wall. In order to construct the Dome's storied roof structure and connect it to the steel framework, crews from American Bridge fabricated thirty-seven falsework erection towers. Each tower was placed circumferentially at the base of the building in order to provide support for the trusses that grew to span 642 feet in diameter. The towers consisted of an inner ring of twelve 200-foot towers, an outer ring of twenty-four 160-foot towers, and a 303-foot center tower. Thirty-six towers were arranged as opposing pairs in twelve pie sectors comprised of 30 degrees, with the thirty-seventh tower placed in the middle of the building in support of the Astrodome's geometric center.[22]

The erection of the steel trusses presented particular challenges, as the tension ring had to remain vertical at 60 degrees Fahrenheit and with the dead loads applied in order to maintain the ring's structural integrity. In order to accomplish this end, jacks were placed at the top of each tower to make incremental adjustments as the erection of the steel progressed.

Throughout the year, the project had become the focal point of local, national, and even international interest. While the media offered unremitting coverage of the building's progress, Houstonians observed the ever-rising structure from vantage points across the city's southern reaches. As the crews from American Bridge welded the trusses into place, the tension ring at the heart of the Dome's structural design began to take form. Weighing 750 tons, the tension ring consisted of seventy-two steel sections of articulated joints in order to allow for the expansion and contraction of the roof.[23]

During the process of constructing the tension ring, Kiewitt strongly recommended that radiographs, similar to medical x-rays, be made of the welds in the tension ring in order to ensure that they were not cracking under the extreme weight of the building materials. Indeed, as the American Bridge crews worked to put all of the trusses and framework into place, a certain risk existed—notwithstanding the extra protection and stability afforded by the erection towers—that a gale-force wind could topple the steel skeleton and injure the construction workers nearly two hundred feet below. Kiewitt had clear reason to be concerned. During the summer of 1963, a high-force wind of 90 MPH had assaulted Victoria, Texas, some 125 miles to the southwest of the construction site. Anything along those lines would have spelled almost certain doom for Hofheinz's lofty municipal dreams.[24]

Kiewitt's insistence on regular radiograph tests may have made the difference in ensuring confidence in the incipient building's structural integrity. As it happened, Hurricane Cindy pelted the Texas coastline with a steady assault of wind and rain in late September, and the framework, with all of its welds fully in place, withstood the onslaught with nary a scratch.[25] On December 2, the tension ring was finally completed, along with the building's support columns. As American Bridge crews anxiously watched, the jack on the central, thirty-seventh, tower was lowered and the tension ring rested atop its steel pillars. To commemorate the occasion, workers placed a pair of Colt .45 pennants atop the roof. Almost immediately, the stress of so much weight on top of the framework began to exert its awesome might, with 220,000 pounds of pressure being transferred onto the stadium's support columns. Consequently, the columns bent slightly—by as much as an inch in some places. The American Bridge crews hastily erected temporary steel supports in order to deflect the load and protect the steel skeleton from suffering any damage. While the incident proved to be a momentary concern, it turned out to be a harbinger of other issues to come. As a result, engineering teams from Roof Structures and Walter P. Moore assembled in January 1964 and decided to cross-brace the columns to further enhance the structure's support. As an additional measure, gamma-ray equipment was deployed in order evaluate the quality of the welds before moving further with the project. Ten welds were found to be defective and subsequently corrected before construction continued.[26]

By early 1964, all of the Dome's spans had been completed and the trusses and framework were fully in place. At this key juncture in the building's construction—with the connections having been welded together and the alignment confirmed—the crews began the laborious and painstaking process of lowering the jacks and eventually removing the erection towers altogether.[27] On January 16 Zimmerman announced that the columns were properly braced and could now support the roof structure without benefit of the erection towers. American Bridge predicted that it would take just under three weeks to lower the jacks and remove the towers.[28] Concerns mounted as the trusses were released from the safety net afforded by the towers. The time had come for Zimmerman's engineering and design to prove its integrity—or, failing that, to collapse on an international stage, once more branding Houston as a hick town under the watchful eyes of a waiting world.

Zimmerman had been known to joke with friends and family that if the structure were indeed going to founder, he wanted to be standing in the middle of the construction site, hundreds of feet below the centroid, to be spared the ultimate humiliation of seeing his work collapse in upon itself.[29] But his gambit was hardly necessary. If Zimmerman truly held any doubts, they were resolved fairly quickly, as the Dome's skeleton held fast. On February 4 the roof was liberated from the erection towers, and the 7.5-million-pound lamella dome came to rest entirely on the stadium walls. After all of the towers had been removed, the stadium had sunk four inches, as predicted by the engineers, under the combined weight of the roof and the framework.[30] For the first time, Hofheinz's original vision of a modern-day Roman Colosseum was beginning to take form. The steel superstructure was finally complete, and the outline of the Astrodome's interior framework remained visible for miles in every direction.

But as events would show, Houston's collective sigh of relief over the building's structural soundness was short-lived. With the steel framework in place, Zimmerman and his engineers tested the structure's plumbness to see if it held true without benefit of the erection towers. And to their great consternation, and eventual panic, the mathematics didn't add up. Simply put, the framework wasn't plumb. In civil engineering parlance, plumbness refers to a structure's state of being vertical, or "true." Today, engineers test a building's plumbness using laser equipment. In the Astrodome's heyday, plumbness would have been tested by deploying a lead weight on the end of a line in order to determine verticality.

During the process of slowly retracting the jacks atop each of the thirty-seven erection towers, Zimmerman's engineering team periodically checked the tension-ring alignment and tested the plumbness of the columns. To their growing dismay, the plumbness results shifted on a daily basis. Not surprisingly, concerns began to mount among the engineers from Walter P. Moore and Roof Structures. Eventually, those concerns spread to the county commissioners, who became increasingly nervous at the mere thought that such a high-profile project might prove to be structurally unsound after years of careful preparation and no-holds-barred politicking. Under this level of scrutiny, Zimmerman's team reconsidered the monitoring data from the plumbness tests, while also examining the design of the supporting columns to ensure that nothing was amiss. Finding nothing of concern—save for the inconsistent plumbness data—Zimmerman gave the order to lower the jacks completely and release the frame to face the elements.[31]

With the jacks having been fully retracted and the framework set free, the engineers continued to monitor the structure's plumbness on a daily basis. Specifically, the team worked to ascertain the degree to which the columns' deviation from plumbness remained constant from day to day. Not only did the results not remain constant, but they varied daily. As the days continued to pass, tensions on the construction site mounted and the county commissioners began to doubt the efficacy of the design. And then it finally happened: Zimmerman's "Eureka!" moment, when he discovered that the plumbness differential was due entirely to temperature effects. He realized that the columns needed to be checked at the same time on successive days in order to ensure that there were no variations in temperature. In short, the plumbness calculations would shift from morning to evening, as the framework moved from sunshine into shadow. Recognizing that his design allowed for temperature effects, Zimmerman exclaimed that "the old girl was behaving just as was predicted!"[32]

Zimmerman's innovative design demonstrated the vital ways in which long-span structures like the Astrodome move almost continuously. The same effects can be understood in terms of high-rise buildings such as the former World Trade Center in New York City, which was engineered to allow certain degree of natural sway in concert with the elements—namely, wind—in order to protect both the engineering integrity and the Twin Towers' occupants. As Gosain points out, "There is no structure that is rigid. They all move—all structures move. The wonderful thing that engineers have accomplished—and especially with such buildings as the World Trade Center or the Etihad Tower 5 in Abu Dhabi—is that they minimize structural movement so that it's not perceptible."[33]

Calculations made after the Astrodome's completion confirmed Zimmerman's hypothesis, as well as the soundness of his design. The engineers' monitoring data demonstrated a temperature differential of 20 degrees Fahrenheit between the interior and the exterior of the building, but also on the exterior from east to west and north to south. Yet another calculation proved that the Dome enjoyed a dead-load deflection of 1.88 inches. The fact that the Astrodome would be air-conditioned raised the possibility of an interior/exterior temperature differential of more than 70 degrees Fahrenheit. Meanwhile, for the design's wind load, the horizontal movement allowed for an incredible 5½ inches of sway. This posed a particular challenge for both the architects and engineers tasked with designing the expansion joint at the edge of the Dome's roofline. The design specifications needed to be prepared for a total movement of 11 inches in order to account for 5½ inches in either direction. To address this issue, the design team devised a maintenance-free solution, which consisted of a screen appended to the tension ring and extending beyond a concrete curb on the edge of the stadium roof. The screen camouflaged the expansion joint, which was afforded with the requisite space to allow for total movement not to exceed 11 inches. Through this elegant solution, the screen and the curb overlap so as not to allow rain to blow into the building's interior; at the same time, the curb's height was designed to prevent rainwater from spilling downward from the edge of the roof.[34]

With the Dome's plumbness crisis having been resolved, the

project moved apace with slightly more than a year to go until Major League Baseball's projected opening day in the Astrodome in April 1965. By April 1, 1964, the crews began lodging the roof's 4,596 skylights into place, with the concrete seat risers to be installed shortly thereafter.[35] With the building's skeleton having been fully completed, the project shifted toward the activities associated with fitting out any multipurpose stadium—although the Astrodome was hardly any run-of-the-mill sports complex.

As with Zimmerman and the team from Walter P. Moore, the project's construction crews were especially enamored with the process of assembling and installing the Dome's gigantic center-field scoreboard. Four stories high and 474 feet wide, the $2 million electronic scoreboard encompassed more than fifty thousand individual light bulbs. Weighing more than three hundred tons, the scoreboard, which would come to be known among sports fans as the Home Run Spectacular, required some twelve hundred miles of wiring.[36] As Gosain has remarked, the scoreboard was designed, with Hofheinz's typical bravado and brash showmanship, "to put the Aurora Borealis to shame!"[37]

The Astrodome's gala opening on April 9, 1965, was punctuated by far more than Mickey Mantle's home run for the visiting New York Yankees. It marked the birth, in many ways, of Space City, Houston's long-sought recognition as a cutting-edge metropolis on a collision course with the twenty-first century. Yet the events of that evening also focused the eyes of the world on Houston's crowning success in remaking itself through high-profile architecture made possible through innovative engineering. The same could be said for the dramatic recasting of the New York City skyline via the World Trade Center and the ascent, not long thereafter, of the Sears Tower in Chicago. For Houston, often cast as a second-tier, backwater city, the impact of the Astrodome's presence may have been even more transformative.

Yet for all of the hoopla, the excitement over the Dome's grand debut was threatened, in short order, by issues involving the glare emitted by the building's skylights and the ill-fated design with natural grass on the playing field—issues that will receive close attention in the next chapter. But on that very first night, the evening's gala festivities were dampened by the fans' postgame experience when they left the stadium only to be greeted by nearly unremitting darkness, save for the light emanating from the Astrodome itself, along with a handful of light standards scattered about the complex's massive parking lot encircling the facility. It was pitch black as entire families, lost amid a sea of nearly forty-eight thousand people, searched in vain for their vehicles in unfamiliar environs. Some attendees even remember people climbing atop the roofs of their cars and shouting out the names of their friends and relations in vain efforts to make their way home.[38] But for all of the opening-night trauma, the need for additional light standards was a relatively minor—and eminently fixable—inconvenience.

Because then—worse yet—there was the matter of the Dome's leaky roof.

From April 1965 through the present, the Astrodome has enjoyed renown for its innovative lamella roof design. But within scant days after the building's resplendent international debut, a series of springtime rain showers revealed the first cracks in the stadium's vaunted reputation as a harbinger of our collective architectural future. Although the press reports during the Dome's first, heady days of public life were almost uniformly laudatory, news stories about the leaks resurrected the cries—heard, most notably, during the political wrangles that trailed the project from ideation and the bond hearings through construction and opening day itself—that the Astrodome would go down as "Houston's folly."

The leaks first revealed themselves to the public on May 18, during a night game between the Astros and the Dodgers. The Astrodome's roof ensured that the torrential rainstorm that fell upon Houston that day would not affect that evening's ballgame. But fans couldn't help but notice the steady leaks soaking various parts of the seating area, as well as two spots on the playing field. The HSA's PR team was quick to get out in front of the story, with spokesman Bill Giles informing the media that the leaks did not represent a "major problem" and that the organization actually "expected" them, given earlier occurrences of unwelcome moisture prior to opening day. Giles speculated that the leaks must have originated from the recent painting of the skylights, although his logic was unfounded, given that the skylights were painted *after* opening day, when outfielders complained vehemently about the glare that they experienced during day games.[39]

Not wasting any time, the HSA dispatched Charles Fritts of the Socony Paint Products Company to inspect the steel support beams on the roof. Fritts located a number of areas in which rust had accumulated on beams and bolts—in some cases the rust was an eighth of an inch thick. Fritts theorized that the steel had not been properly wire brushed in order to remove scaling, which refers to the hard mineral coating that accrues on the exterior during the oxidation process. He recommended that the rust be immediately removed, followed by the priming and repainting of the beams in short order. Fritts's logic notwithstanding, the HSA quickly reconvened its engineering brain trust in order to address the increasingly tense situation. With Bass from Roof Structures and Bill Glaze from Walter P. Moore in tow, chief architect Robert Minchew walked the Dome's rooftop to inspect the condition of its steel supports. Bass and Glaze were particularly concerned that, without bold action, lasting structural damage would occur. According to Glaze, "within five years too much damage" would result in the need for "extensive repair and replacement." Glaze and the other engineers recommended the cleaning of plugged weep holes in the skylights, the removal of scaling as Fritts had suggested, and repainting the entire steel lamella roof, as well as the interior steel, in an effort to prevent further corrosion. In Glaze's thinking, the weep holes, which are designed to allow ventilation in order to dry the structure, were failing in their fundamental purpose.[40]

But after another heavy rainstorm, the roof leaked yet again, necessitating an inspection by J. R. Watson of Roof Decking, Inc., who found six holes located in horizontal joints. Watson speculated that the holes were caused by earlier efforts to repair the leaks and were aggravated by the engineering design that allowed the Dome's roof to expand in response to the elements. Not leaving anything to chance, Minchew conducted yet another inspection and discovered that the vinyl sealing gaskets in several skylights had failed. Minchew recommended a new design that seemed to pass his leakage tests, although events quickly proved otherwise, as moisture continued to plague the Dome. Alan Farnsworth of Lott-Drake finally hit upon a solution after hypothesizing that the leakage resulted from multiple causes, as opposed to a single problem. In Farnsworth's estimation, torrential rainfall would overcome the weep holes, resulting in spillage into the interior frame and, ultimately, into the stadium itself. Farnsworth recommended a coat of neoprene to waterproof the skylight framing across the entirety of the roof, and mercifully the leaks stopped, forcing the Astrodome's growing number of critics to look elsewhere in order to promote their misgivings about the Eighth Wonder of the World.[41]

The Dome's critics notwithstanding, the resulting stadium was titanic, covering 9.14 acres, with an outer diameter of 710 feet and a clear roof span of 642 feet. The seating capacity was remarkable for that era, accommodating 45,772 for baseball, 52,383 for football, 66,000 for boxing, and 55,000 for conventions. During its heyday, the Astrodome was cooled and heated by drawing upon equipment with some six thousand tons of cooling capacity and circulating approximately two million cubic feet of air per minute, not to mention another two hundred thousand cubic feet of fresh air intake per minute.

The Dome's construction had required more than 250,000 cubic yards of excavation, forty thousand cubic yards of cast-in-place concrete, and twenty-five hundred tons of reinforcing steel bars. The structural steel of the general stadium frame required six thousand tons of steel, along with three thousand tons associated with building the dome itself. More than twenty-five lineal feet of prestressing tendons were required in order to support the structure, which stands eighteen stories tall.[42] After the Astrodome's completion in November 1964, its total building cost was computed to be $35 million, which amounts to approximately $264 million in today's dollars.[43]

Most significantly, the Astrodome's gala opening ensured that Major League Baseball finally enjoyed a resounding success in Houston, with the media juggernaut associated with the stadium skyrocketing Space City from a regional oil patch and cattle town into an international player. Astros ticket manager Dick McDowell was genuinely astounded by the Astros' first-year attendance marks, noting that "before the season we figured on an attendance of between one and a quarter and one and a half million." At season's end, the Astros' attendance far surpassed McDowell's predictions, coming in at 2.1 million. Even more impressively, nearly half a million visitors paid one dollar each to tour the facilities, offering clear testimony to the building's capacity for capturing the imagination during those heady, early days of its existence. Meanwhile, the HSA, for its part, paid a pittance in county taxes and yet realized a mighty first-year profit of $8.5 million.[44]

In the years after the Dome's grand opening, one of the stadium's staunchest, and perhaps most prominent, critics was Bud Adams, the notoriously cantankerous owner of the Houston Oilers. His ongoing issues with Hofheinz would become the stuff of Houston business legend. During the first few years of the Dome's existence, Adams pointedly refused to sign a lease with Hofheinz. As Oilers vice president Mike McClure recalled, "Bud was one of the original members of the Houston Sports Association with Judge Hofheinz. But when it came time to negotiate a deal with the Oilers to play in the Dome, Hofheinz wanted a ridiculously high 17 percent rent from Adams."[45] Adams famously quipped that if the Dome was the "Eighth Wonder of the World," Hofheinz's proposed lease was "surely, 'the ninth.'"[46] In 1968 Adams bought out his lease with Rice Stadium and, having briefly buried the hatchet, signed a ten-year deal with Hofheinz that enabled the Oilers to play in the Astrodome.[47] During the ensuing press conference, Adams was all smiles, remarking that "much has been made of a so-called feud between Judge Hofheinz and me. I would be remiss if I did not dispel such rumors, for they are exactly that, rumors. We are both businessmen and naturally seek the best terms we each can obtain."[48]

By the 1980s, as the Oilers finally made inroads into the NFL's upper echelons on a consistent basis, Adams was finally able to leverage the team's big-time football clout to create real energy behind his agenda. Oilers management had long criticized the

Astrodome's audience sightlines as being substandard—namely, involving the fifty-yard-line seats, which were furthest from the field of play among the lower boxes, while the end-zone seats, typically considered to be the most unfavorable in terms of viewing the game, were closer to the action. Worse yet, by the 1980s the Dome held the dubious honor of having the league's smallest seating capacity, accommodating a mere fifty-two thousand fans. For Adams, the most problematic aspect of his team's occupancy of the Astrodome was having to play second fiddle to the Houston Astros, the building's primary tenant and its annual resident for no fewer than eighty-one home games, barring any playoff appearances.[49]

By 1987 Adams was ready to make his move. He began his effort to rattle the HSA management—and, ultimately, Houston's civic leaders—by threatening to relocate the Oilers to Jacksonville, Florida, unless Harris County agreed to undertake considerable improvements to the Dome, which had recently marked its twenty-second year in operation. In exchange for the improvements, Adams vowed to keep the Oilers in Houston for at least another decade. Adams demanded the addition of ten thousand more seats, a new AstroTurf surface for the Oilers' use, and, perhaps most significant in his overall game plan, the construction of sixty-five luxury boxes to put the Oilers on par with other NFL franchises.

Adams's timing, as it turns out, couldn't have been better. After languishing for many years in the shadows of the "Luv Ya Blue" era, the Oilers began to right their ship in the late 1980s, winning steadily during their "House of Pain" period as one of the league's most consistently successful squads.[50] As Larry Dierker points out, the Oilers had gone from being a junior partner in the Astrodome's fiscal outlook to a key player in ensuring its financial success. "The Astros held the master lease and were in no position to give up the income they received from subleasing the stadium to Bud Adams's team," Dierker writes. "They caved, and that was that."[51] In short order, Harris County acquiesced to Adams's threats and floated a $67 million bond in order to fund the improvements as stipulated by the Oilers' owner.[52] Ironically, the renovations would be more expensive than the entire cost of the original project during the mid-1960s.

The Astrodome's extensive renovation occasioned Zimmerman's return to action. Although he had retired from Walter P. Moore in 1982 after serving for many years as the firm's chief engineer and as vice chairman of the board, Zimmerman continued to serve as the organization's much trusted quality-control consultant, regularly leveraging his experience as Walter P. Moore continued to build its reputation as one of the world's leading engineering firms for stadiums and other long-span projects. The Astrodome's renovation in the late 1980s was led by Gosain, Zimmerman's protégé. While Gosain always enjoyed any work associated with the Astrodome, the renovation to meet Adams's demands made for "the most excruciating project," he later recalled. The specifications for the renovation strictly called for no breaks in the existing schedules for such major tenants as the Astros, the Oilers, and the Houston Livestock Show and Rodeo. In addition to the tightness of such a convoluted construction schedule and the reality of working around more than one hundred home games for the Astros and the Oilers, the project had a design and construction timeline of a scant thirty-two months. The contract also precluded the loss of any revenue due to unusable seats as a result of the construction process.[53]

A variety of dramatic structural changes had to be made in order to meet the bond specifications. The renovation project required the addition of four large circular stairwell structures, complete with accessibility ramps, around the Dome in order to accommodate progressive shifts in building codes since the 1960s. To accommodate the ten thousand additional seats stipulated by Adams, a number of interior structural alterations were required. Because the open depths above the Astrodome's left-, right-, and center-field bleachers were selected for the new seats' placement, a variety of structural concerns had to be addressed. In order to begin, the renovation required the removal of much of Judge Hofheinz's opulent private quarters in the upper reaches of right field. In addition to the Astrodome's chapel facilities, Hofheinz's fabled bar, putt-putt golf course, private club, and other amenities had to be gutted to afford space for the expanded seating capacity.[54]

Worse yet, the renovation sealed the doom of the stadium's famous exploding scoreboard. For many Houstonians, the dismantling of the Home Run Spectacular easily marked one of their most despondent moments in the Dome's storied history. "If the Houston Astrodome was the brainchild of flamboyant Judge Roy Hofheinz," Michael L. Graczyk lamented in the *Los Angeles Times*, "the 40,000-light scoreboard that spanned nearly 500 feet of the stadium's back wall could be seen as the twinkle in his eye."[55] On September 6, 1988, the forty-five-second Home Run Spectacular sequence exploded into life for the last time before going dark forever at the conclusion of the Astros' home game against the Cincinnati Reds.

During the design phase, the renovation specifications called for Gosain to consider any structural changes that the building might have experienced during the previous two decades, as well as the effects of adding the weight associated with ten thousand seats onto the Dome's vertical columns and its reciprocal effects upon the tension structure that sustains its engineering integrity. "There were numerous technical challenges," Gosain recalls. "The Dome's roof was a major concern because we had to protect the columns that supported it, while recognizing that the tension support for the dome has increased due to differential settlement." With some twenty-two years having passed since the building's completion, the level of settlement had to be accounted for in order to consider the effects of adding the weight of the additional seats and the attendant "people generated sway loads." For Gosain, the principal question was clear: "Will the settlement be even and uniform or not uniform?" To address this issue, "We did very detailed studies. We took it upon ourselves to start generating a computer model with the new technology that had evolved since the 1960s to assess whether the tension ring, given the level of differential settlement over the years, would exert any distress on the Dome's roof structure."[56]

Gosain's ensuing series of structural integrity tests revealed that several tension-ring members had become stressed with age.

Not wanting to take any chances with the tension ring's role in maintaining the Dome's safety and stability, Gosain devised an ingenious means for adding seats without adding any additional stress to the tension ring. It was a moment of incredible creative instinct, much like Zimmerman's earlier inspiration in conceiving the innovative knuckle and star columns. First, Gosain recalls, "We made the decision to enlarge the footings in the area of the building associated with the renovation to minimize the differential settlement." This aspect of the renovation proved to be an essential undertaking, given that the addition of ten thousand seats in that particular area of the Dome necessitated the alteration of key structural columns in order to allow the requisite space for concession areas, restrooms, and walkways to afford fans with passage to the new seating in the building's upper reaches. "There were some serious challenges," Gosain remembers. "We had to essentially cut columns off and come up with new transfer systems. Cutting a column is a very tricky thing." Moreover, "several beams had to be strengthened; transfer girders and footings had to be augmented because these areas were never designed to be concourse levels with public access, so they all had to be upgraded to support the load of the people."[57]

Second, and even more impressively, Gosain had to devise a massive balcony system to span the open space previously occupied by the Home Run Spectacular. But he had something far more ingenious in mind than merely cramming ten thousand seats among the Dome's center-field rafters. In order to protect the integrity of the tension ring, which was vital to ensuring the structural soundness of the existing building, Gosain formulated a plan for building the world's first retractable upper-deck seating. To accomplish this feat, Gosain tasked his mechanical engineers with preparing a winch and pulley system, supplemented with a specially designed hydraulic mechanism, for extending the primary balconies that would account for the majority of the seats. In Gosain's plan, there would be twenty balcony sections overall, each with its own retractable ten-foot-wide section, to bring the additional seating capacity to ten thousand.[58]

The retractable seating proved to be especially valuable in meeting seating expectations for the Dome's different baseball and football seating configurations. For baseball, the seats in the new balconies could be retracted so as not to interfere with fan sightlines. For football, the seats would simply be lowered below the primary balconies resulting from the renovation, extended via the winch and pulley system, and then retracted again and held in place by a series of pins in order to accommodate baseball games. Working with Zimmerman in his retirement, Gosain ensured that the team from Walter P. Moore learned from their experiences back in the 1960s when contractors and subcontractors—not to mention many politicians, civic leaders, and businessmen jockeying for position—succeeded in delaying the Astrodome's construction over a period of several of years. "We put everything down on paper," Gosain points out. "All the existing framing, the plumbness, the alignment. Our documentation was put together very much indeed so there could be no excuse on the part of the contractor to create delays."[59]

Gosain's extensive documentation and planning for nearly every possible outcome prepared the engineering team to meet the construction challenges as they arose during the project's abbreviated timeline. Looking back on the project, Gosain rather humbly describes his remarkable efforts to address an exceedingly complex structural problem. "That's what engineers do. They rise to the challenge, meet the challenge, and move on to the next thing."[60] But the extensive renovations were all for naught, of course, as Adams eventually made good on his threats and moved the team anyway, relocating the Oilers to Tennessee in time for the NFL's 1997 season. The team was later renamed the Titans.

For his part, Gosain's work as lead engineer on the renovation project demonstrated Walter P. Moore and Associates' longstanding and influential role in the life of the building. Thinking back on his experiences as Zimmerman's protégé and most trusted colleague, Gosain clearly recognizes the incredible place that the Astrodome holds in the history of his firm, as well as in his own life and career. As Zimmerman's spiritual and professional successor, Gosain is still called upon as a consultant in matters relating to the Dome, and he realizes, much to his own despair, that if the stadium eventually succumbs to the wrecking ball, he will very likely be called upon for the last time to share his expertise in the service of its demise.

As with Gosain, the Astrodome was, most assuredly, the highlight of Zimmerman's career, although he would be the first to admit that it was an engineering achievement to be shared by many, especially the building's architects and the outstanding teams assembled by Roof Structures, American Bridge, and Walter P. Moore and Associates. Over the years, he would be interviewed about the project. Invariably, Zimmerman would conclude his remarks by lapsing into a sentimental fondness. "It was the biggest and finest of its kind around," Zimmerman would say, thinking wistfully about his signal role in engineering what, for a time at least, some folks called the Eighth Wonder of the World.[61]

5

The Grass Isn't Always Greener
AstroTurf and the Sports Purist Backlash

The Dome's majesty began to tarnish almost immediately after the Astros' exhibition game against the vaunted New York Yankees in April 1965. Within a matter of weeks, the stadium's leaky roof made itself known, literally dampening the much-ballyhooed festivities associated with the Astrodome's early months as a Major League ballpark. But long before fans began to notice the unsightly watery blemishes pooling in the stands and on the playing field during inclement weather, the players realized an even more glaring issue—namely, the glare that they experienced during day games when gazing at the skylights pocking the building's lamella roof. Journalist Lowell Reidenbaugh spoke for many when he referred to this design oversight as a "glaring fault."[1]

The glare from the skylights was apparent from the first moments in which the players stepped onto the field. On Wednesday, April 7, the Astros held their first practice in order to acclimate to the Dome in preparation for a scrimmage against their Minor League affiliate, the Oklahoma City 89ers. In short order, players from both teams realized that they could scarcely make out fly balls, even easy popups, as they passed in front of the maze of girders and skylights some two hundred feet above the playing field. Worse yet, the late afternoon sun wreaked havoc on the fielders attempting to negotiate the blinding glare emitted by the skylights. Astros outfielder Jim Beauchamp left the field in frustration, remarking to the assembled media, "First you see it, then you don't." After the first day's workout, Astros general manager Paul Richards hypothesized that the HSA could minimize the glare by activating the stadium's indoor lighting system during the afternoon to counteract the sun.[2] Events would prove Richards to be very, very wrong.

The next afternoon, Thursday, April 8, an intrasquad scrimmage between the Astros and the 89ers was halted after seven innings because Astros manager Luman Harris was concerned for his players' safety in advance of the next evening's gala home opener against the Yankees. Ron Davis, the 89ers' center fielder, lamented that he "caught two fly balls out of about 10 or 12." He noted that "outdoors, you can shade the glare with your glove. But here the glare with your glove is so strong it just surrounds the glove." Fearing that he would be hurt by an ordinarily catchable fly ball while patrolling the outfield, Davis took to wearing his batting helmet to avoid injury. Astros outfielder Al Spangler bluntly remarked that "a routine fly ball is no longer routine."[3] Watching the action on the field, *Houston Chronicle* sportswriter Mickey Herskowitz couldn't believe his eyes. "The glare was blinding," he remarked after watching outfielders as they squinted in the direction of the skylights overhead before cowering so as not to "get hit in the nose."[4]

Attempting to remedy the problem as soon as possible, the HSA gathered numerous pairs of sunglasses in an effort to safeguard the players against the unexpected dangers of playing inside the Astrodome. With the sunglasses providing only mild relief from the sun's glare, Richards announced that "it's impossible to play under these conditions." Yet at the same time, he recognized that a reasonable solution could be found. And why not? As Richards himself pointed out, "I know that people who can build a wonderful stadium like this can solve this one little problem."[5]

As it happened, the issue of the glare from the skylights had been diagnosed long before the 89ers came to town. Architect Hermon Lloyd noticed the problem after installing the first few hundred skylights during the construction phase and dutifully brought the issue to the HSA's attention. "I told the HSA what might happen," he recalled, but "they seemed to think that it was a situation that would be easily resolved." For Lloyd, the solution seemed to lie with a simple alteration to the players' equipment; he even went so far as to suggest that the Dome employ "colored" baseballs in order to remedy the issue. Architect S. I. Morris wasn't so sure. In Morris's mind, a more permanent solution would be necessary, although Hofheinz wasn't having it. The judge was loath to undertake any wholesale changes to the shiny new stadium—especially anything that might result in harm to the natural grass playing surface. After all, a special strain of Tifway 419 Bermuda grass had been carefully selected for use during the Dome's inaugural season. Meanwhile, the HSA's Bill Giles recommended the deployment of a massive canvas to cover the roof during day games, which could be subsequently removed to allow the natural grass playing field to receive its requisite daily dose of sunlight.[6]

Widespread calls for blacking out the skylights came as early as the Astros' gala exhibition games against the New York Yankees and the Baltimore Orioles during the Dome's first weekend of business. Hofheinz was quick to respond to criticism associated with the glare, promising to exhaust all solutions before painting the skylights. As Jason Chrystal observes, "Blacking out the sunlight would kill all the grass and reduce the playing surface to dirt and dust." The experiment of growing natural grass indoors was already showing clear signs of ineffectiveness. "In the outfield," Chrystal adds, "the grass had grown unevenly and turned brown in some areas. Immediate speculation centered on the idea of getting synthetic turf to replace the natural grass." Predictably, Hofheinz held his ground, promising to address every option in order to afford baseball's indoor palace a natural grass playing surface. "We are aware of the advantages of synthetic or plastic type grass," he remarked, "but we haven't given up on growing natural grass in the Astrodome."[7]

With the Astros' first day game scheduled for April 25, Hofheinz worked under a highly constrictive timeline. In the meantime, the media frenzy about the Dome's glaring problem took on a life of its own, and the HSA became inundated with thousands of letters from fans and well-meaning citizens across the nation. A host of solutions was suggested, including the oft-cited notion of using colored baseballs to establish much-needed contrast for fielders attempting to decipher the flight of the ball among the effects of the unremitting sun and the building's steel girders. At his wit's end, Hofheinz hired a special team of consulting engineers from DuPont who traveled to Houston to produce a solution. Working on short notice with their lab team back in Wilmington, Delaware, the DuPont engineers were unable to devise a remedy for the glare. Their failure, in retrospect, was hardly surprising, given the scarcity of variables. Colored baseballs, sunglasses, and the idea of a giant canvas were short-term solutions at best. In spite of Hofheinz's objections, the only genuine pathway to reducing the sun's glare was to modify the Lucite panels.[8]

As the Astros' first day game grew ever closer, Hofheinz vowed to take charge after the folks from DuPont were unable to fashion a solution. Claiming that several greenhouse directors had advised that painting the skylights would not adversely affect the Dome's specially designed natural grass playing surface, Hofheinz called an end to his self-imposed mandate against altering the building and ordered the painting of the Lucite panels. On April 20 a crew of ten painters ascended the lamella roof and began applying gallons of "off-white" acrylic paint to the skylights. After three days of work, the crew had applied more than seven hundred gallons to the Dome's 4,596 skylights. The HSA spent $20,000 on the process—a far cry from the expense that would have been necessary to cover the building's ceiling via other means.[9]

In a press conference, Hofheinz employed his well-honed showman's bravado in crafting his message: "We're reasonably certain that this will stop the glare," Hofheinz announced, while explaining that the paint would still allow sunlight to travel into the Dome, albeit at a significantly reduced rate. The judge described the paint as a "permanent coating" that would "make the Dome glitter on the outside and glow on the inside," even going so far as to boast that the painted skylights would play a role in "enhancing the stadium's beauty." Proclaiming that the paint would reduce the glare by 25 to 40 percent, Hofheinz took great pains to suggest that natural grass might still be possible in the indoor stadium, as promised by his greenhouse consultants, but hardly anyone believed him. Writing in the *Houston Post*, Red Smith made the case for an artificial playing surface: "If baseball was going to be played under an artificial sky with artificial lighting in artificial temperatures, why bother the Almighty about furnishing grass when man could do it just as well, if not better?" As Smith was quick to add, "One worm in the apple shouldn't obscure the fact that something truly revolutionary has been accomplished." In stark contrast with Hofheinz, Astros publicity coordinator Bill Giles had already given up the ghost, admitting that the HSA was ready to install a temporary natural grass surface or finish the season with a dirt playing field.[10]

As Barbara Moran notes, in the wake of the twin fiascoes of the skylights' unremitting glare and the building's leaky roof, the Astrodome was quickly "becoming a laughingstock" when it should have been the toast of the mid-1960s sporting world.[11] For Hofheinz and the HSA, the withering and subsequent death of the grass may have been the unkindest cut of all. The famous strain of Bermuda grass had been diligently selected by botanists and turf-grass experts at Texas A&M University, where the Tifway 419 Bermuda grass had been bred deliberately for deployment in the Dome because of its capacity for carrying out photosynthesis under the constraints imposed by growing indoors.

As Murry R. Nelson points out, the Astrodome's climate-control system seemed to offer the right kind of environment for Tifway 419 to flourish, especially given the grass's ability to receive sunlight through the Dome's semitransparent Lucite panels.[12] One of the leading proponents of turf-grass management, Phillip Jennings Turf Farms, has long lauded Tifway 419 as one of the most durable hybrid Bermudas because of its capacity for rapid growth, its ability to tolerate close mowing, its disease resistance, and its quick recovery from the kinds of injury associated with a protracted professional sports season.[13] If not for the sun's glare affecting the field of play during day games, Tifway 419 might have held its own as the natural grass of choice in the Eighth Wonder of the World and its multipurpose successors. But it was simply not to be.

After the process of painting over the skylights was completed, the days of Hofheinz's once vaunted natural grass playing surface were truly numbered. "Bare patches of dirt appeared" in the Astrodome, Moran writes, "leaving the outfield hard and rutted. Groundskeepers resorted to spraying the field with green paint, and any ball hit to the outfield was stained green."[14] In addition to painting the playing surface, the HSA also took to peppering the field with a "green sweeping compound" to effect the appearance of grass for television audiences.[15]

The HSA brass had been warned years before about the problematics of nurturing a natural grass surface under the Dome. As construction workers hoisted the building's massive framework, one of the architects, speaking anonymously, offered a damning report in which he proclaimed that the notion of growing grass indoors was a farce. "If you pour in enough air conditioning to cool the customers, then you do not have enough heat to grow the grass." He added that "somebody is being kidded" if they believe anything to the contrary. Not surprisingly, Hofheinz was incensed by the report, describing the Astrodome as a "prestige project" in which no cost was being spared to transform the impossible— such as growing grass indoors—into the possible in his future-oriented, space-age stadium.[16]

But now, in spite of his earlier misgivings about resorting to artificial turf, even Hofheinz had had enough. Tal Smith, a special assistant to the Astros in 1965 and later president of the team from 1994 through 2011, recalled that "Hofheinz came into my office one day and said, 'I don't care what you do. You've got unlimited resources. Do whatever you have to do, but find a solution to the field problem.'"[17] In many ways, the solution was patently obvious, just as it had been when the HSA was confronted with the issue of glare. In the case of the skylights, the only long-term solution was to paint them to avoid further affecting the field of play during day games. With the matter of the Dome's rapidly deteriorating natural grass surface, a solution was already available and waiting for the Astros to come calling.

The history of artificial playing surfaces reaches way back to 1949, long before the Astrodome's grass began to wither and die because of a sudden shortage of available sunlight. More specifically, it started with a joint venture between Monsanto and the American Viscose Corporation that resulted in the creation of Chemstrand, a company that specialized in synthetic fibers. While DuPont had emerged as the industry's standard-bearer because of its pioneering work in nylons, companies like Chemstrand entered the marketplace in an effort to take advantage of the rapidly growing human-made-fibers business. Chemstrand began as a manufacturer of conventional indoor carpeting, but the firm's leaders were determined to find their niche in the burgeoning field of outdoor carpeting. When a heavier strain of Chemstrand's synthetic fibers proved to be both durable and water-resistant, a viable outdoor carpeting was born.[18]

In 1958 the push for creating an artificial playing surface gained momentum and credibility when the Ford Foundation offered $4.5 million in grant funding to establish the Educational Facilities Laboratories (EFL) with group's mission to "encourage research, experimentation, and the dissemination of knowledge regarding educational facilities." In an early research report, the EFL found that inner-city schoolchildren suffered from a lack of green space, concluding that "whoever invents for rooftop and playground a material that looks like grass and acts like grass, a turflike substance on which a ball will bounce and a child will not, a covering that brings a slice of spring in Scarsdale to 14th Street in April, will have struck a blow for stability in the big city." The EFL's report ended with a prophetic "NOTE TO INVENTORS: The non-educational market should be substantial."[19]

The folks at Chemstrand wasted little time in working to modify their outdoor carpeting for the sports marketplace. As chemical engineer Ed Milner recalled, "Our fundamental research people started measuring things like 'How do balls roll on natural grass?' And 'How do balls bounce?' And 'How much traction to you need to do the things that you do in sports?' And 'How much cushioning do you need when you fall down?'" Chemstrand subsequently transformed its labs into a turf-testing center, even going so far as to pound their synthetic fiber with metal plates, subject it to steam ovens, and bake it in open sunlight to ensure its long-term durability.[20]

Artificial turf would finally see its first full-scale installation in a sporting environment in 1964, when Chemstrand installed ChemGrass, as they originally called their synthetic fiber, at the Moses Brown School in Providence, Rhode Island. Founded in 1784 by Moses Brown, a Quaker abolitionist, the boys' and girls' preparatory school is one of the nation's oldest and most traditional prep schools—and an unlikely place, by any measure, to be the first home for artificial turf. In 1965 Campanella Field, home to the school's football, field hockey, lacrosse, and soccer teams, became the first athletic facility to install ChemGrass as its playing surface. Tal Smith subsequently traveled to Providence, where he came face-to-face with the solution to his problems back at the Dome. "It was green. It had fibers. It looked like grass," Smith proclaimed. The answer to his playing-field dilemma was finally at hand.[21]

For Hofheinz, ChemGrass was appealing on two principal levels. First, he was familiar with the artificial surface, having experimented with using it at Colt Stadium a few years earlier. Second, ChemGrass required significantly less preparation and installation time than Tartan, the other leading artificial surface during that era. Besides, ChemGrass offered a removable carpet, perfect for the Astrodome's multipurpose usage, that could fairly easily be mounted by connecting the nylon monofilament material to a wooden cleat bolted to a concrete anchor.[22]

When Hofheinz sought a solution to his highly publicized natural grass problem, the manufacturers of ChemGrass were eager to oblige. As the ballpark design expert John Pastier notes, "The Monsanto Chemical Company installed roughly 100,000 square feet of its evergreen flooring and named it in the Dome's honor. Thus was AstroTurf baptized under crisis conditions." Given the Dome's post–opening day woes, artificial turf made all the sense in the world. As Pastier points out, "Being synthetic, it could not die: being integrally colored, it stayed green. It needed no water, and since it did not engage in transpiration, it reduced the dehumidification demands on the air-conditioning system."[23]

With a solution at hand, Hofheinz wasted little time in bringing ChemGrass to the Astrodome. During the off-season, Monsanto installed its artificial surface, rechristened AstroTurf-8, in the stadium's infield and foul territories, with plans to convert the outfield to an artificial surface by midseason. Monsanto worked double-time in order to produce enough synthetic fiber to fulfill the Dome's needs. Recognizing the import of meeting the

Astros' needs and taking advantage of the media glare associated with the Astrodome, Monsanto ramped up production, working days, nights, and weekends in order to bring the job to fruition. As Milner remembered, "Those guys on the line busted their buns" carrying out a manufacturing process involving nylon pellets mixed with pigment and then melted at nearly six hundred degrees Fahrenheit. Afterward, the molten nylon is extruded in order to produce lengthy strands of nylon, which are cooled and woven on looms in the same fashion in which carpet is produced. The resulting turf arrived at the Astrodome in two-hundred-foot-long strips that weighed some three thousand pounds each.[24]

In January 1966 Hofheinz scheduled a workout in the newly carpeted Dome in order to test the artificial turf's durability and gauge its reactions under simulated playing conditions. For the players, AstroTurf proved to be a welcome relief from the uneven dirt surface that had plagued the latter months of the 1965 season. The Astros in attendance were heartily satisfied with the ball's natural bounce on the artificial carpet. Even Rusty Staub allowed that "it's got to be better than our field last year." Given his mandate from the judge to find a workable solution to the team's playing-field woes—not to mention having weathered the earlier problems associated with the leaky roof and the skylights' unremitting glare—Tal Smith was nothing short of elated. "With the installation of AstroTurf," he announced, "we will have eliminated the last pitfall in conjunction with the stadium."[25]

AstroTurf made its Major League debut on March 19, 1966, during an exhibition game between the Astros and the Los Angeles Dodgers. While the players complained about the unsecured dirt beneath the artificial surface, one reporter giddily quipped that "the infield looked and felt like a billiard table." For Hofheinz's part, the grand showman could hardly contain himself when afforded the opportunity to share the Dome's latest innovation with the national press. "Let's face it," he boasted, "they had to pick the Dome as the first place for artificial grass. This was the only showcase. By tomorrow, every person in Houston is going to start thinking about using this stuff for his backyard. In another few years, all the outdoor stadiums will have the same thing on their playing fields." At the end of the press conference, Hofheinz invited the assembled media to test out the AstroTurf for themselves before turning over the proceedings to the Astros' infielders, who briefly worked out for the reporters. Astros third baseman Bob Aspromonte noted an extra zip on the batted baseball as it shot across the infield, adding that conventional cleats might need to be modified in order to afford players with more certain footing on the artificial surface.[26]

The media hardly had to wait very long to witness the trials and tribulations of playing on AstroTurf. In the ensuing exhibition game, the Dodgers committed three defensive miscues, only two of which were officially scored as errors, during their debut on the artificial playing field. Although they won the contest 8–3, the fireworks began for the Dodgers in the bottom of the first inning when LA's first baseman Wes Parker was overmatched by a blazing grounder off the bat of Joe Morgan. In the fourth, Parker misjudged yet another raging groundball, followed by second baseman Nate Oliver, who misplayed a grounder hit by Astros catcher John Bateman. It may been an inauspicious debut, but Hofheinz was hardly one to back down. As promised, he saw to it that the Dome's outfield was outfitted with synthetic fibers by June 1966. He hardly minded the attendant publicity generated by his new playing surface, and besides, he reasoned that AstroTurf would save him $4,000 to $5,000 a year in maintenance expenses involving watering, mowing, and fertilizing natural grass.[27]

Before long, the Astros brass realized yet another benefit from AstroTurf, which evolved into an unforeseen home-field advantage for the Astros. The team had already seen visiting clubs cower in the face of the Dome's deep power alleys and cavernous dimensions. But AstroTurf provided yet another advantage in terms of the sheer number of ways in which it served to speed up the pace of the baseball and the game. Thanks to AstroTurf, slick-fielding infielders could turn brisk double plays, while speedy outfielders could run down fly balls in the far reaches of the Dome. In short order, the Astros' new stadium was quickly emerging as a pitcher's park of the highest order.

Meanwhile, visiting fielders not used to the give and take of the building's artificial playing surface would find themselves at tenterhooks in the Astrodome's unfriendly confines as they misplayed what might normally have passed as routine grounders into multibase errors. In the 1980s and 1990s, as the Astros went from being one of the National League's perennial losers to a league-leading mainstay, AstroTurf was often credited as the team's secret weapon, as visiting teams, having grown used to the proclivities of natural grass in their cozy traditional stadiums, ventured onto the Astrodome's slick, unforgiving carpeting and watched their home runs transform into harmless fly balls in the Dome's vast environs.

Once disparagingly described by Hofheinz as "undertaker's grass," in reference to the gravesite deployment of ersatz plastic grass, artificial turf had arrived to stay in Houston by the conclusion of the 1966 Major League Baseball season. And the Astrodome, for all intents and purposes by virtue of the circumstances of its construction, had birthed it. The 1966 edition of the HSA's Astrodome media guide took great pains to propagandize the value of AstroTurf, describing it as a "unique surface, which may some day become the regulation surface for all of baseball." Astros manager Grady Hatton Jr. is subsequently cited in the media guide, remarking that AstroTurf "puts the icing on the cake. The Astrodome now becomes a real Utopia for baseball. No wind, no sun, no rain, no heat, no cold, and now no bad bounces. Now if we can just get the umpires perfect, we will be in great shape." Affording Hofheinz with the last word on the matter, the Astrodome's media guide lauds the judge for making the Dome "the new showplace of the world." According to Hofheinz, ever the showman, "Everything about the Astrodome is unparalleled and trail-blazing. We feel the addition of this new playing surface, a product of chemistry, not only enhances our own facilities here, but also should launch a new and wondrous era in recreational engineering. The Astrodome is honored to be the site of this extraordinary experiment."[28]

But the Dome was only the beginning, of course. The rate at which usage of artificial turf grew was astounding by any measure. During the following year, AstroTurf saw its first installation in an outdoor facility, at Indiana State University's Memorial Stadium. In 1968 the first full-scale AstroTurf manufacturing center was opened in Dalton, Georgia, opening the floodgates for a new technology that was suddenly in high demand in spite of its growing number of detractors among baseball traditionalists. The first World Series game played on artificial turf occurred in 1970 when the Cincinnati Reds played the Baltimore Orioles at Riverfront Stadium. The NFL's most celebrated contest joined the ranks shortly thereafter, when the Miami Dolphins faced off against the Minnesota Vikings at Super Bowl VIII at Houston's Rice Stadium. Yet for many Americans, AstroTurf owes its genesis not to the Astrodome but to prime-time television, thanks to ABC's *The Brady Bunch*, which prominently featured artificial grass in the family's backyard.[29]

For sports purists, the age of AstroTurf spelled the end of America's nostalgic fondness for the fields of dreams of yesteryear. Worse yet, it heralded a new era of sports-related injuries that has never truly ebbed. As Pastier observes, "Because it was not as resilient as grass, it increased player fatigue and wear on leg joints. Because it did not give way like grass, it increased the frequency and severity of knee injuries associated with twisting and sudden stops." AstroTurf has also proved to be especially perilous in warmer climes, Pastier adds. "When used outdoors, it proved a fine solar heating device, producing field temperatures as high as 130 degrees." As Pastier concludes, "It would be nice to say that this miracle material ended the woes of indoor baseball in Houston, but it merely substituted new ones and eventually spread them throughout much of the sporting universe. Stadiums that did not otherwise need it installed AstroTurf or 3M's Tartan Turf to simplify maintenance or to promote the faster game that the speedy surface allowed."[30]

Yet for the most die-hard of sports purists, it was all about the aesthetics of natural grass. Outfielder Dick Allen famously proclaimed his distaste for AstroTurf, remarking that "if a horse won't eat it, I don't want to play on it."[31] And to think that this much-maligned artificial surface exploded onto the national stage via

Hofheinz's brazen effort to appease baseball traditionalists while professing his vision for the sport's most nontraditional of venues.

But it was all for naught, of course. The Astrodome had now once and truly become the bane of baseball purists' existence. Out of the incredible hoopla associated with the building's grand opening in April 1965, the stadium had emerged as a working symbol of a crass and unwelcome future for die-hard fans. With the Dome's climate-controlled, air-conditioned environment, its slickly produced electronic entertainment, its over-the-top creature comforts, and its signal role in the invention and mass proliferation of AstroTurf, Hofheinz had fully unleashed the era of the brash, unapologetic multipurpose stadium on an uncertain world.

SPACE CITY

Fractious Dome Futures

On May 21, 2013, the National Football League awarded Houston the hosting rights to the 2017 Super Bowl, the most watched sporting event in North America. The Houston media erupted in excitement as the news broke, but a subtext of the enthusiastic coverage was speculation about the Astrodome's future.

A *Houston Chronicle* editorial celebrated "the things Houston will gain by 2017," but the editors somberly lamented "the big one we'll probably lose—the Astrodome." Still, plans were put on the table to repurpose the Astrodome into an open-air, park-like area that the editorial suggested might transform the Eighth Wonder of the World into a facility that "would play an important support role for the Houston Livestock Show and Rodeo, tailgating, and all sorts of events."[1]

Editorial support for such a renovation plan was undermined by a regional culture that preferred new to old, a transient population, the lack of high-profile advocates, and the necessity of tax support to ensure a successful conversion process. The issue of a population transplanted from elsewhere was problematic. Despite Houston's high level of transients, people who were not embedded in the city or the region, the greater Houston area was often successful because the metropolis optimistically welcomed and generally attracted high-quality talent and, while doing so, looked forward rather than reflecting back on its history, however impressive that history might be.

When Houston won the 2017 Super Bowl bid, NFL officials invited the civic leaders Rick Campo, CEO of a Houston-area real estate firm, and David Crane, CEO of NRG Energy, to step up to the podium to celebrate Houston's achievement. Unlike Roy Hofheinz, neither had spent his childhood years in or near Houston, yet their energetic leadership was instrumental in putting a successful Super Bowl bid together. Campo's career unfolded in Oregon and California before his relocation to Houston, while Crane's pedigree was from the East Coast. A power base with fewer visceral ties to Houston had emerged in the twenty-first century, although many old-guard power brokers maintained a nostalgic respect for the aging facility that had helped to make Houston better known on a national stage.

In the 1960s and 1970s the Astrodome served as the most recognizable symbol linking Houston to a culture that embraced high-technology solutions to its problems rather than relying on its old-tech oil and cattle roots. Astrodome construction helped to shift how Houston thought about itself and how outsiders perceived Houston. By 2014, big petroleum still dominated the regional economy, but technology rather than old-style, muscle-oriented wildcat drilling had become an integral part of this previously old-tech industry.

Furthermore, metropolitan Houston had seen major technology companies established. As one example, the Harris County–based computer company Compaq challenged the hegemony of IBM in office-based computing, selling more personal computers than the multinational giant during the 1990s, and at a time when America's reliance on computing and an information-based economy gained intense momentum.

The rise of the space program in the 1960s, 1970s, and 1980s further elevated Houston's technology-based stature, as did pioneering medical research that unfolded after the Astrodome was unveiled. Dr. Denton Cooley, as an example, performed the first implantation of an artificial human heart in 1968 at the Texas Heart Institute, a remarkable milestone that added to Houston's reputation as a cutting-edge city. The pioneering cardiac work of Cooley and Dr. Michael DeBakey continued in Houston for decades, with Memorial Hermann Medical Center also emerging as a world-class location for a variety of medical procedures. In a broad range of endeavors, Houston had successfully transitioned from a city that was perceived to be a low-tech cattle and oil hub to a locale that was every bit as cutting edge as its modern sports facilities.

Nevertheless, as the Super Bowl decision was made, the Astrodome was shuttered to the public, but its symmetrical beauty could be seen from nearby highways. It was portrayed in local and national media as an aging relic that had fallen into a state of severe disrepair. Several code violations had rendered the facility unusable for large-scale public events, although it had served admirably as a shelter for the victims of Hurricane Katrina in 2005, most of whom were transported to Houston after being initially housed in New Orleans' Superdome.

The Superdome proved to be inadequate for sheltering Katrina's victims after hurricane-force winds damaged major portions of its outer shell, yet it was rapidly renovated while the New Orleans Saints played out their entire 2005 schedule in other venues outside of New Orleans. The lion's share of the $185 million renovation costs, approximately $115 million, were paid by the Federal Emergency Management Agency (FEMA), not out of local or state revenues, with the NFL kicking in $15 million and the balance coming from Louisiana sources. As the New Orleans facility prepared to reopen, Bill Curl, spokesman for the Superdome facility, proudly boasted that "never in the history of stadiums in the USA has a facility been so heavily damaged and rebuilt in one year."[2] The success was sufficiently impressive that the luxury auto manufacturer Mercedes-Benz entered into a naming rights agreement with Superdome officials, who rechristened the facility the Mercedes-Benz Superdome in 2011. In addition, the NFL chose this facility to host the 2013 Super Bowl.

As the New Orleans dome received widespread public acclaim for its rapid and dramatic revitalization, the Houston facility that had served as an inspiration for the Superdome's construction sat unused, with little evidence that its situation might change. With maintenance scaled back to a bare minimum, it continued to fall into further disrepair, although, unlike the Superdome in nearby Louisiana, its overall structural soundness was never in question.

In 2000 Houston had broken ground on a new multipurpose

stadium, a necessary step to attract a new NFL team. As the construction unfolded, the Astrodome had no ready-made advocates with the necessary deep pockets to refurbish it, so attempts to preserve the structure remained elusive. In an attempt to summarize Houston's architectural legacy, preservationist Anna Mod asserted that, quite frequently, "the buildings [of Houston] that unabashedly ushered in a future of such promise are often those most threatened by neglect, insensitive alterations, and demolition."[3]

Not everyone believed that the Astrodome should be preserved. Among its better-known critics was Pulitzer Prize–winning author and Texas native Larry McMurtry. He wrote that Houston is "the kind of boom town that will endorse any kind of municipal vulgarity so long as it has a chance of making money," slamming the exterior design as one that "looked like the working end of a gigantic roll-on deodorant," even if, quite ironically, the air-conditioned facility served to decrease perspiration among Houston's citizens.[4]

As new construction unfolded in close proximity to the Astrodome, it became abundantly clear that the first large-scale indoor sports facility would no longer be the central meeting place for Houstonians and nearby visitors. Despite that, construction chugged along, while the Astrodome remained a useful community asset. WrestleMania unfolded in the Dome on April 1, 2001, to a crowd of 67,925 screaming fans. Musician George Strait attracted an audience of 68,266 in 2002, an Astrodome record for paid attendance. The Livestock and Rodeo Show remained in the Astrodome in 2001 and 2002, but the giant event that had grown exponentially as a result of its move to the Dome was shifted to the shiny new stadium next door by 2003. The Livestock and Rodeo Show continued to book the Astrodome for a multievening event called the Hideout, which turned the floor of the Dome into a giant bar with dancing and live entertainment. The Hideout continued in the Astrodome through 2008, with the last event unfolding on Saturday, March 22, with Houston native Johnny Bush, a country singer, as the final lead musical act to play on the floor of the giant indoor venue.

Few people realized that this would be the last-ever regularly scheduled public event to take place inside the Astrodome. Livestock and Rodeo Show officials expected to use the venue for the Hideout again in 2009, but code violations uncovered later in 2008 blocked the facility from maintaining the certificate of occupancy necessary to remain in use for public events. Initially, $250,000 would have addressed these early code violations, but as time unfolded, limited caretaking gradually increased the cost, with no one willing to absorb the expenses.[5] Plans were subsequently announced to convert the Dome into a luxury hotel, but the international meltdown of the financial services industry created an increasingly cautious investment environment. The economic downturn prompted the abandonment or postponement of numerous large-scale real estate projects, including private investment in the Astrodome.

Livestock organizers continued the Hideout event in 2009 but moved it into a giant temporary tent that was positioned near the Astrodome. A party-like event, one that was somewhat reminiscent of the weekend parties that Roy Hofheinz organized as an enthusiastic teen, unfolded without the Astrodome for the first time in years. The massive fabric structure was ironically similar to the large Ringling Bros. Circus tent that Hofheinz visited in Beaumont as a young boy, likely the first grand indoor event ever experienced by the famed maestro of the Astrodome's complex construction. Although the Hideout's theme was country western, not the up-tempo jazz preferred by Hofheinz during the 1920s, the shift from dome to tent was sadly ironic to anyone who might consider the long, complex, and winding biographical trajectory that inspired Hofheinz to take the lead in the Astrodome's construction.

Bud Adams, Hofheinz's peripatetic nemesis, had long since left the Bayou City for a more lucrative stadium deal in Tennessee. He departed Houston shortly after the 1996 season. After $67 million in taxpayer dollars were poured into an Astrodome renovation, a facelift that Adams requested, he was unhappy that his subsequent call to build a brand-new, more lucrative, taxpayer-funded stadium in Houston for his team failed to gain sufficient political traction, with Mayor Bob Lanier serving as a powerful opponent of further taxpayer subsidy for the Oilers. Adams had planned to leave after the 1997 season, but Houstonians, knowing their team would be heading elsewhere, understandably stopped spending their money to watch the lame-duck Oilers in 1996, generally abandoning support for the team.

After sparse attendance in 1996 the league and Adams wisely arranged a hasty departure to avoid a highly embarrassing farewell tour. Houstonians recognized that they were losing their NFL franchise to a much smaller metropolitan area and understandably felt slighted by Adams's decision. As the team moved to Tennessee, *Houston Chronicle* sportswriter Ed Fowler produced an acerbic tome entitled *Loser Takes All*. Fowler portrayed Adams as a self-centered and mercurial owner, while suggesting that a difficult road would lie ahead for any city that might have to work with him.

To attract a new NFL team, Houston's taxpayers eventually agreed to build a brand-new stadium at a cost of $352 million, one with considerably larger capacity than the Astrodome. The construction allowed Houston, the nation's fourth most populous city, to leap in front of Los Angeles, the nation's second-largest city, to bring professional football back to the Bayou City. Reliant Stadium, as it was initially called, was the first enclosed stadium with a fully retractable roof to be constructed for any NFL team. Unveiled in 2002 as home to the newly formed Houston Texans, it seated 71,054 fans, approximately 20,000 more than the Astrodome's initial capacity and about 10,000 more than its expanded capacity. The enhanced seating numbers and retractable roof design proved to be more desirable for the power brokers within the Houston Livestock and Rodeo Show than what the Astrodome might offer. The impressive facility was built adjacent to the Dome, and its towering presence suggested that the Astrodome's useful days might be numbered, although plans for the Dome's long-range future were not immediately confronted.

The structural soundness of the newly constructed facility was challenged in 2008 when Hurricane Ike damaged Reliant Stadium's retractable roof structure. In response, the NFL juggled the team's home schedule for that season while forcing the Texans to play with the roof open for a year, although subsequent repairs brought the facility back to its initial state-of-the-art condition. Nevertheless, the Astrodome served as a staging facility for emergency workers as hurricane-force winds bore down on the region, with no structural damage whatsoever reported to the aging Dome. Although nature's brutal assault could not bring down the Astrodome, other factors would contribute to its demise. Even though it was structurally sound, the larger capacity and shiny newness of the nearby facility, since renamed NRG Stadium, kept the Astrodome offline and out of use.

Harris County taxpayers resisted spending money to revive and maintain the historic facility, and attempts to lure private funding to renovate the Astrodome were never successful. As a result, gradual decay developed into code violations that rendered the Astrodome useless as an entertainment venue. Those with fond memories of its prior greatness resisted various proposals to tear the landmark down, as has been common in most other American cities. The Astrodome was most recently used as a temporary storage shed for seats, turf, and other large items used within the newer nearby facility, although in 2004 it achieved a brief moment of nostalgic fame as a set location for the Hollywood film *Friday Night Lights*.

While the renovations that Bud Adams demanded served to undermine some of the unique qualities of the venue, the modification plan of the Oilers' owner was not the sole reason for the Astrodome's demise and eventual replacement. Roy Hofheinz focused on creating a unique and thoroughly modern facility that was state of the art when it was constructed. Its unparalleled use of new technologies was one reason among many why visitors were so impressed with it in the 1960s. However, ongoing technological advances constituted a sort of poison pill that undermined the awe-inspiring novelty of the Astrodome.

Without major infusions of cash, routine and ongoing technology upgrades would be impossible to sustain for those charged with oversight of the Dome. As a result, newer and shinier stadiums served to chip away at the initial luster of the Astrodome. Over time, it was less of a novelty, and gradually it became more of a relic. Roy Hofheinz's health declined in the 1970s, with a stroke confining him to a wheelchair. After he passed away in 1982, the facility lacked a high-energy ambassador, someone who might continue to maintain the Astrodome's opulence with his unique flair, enthusiasm, and creativity.

In 1988, Bob Wood, author of *Dodger Dogs to Fenway Franks*, a book described as "the ultimate guide to American's top baseball parks," assigned a grade of D, an abysmal score of sixty, to the Astrodome for its overall atmosphere. Wood described the employees, the food, and the general ambiance as substandard, calling the venue "just another dome, only worse."[6] He slammed the unenthusiastic attitude of the vendors, the overall artificial environment, and the lack of fan emotion during game day. Although he lauded the architectural beauty of the exterior and what was then the innovative touch of inserting television monitors above concession stands so that patrons would not miss on-field action while loading up on food, he ranked the Astrodome dead last in his overall evaluation of twenty-six Major League ballparks.

Houstonians still regarded the Dome with a degree of respect despite its imperfections. As the Dome's twenty-fifth anniversary was celebrated, retired Astros pitcher and local sports icon Larry Dierker described his initial visit to the Astrodome as a moment with "a sense of unreality to it. I felt like I was in a futuristic dream—like I had walked into the next century."[7]

Despite extensive publicity related to the twenty-fifth anniversary, attendance was not nearly as strong in 1990 as it had been in seasons past. In that season, the Astros attracted just 1,310,927 fans. Only Cleveland's and Atlanta's baseball teams had weaker overall attendance records. A year later Astros attendance slipped to 1,196,152, and by 1992 the Astrodome's 1,211,412 attendance figure was the lowest of any team in Major League Baseball. The slippage was not the result of a decline in the popularity of indoor facilities, however. In those three seasons, Toronto's SkyDome led professional baseball in total attendance, surpassing the four million mark twice.

Nevertheless, the unveiling of Baltimore's Camden Yards in 1992 ushered in a seismic shift in ballpark design, one that focused on old-style nostalgia, with the unique retro ballpark achieving an impressive second place in overall attendance, attracting 3,567,819 fans despite having a much smaller capacity than Houston's Astrodome or Toronto's SkyDome.

The retro ballpark was the brainchild of Eric Moss, a Syracuse University graduate student whose passion for sports-related architecture was palpable. The new design allowed patrons to enjoy a variety of modern amenities while basking in the quaint and presumably more innocent ambiance of a turn-of-the-century ballpark, even though the new construction was merely a modernized replica of that bygone era. Essential to the design were features such as natural grass, quirky and unique elements such as ornate custom ironwork melded with old-style brick or stonework, integration of a more subdued and traditional palette of colors than was evident in the Astrodome, unique outfield dimensions, and less generous foul areas that brought the highest-paying fans closer to the on-field action.

Ballpark design was just one issue confronting supporters of the Astrodome, however. Without the enthusiastic, overbearing, and autocratic leadership of Roy Hofheinz, the Astrodome had slipped in its fan-based service, and its menu offerings were less than desirable. The Houston Sports Association had farmed out its food services to the Harry M. Stevens Company, a firm that also managed the concession stand operations at New York's Shea Stadium and San Francisco's Candlestick Park. The quality of the company's offerings was so bad that *San Francisco Chronicle* reporter Lowell Cohn was prompted to assert that the hot dogs "tasted as if they'd been hanging around a meat locker since the days of Carl Hubbell," a New York Giants pitching standout who faced Babe Ruth and Lou Gehrig during the 1930s.[8] In stark contrast to the culinary vision of Roy Hofheinz, the dining options of the Astrodome led Houston reporter Ken Hoffman to bluntly assert that "eating is not among the pleasures of watching a game at the Astrodome. Fans don't dine at the ballpark. They either hit a restaurant before the game, or wait for a midnight refrigerator raid at home."[9]

Regardless, Houston officials clung to the belief that the Astrodome still had the capacity to awe out-of-towners, even if the food quality was poor, customer service was lacking, and more advanced technologies were available in venues elsewhere. The unveiling of newer facilities further chipped away at its overall luster, but Houston officials were confident that they could continue to push the Astrodome as a national attraction. They successfully pitched the Astrodome as a venue for the 1992 Republican National Convention and unsuccessfully embarked on an effort to bring the NFL's Super Bowl to the venue.

The attempts to bring the Astrodome to national prominence in the late 1980s and early 1990s gave way to a push to replace it. As the NFL began to produce more futuristic facilities with fancy, upscale retailing space and other profit-generating amenities, Major League Baseball fans responded with passion and enthusiasm to the retro-ballpark trend. The immense popularity of Orioles Park at Camden Yards propelled other team owners to copy the retro concept, generally at substantial cost to each region's taxpayers.

Retro-ballpark construction, as it permeated city after city, including an array of smaller, Minor League towns, rendered the circular ballpark much less desirable to both casual and die-hard baseball fans. Casual fans, in particular, enjoyed the vast retail spaces woven into the bowels of these retro facilities. New, more favorable leases were extended to team owners, with taxpayers generally subsidizing a large portion of the construction, while teams were generally given more access to ballpark revenue streams as part of the negotiations.

Visiting patrons were often willing to pay more to enjoy a re-created past, however imperfect, and to share a feel-good mood. Team owners cleverly integrated statues of past heroes and other symbols of an earlier era into the design as a strategy that enabled teams to successfully monetize regional nostalgia. The visit to yesteryear offered all the modern amenities of the twenty-first century while encouraging consumers to conjure up an idyllic past that may or may not have ever existed.

The retro trend helped to further popularize ancient ballparks such as Boston's Fenway Park and Chicago's Wrigley Field, allowing those teams to raise ticket prices substantially, although the greed of some team owners in newly designed retro ballparks left a percentage of the priciest seats empty. In one of the most blatant examples of predatory pricing, the ticket price for a single seat located behind home plate in the new Yankee Stadium was set at a whopping $2,500 for a regular season game.

As the retro trend unfolded, the newly constructed ballparks diminished the value of circular ballparks such as New York's Shea Stadium, St. Louis's Busch Stadium, Pittsburgh's Three Rivers Stadium, and the Astrodome, relegating them to second-tier status. Quaintly designed, smaller ballparks were allowing team owners to raise ticket prices since sellouts of these smaller venues were more achievable and holding back on a ticket purchase could mean being frozen out of attendance for any given game. Larger, cavernous, "all-purpose" facilities like the Astrodome struggled to attract fans, since patrons could generally choose to buy a ticket on game day without any fear of being turned away.

The Astros management saw this trend increase the profitability and the franchise value of rival baseball teams while their bottom line remained stagnant. As a result, they pushed for a new retro facility for Houston. With the loss of Houston's football franchise fresh in the minds of the voters, fearful taxpayers, worried about the loss of a second major professional sports team, supported a referendum to build a new baseball field for the Astros by a narrow 51 to 49 percent vote.

Rice University sociology professor Steven Klineberg attributed the departure of Houston's NFL team as a key factor in the measure's passage, stating that "if Houston had lost a baseball team and a football team in a period of 12 months, that would have hurt, especially in a city that loves sports so."[10] To convince voters, the measure called for car rental and hotel taxes to fund the construction, meaning that county property taxes would not be affected, ensuring that visitors would pay a large share of the construction costs.

The $248 million retractable-roof ballpark, initially named Enron Field after the energy behemoth signed a $100 million, thirty-year naming rights agreement, was unveiled on March 30, 2000, in an exhibition match, fittingly, against the New York

Yankees. The ballpark included natural grass, wide concourses, and vast retailing areas, and, like other retro ballparks, it incorporated old-style architectural touches. The design achieved its desired effect as a retail-based profit center, with *Houston Chronicle* reporter David Barron asserting that "when fans weren't cheering, they were eating and drinking, and when they weren't eating and drinking, they were buying."[11] The Enron moniker was temporary, as a managerial scandal within the company and its subsequent bankruptcy forced the renaming of the ballpark. Minute Maid, a subsidiary of the Atlanta-based Coca-Cola Company, acquired the naming rights in 2002, once again in a thirty-year deal worth $100 million. By 2004 the Astros had unveiled wireless access, a feature never offered within the Astrodome.

The Astrodome's focus on technological novelty ensured that others would try to build facilities that might be regarded as newer, shinier, and more impressive than the Dome years later. When the facility was initially christened, Houston's emergence into the professional sports world was dramatic, attention grabbing, and unique. Retro ballparks, with their faux-ancient façades, nevertheless contained an array of modern amenities, many of which had been unavailable when the ultramodern and cutting-edge Astrodome was unveiled. They offered mall-style food courts, spacious retailing areas, high-definition scoreboards, high-tech luxury skyboxes, and club-style restaurants. What was incredibly impressive in 1965 became less so as time took its toll on Houston's revolutionary structure and as technological innovation moved inexorably forward.

Even though no other indoor structure as large as the Astrodome was as rigorously tested to withstand sonic booms, hurricane force winds, and a vast range of natural and man-made hazards, by the twenty-first century, sports fans were more concerned with amenities such as convenient access to wireless technology and trendy features that were not even under consideration when the Astrodome was planned and built. The road to an obsolete Astrodome was a gradual one; for almost two decades, the first enormous indoor sports facility had been regarded as cutting edge. Modern features were woven into newer ballpark designs, even if the Astrodome was still regarded as unique and every bit as impressive as some of the sports palaces that were constructed during the 1970s. However, as digital technology permeated the cultural landscape of the 1990s, for all but a small core of individuals, the Astrodome was no longer regarded as awe inspiring.

It took a while for the Astrodome to lose its dramatically unique stature. A decade after the Astrodome was christened, new indoor facilities were completed in New Orleans and in the Detroit suburb of Pontiac. A year later, in 1976, the Kingdome was unveiled. This sixty-six-thousand-capacity stadium was under construction before a professional sports team had even committed to Seattle, its host city. By the early 1980s Minneapolis and Indianapolis introduced indoor structures to house their local sports teams. A massive indoor sports stadium was no longer a novelty. This undermined the ability of the Astrodome to attract out-of-town visitors. It no longer provided Houston with a landmark that was a topic of enthusiastic conversation elsewhere.

As technology advanced, other facilities, both indoor and outdoor, featured massive scoreboards. Though none were as large as the Astrodome's behemoth, the dramatically improved resolution of these newer big screens rendered the massive Astrodome scoreboard less unique and perhaps limited resistance when the giant board was finally replaced to make way for more seating capacity to temporarily satisfy Bud Adams.

In addition, other owners copied Hofheinz and his most innovative ideas since luxury was not a patentable commodity. As an example, some teams erected lavish skyboxes that rivaled what Hofheinz tried to achieve. After Arrowhead Stadium opened in 1972, Kansas City Chiefs owner Lamar Hunt chose to appoint what he dubbed the "Gold Suite," his personal skybox, with rare sixteenth- and seventeenth-century art and antiquities, making a status statement that attempted to surpass what had unfolded in the Dome.[12] The Astrodome established a luxury-based trend that made skyboxes a mandatory feature in present-day stadiums, and the concept of putting multiple restaurants within a sports facility was transplanted elsewhere, too. As others emulated the dramatic opulence that Hofheinz had pioneered, the sizzle that made the Astrodome special further diminished.

A variety of plans emerged to try to save the Astrodome. Some were absurd, some may have had the potential to work, but no plan appeared to be feasible with private funding alone. Among the ideas were conversion of the Dome to a conference center, a luxury hotel, a gambling casino, a movie studio, a shopping mall, an indoor skiing/winter sports facility, a giant water park, a massive fitness center, an indoor soccer field, and a mixed-use facility that would serve multiple purposes and constituencies.

In 2004 plans were unveiled to turn the Astrodome into a thirteen-hundred-room luxury hotel. While this seemed to be a promising option, a combination of financing difficulties and stalled negotiations with the Houston Texans and rodeo officials hung up progress. By August 2008, Larry Shaffer, the Livestock and Rodeo Show COO, bluntly stated that "last time, we were looking at a lease that violated our rights all over the place. Now, a lease is being developed to protect our rights." Texans president Jamey Rootes also indicated "a willingness to finalize agreements that protect the rights of all parties and allow for the successful redevelopment of the Reliant Astrodome." Both rodeo and Texans officials raised concerns about ambush marketing and naming rights deals while expressing concerns that the nearby facility could siphon off revenues from the adjacent stadium.[13] Despite having approval to move forward and a proposed lease agreement on the table as early as May, the Astrodome Redevelopment Company was at a decided disadvantage in navigating a financial deal without a finalized lease agreement in place. Even with a delay, rodeo and Texans officials finally indicating a willingness to step up, and it appeared as though a contract might be hammered out that would allow the plan to be linked to a private sector lender.

However, on September 15, 2008, panic struck Wall Street. Lehman Brothers, a major player in commercial investment, faced economic free fall and filed for bankruptcy. This created a cascading implosion of investment capital with dramatic global implications. Economic hard times from September 2008 onward sabotaged the potential for private sector support for Astrodome renovations, with investment capital becoming increasingly tight as the global economy sputtered and slowed. Even with the economic meltdown, the Astrodome Redevelopment Corporation did not back away from its willingness to commit $150 million to preserve the iconic structure, but Scott Hanson, president of Astrodome Redevelopment, admitted that the credit crunch placed the project in peril.

The shaky economic climate was reported to have pushed capital requirements to begin such renovation into the $225 million range, a daunting figure. To be in a position to seek financing at this level, final, detailed construction drawings, estimated to cost $10 million to fully complete, would be required, but without a green light on a lease agreement, such an expenditure could be futile. As December rolled around, the leadership of the Texans and the rodeo could not be convinced to sign off on a lease agreement that might push the proposal forward, though they indicated a willingness to negotiate further.[14] The project stalled and went nowhere as a shaky economy and tighter credit standards gripped the nation.

After years of inaction, Dome advocates pushed to raise public funds instead. A November 5, 2013, referendum to convert the Astrodome into an energy-efficient convention and events center that would be surrounded by parkland, dubbed the "New Dome Experience," was put on the ballot, with $217 million in taxpayer support required for full completion of the project. With limited campaigning, the measure failed by 53 to 47 percent, an outcome that put the Astrodome's future on exceedingly shaky terrain. Of the more than 4 million Harris County citizens, only about 250,000 voted, slightly more than 6 percent of the total population.

Although Houston's economy was frequently touted as "booming" in spite of a fragile and more sluggish national economy, passage of the Astrodome referendum was an uphill battle, in part because of shifts in demographic patterns. Increasing poverty rates may have convinced some citizens that saving a stadium that did not have a specific tenant or a tangible private sector partner was a luxury too rich for Houston. Despite rising median household incomes in the region, 23.8 percent of Houston's citizens were at or below the poverty line, typically working in low-skilled, low-benefit jobs and unlikely to support any measure that appeared to be tied to affluence and wealth.[15] In addition, a Brookings Institution report that showed suburban poverty increasing at twice the rate of poverty in cities suggested that Harris County suburbs, too, might be less likely to support such spending than prior generations had been.[16]

Many citizens—29 percent, to be exact—regarded traffic and road conditions as the region's most pressing need, even outpacing concerns about the economy and crime. As the vote unfolded, more than half of Harris County's citizens aged sixty-five and older were white, but demographic patterns were fast changing. The younger demographic, twenty and under, was more than 50 percent Hispanic, and one-fifth were African Americans.[17] Although Roy Hofheinz routinely earned high levels of support from the minority community while building the Astrodome, the younger voting demographic was largely unaware of his commitment to civil rights or his support for minority causes during his service as mayor and after, with many younger voters possibly altogether unaware of who Roy Hofheinz even was.

Another key factor, however, was a political climate that was less receptive to funding bond measures, which served to siphon middle-class votes away from the project. Highly ambitious commitments made in the previous year's election cycle had prompted a more cautious environment in 2013. In 2012 Houston voters approved a whopping $2.7 billion in bond initiatives, including a $1.9 billion school renovation and construction proposal that was described as "the largest bond for a Texas school district in at least a quarter of a century."[18] Experts suggested that a fiscally conservative backlash described as "bond fatigue" may have unfolded. University of Houston political scientist Brandon Rottinghaus explained that "the voters may be wary of going back to what they consider a dry well." Rejection of a $69 million measure to build a new high school stadium in the football-crazy Houston suburb of Katy, just one year after the team was crowned Texas state champion, seemed to solidify evidence that the voters wanted fiscal austerity in the wake of high bond commitments a year earlier.[19]

Astrodome investments were made by legislators, but the funds allocated seemed aimed at addressing issues that were more likely to bring down the overall cost of demolition than to encourage a tangible renovation plan. As an example, in October 2013, before the referendum was voted on, an $8 million measure was approved by the Harris County commissioners to demolish exterior parts of the facility while removing some of the asbestos that was used inside the structure when it was built. Ticket booths were dismantled and hauled away, as were the circular exit ramps that had been added to the facility to make entry and exit more efficient, particularly for visitors with disabilities. In addition, electrical substation transmission lines were removed, as were some signs that had the potential to be sold later as memorabilia.[20] While asbestos removal might be helpful for anyone attempting a renovation project, cheaper asbestos encapsulation might have been undertaken if long-term renovation was a more desirable scenario.

The timing of the well-publicized Astrodome expenditures provided another benefit to demolition advocates. It gave some cautious voters a sense that Harris County taxpayers might be funding much more than the $217 million proposal if renovation funds were approved, possibly offering less certain citizens an incentive to vote against the plan.

Those charged with Astrodome caretaking were in a strange box regarding its day-to-day management. If they succeeded in obtaining funds to offset some of the maintenance expenses, the renovations might diminish some residents' emotional attachment to the Dome. As an example, the $8 million allocated to the Dome was partially offset by $1.5 million that was raised in an auction of Astrodome merchandise and memorabilia, but as chairs, signage, and some of the more coveted items were dragged out to become household furnishings, what remained was a more antiseptic facility with less evidence of the memories that inspired some people to want to hold on to the old structure. Nevertheless, given the profits earned in the first auction, the Harris County Sports and Convention Corporation indicated a willingness to hold at least one more auction, with some remaining remnants of the stadium to be offered for sale.[21]

Houston's ongoing and unyielding commitment to modernity, a quality that allowed the Bayou City to achieve many great strides, further undermined the logic of investing millions of dollars in preservation, as did the strategic imperatives that prompted Houston to build two new sporting venues to replace the Dome. Whether in Houston or elsewhere, the move to build new facilities involves long, protracted, and strategically focused media campaigns that can be savagely critical of an old facility and its many limitations. However, this is typically a necessary step to convince a wary public to step up and spend millions upon millions of dollars to fund these new projects.

Although these ongoing, high-profile campaigns can be highly effective in steering leaders and citizens to support new venue construction, the overarching process, as it plays out, gradually conditions both leaders and the broad public to diminish their respect and admiration for what may have been unique and might be worth preserving in an older facility. What tends to emerge as a stadium faces replacement are calls for demolition, with opposition from a small core of less unified preservationists with limited financial resources and weak political connections. This group may exude enthusiasm, and may even work to coordinate their efforts, but typically they can be isolated and marginalized with relative ease by those with greater power, resources, and influence. As the full costs of renovation and preservation are revealed, the degree of marginalization tends to intensify.

In Houston, a group that has come to be known as the Domers emerged, along with a small core of preservationists. They attempted to convince Houstonians to preserve and repurpose the Astrodome so that its history and legacy would remain intact. Craig Hlavaty, a *Houston Chronicle* journalist and blogger, wrote about the passion that the Domers had for preserving the Astrodome as proposals were offered that might somehow save the Dome. Shortly after Houston won its Super Bowl bid, Hlavaty wrote, "With all the new attention that Houston is getting, wouldn't it serve us well to show the world that is knocking on our door that we don't demolish everything, and that yes, some things are worth saving? That we can make beauty out of something that grew ugly? Or should NFL commissioner Roger Goodell make that call because he thinks we need 2,500 more parking spots?"[22] Hlavaty has been an enthusiastic supporter of renovating the Astrodome, appreciating its external beauty and its unique place in Houston's history. Even when writing about the Houston T-shirt scene, Hlavaty manages to weave in an Astrodome theme, stating that "most every shirt company in Houston has an item devoted to the Astrodome, as all things Dome are now more popular than ever due to the recent wrangling about the stadium's future."[23]

Although the *Houston Chronicle* was typically cautiously respectful and in several instances supportive of Dome preservation efforts, its popular feature writer Ken Hoffman became a vocal advocate for its demolition. He initially recommended turning the Dome into a giant casino, one that would attract both visitors and money. By 2010 Hoffman argued that "nobody needs the Astrodome anymore," then suggested chopping it up and selling the pieces before tearing it down. He ridiculed Houston's emotional attachment to the Dome, asserting that it was smelly, loaded with mold, and likely inhabited by large rats and stray cats. Hoffman mockingly concluded that "if they could tear down Yankee Stadium, the RCA Dome, Giants Stadium, Texas Stadium—places where championships lived—what's the deal with us and the Astrodome?"[24] Days after the Astrodome referendum failed, a Houston resident's letter suggesting that Houston "lost an opportunity to make the Dome something we can use and share, again" prompted Hoffman to caustically respond, "Harris County officials are not obligated to tear down the moldy, useless, condemned Dome. They can continue to let it sit and rot, like they have for the past 15 years, at the cost of millions of dollars down the toilet."[25]

While Hlavaty's enthusiasm for the Astrodome may have energized Domers and preservationists, Hoffman's overall audience reach was considerably larger. He appeared on radio often and produced a nationally syndicated restaurant column, and his writings were routinely placed in prominent locations within the *Houston Chronicle*. Hlavaty's blogs were afforded an energetic license that was less visible in the print copy of the newspaper, but, simply put, Hoffman's high-profile platform had greater capacity to push the public policy needle against preservation than the less visible advocacy of Hlavaty and others, even if such advocacy frequently contained higher levels of enthusiasm.

The Livestock Show and Rodeo officials confronted the Astrodome issue with caution and reluctance, understanding that it was a beloved Houston icon. They resisted endorsement and any demonstration of enthusiasm for proposals that had the potential to repurpose the Dome in a manner that might become permanent. However, as the Super Bowl bid approached, rodeo officials joined with Texans team officials and began to more aggressively push an agenda that would result in demolition. The rhetoric regarding the Astrodome's future remained cautious, but rodeo officials' releases overtly suggested an outcome that would lead to demolition.

They collaborated with the Texans football team to ensure that the newly constructed stadium remained a crown jewel that would serve their mutually beneficial goals involving revenue generation. As rodeo officials and the Texans worked together, a future that might preserve the Astrodome was not part of any plan that they pushed forward. As an example, in 2013, as the Super Bowl bid was under consideration, the two organizations commissioned a study that concluded that the demolition of the Astrodome and conversion of the land to sixteen hundred parking spaces could be done at a cost of $29 million, a figure that was less than half of all previous estimates. A 2012 study had cited a $64 million cost, while a 2010 study had pegged demolition at $78 million.

In releasing the report, Leroy Shaffer, the Livestock Show and Rodeo's chief operating officer, indicated that it was intended to be "helpful" and gently explained that "we're not recommending this over any other option."[26] County officials challenged the validity of the estimates, but Shaffer addressed the unexpectedly low demolition costs by asserting that rodeo officials and the Texans had carefully vetted the findings "three times, and I can assure you there is nothing left out of this study."[27] The parking lot conversion proposal was further encouraged by NFL commissioner Roger Goodell, who, despite stating "that issue is for the community to decide," asserted that adding extra parking spaces "would enhance Houston's [Super Bowl] bid."[28]

By 2014, with the 2017 Super Bowl bid a known success, the failure of the 2013 referendum prompted skepticism about preservation efforts and a more critical tone from rodeo officials in general. They pushed harder in their public statements to highlight and emphasize the decaying condition of the Astrodome as plans for its future were discussed. In May an anonymous rodeo official told reporters that the organization was eager to find an "acceptable resolution to a closed and rotting building that sits at the center of their operations."[29]

On June 10 rodeo and Texans officials unveiled a $66 million plan created by Gensler, an architectural firm, and Linbeck, a construction company. The proposal would raze the Astrodome and fill the remaining hole to ground level, replacing the structure with parkland. To recognize the Astrodome as a part of Houston's history, the center of the park would hold a newly built and much smaller replica of the Astrodome, while the parkland would be edged by a circle of seventy-two columns that would be shaped to appear like the outer beams of the Dome's wall. Rodeo officials indicated a willingness to provide financial support for the plan but did not disclose an amount. Larry Shaffer confidently asserted, "We think they came up with a tremendous idea, and it's the one thing we don't have out there right now. . . . This puts a park right in the center of our NRG park complex."[30]

The concept appeared to borrow from an idea developed by a University of Houston graduate student, Ryan Slattery. He envisioned turning the actual Astrodome facility into an open park area and recreation space, with the exterior walls removed and the supporting steel beams letting light and air pass through. His plan, unlike the minidome concept, would have preserved the iconic Astrodome roof, leaving vegetation to grow under it. If Slattery's plan was implemented as envisioned, the space could be used for tailgating during football season, grazing during the livestock show, and a variety of other purposes as the calendar dictated. Slattery's proposal appeared to be the least objectionable option, although home-prepared tailgate food might reduce game-day profits somewhat. Slattery did not have the resources or the expertise to provide a good-faith estimate of the cost for his concept, but it appeared to be a cheaper option than any plan that would involve air conditioning and indoor construction. It also gained a degree of support because a parkland project called Discovery Green in the downtown area was a popular public-private partnership that received praise from many Houstonians.

The thirty-seven-page minidome proposal presentation prepared for the rodeo and the Texans included an overhead photograph of the actual Astrodome, not its miniature replica, within close proximity to NRG Stadium. The image was marked with bright red arrows and bold graphics stating that "the Astrodome impedes circulation along two major axes of Reliant Park." After it was noted that the facility's name had shifted from Reliant to NRG Park in March, the organizations making the presentation indicated that the concept had been in the works for some time: since January. The graphic also provided fodder for those who believed that rodeo and Texans officials never wanted to preserve the Astrodome. After all, the Astrodome had not moved since its unveiling in 1965. The "impedes circulation" argument could have been made more than a decade earlier, before tangible private sector proposals were solicited.

Swamplot, a Houston-based real estate blog with a penchant for isolating insider information, evaluated the evidence and speculated that this latest proposal had the potential to backfire on its authors, pointedly asking, "What would happen if the until-now-growing sense among many Houstonians that everything possible has been tried and somehow mysteriously 'won't work' (*blow up the place already, I'm tired of hearing about it!*) gave way to a realization that the same two parties may have, in fact, been responsible for bungling, blocking, discouraging, sabotaging, and outright vetoing every single proposal for saving or revamping the Astrodome over the last dozen years?"[31]

Harris County judge Ed Emmett, a longtime advocate for Astrodome preservation, called the proposal "silly," while the *Houston Chronicle* suggested the repeated silences that had followed other proposals "was long taken as evidence that the Texans and Rodeo were playing the long game, waiting for voters to grow exhausted with the whole process until they finally throw up their hands and say: Demolish this thing already!" The editors attacked the idea of razing the Astrodome, asserting that "we cannot establish a solid future if we consistently uproot our past. Houston must be a place that is willing to invest in itself—a vision that men like Roy Hofheinz had."[32]

After the 2013 referendum failed, little push was made by leaders to address problematic renovation funding issues, while few political leaders, save Judge Emmett, were willing to challenge the rodeo and Texans to step up and make an effort to salvage the Astrodome. Instead, the common assertion from those in a position to broker any deal was that because of the failed referendum, any long-term solution would have to come from private sector funds. To succeed, however, any private sector plan would require ongoing revenue streams. Such required revenue streams were likely raise the ire of rodeo and Texans officials since their goals were predicated on profit generation, too. Not surprisingly, this tangle of competing interests created a dysfunctional negotiating landscape.

A proposal to enter into a public-private partnership that included a smaller up-front subsidy than that rejected by the taxpayers in 2013 might have succeeded if linked to a well-honed, reasonable, and prudent private sector funding plan. But getting the rodeo leadership on board and the Houston Texans to support anything that might compete with their revenue streams appeared to be a nonstarter. Unless the two biggest players were somehow brought in on potential revenues, or a coalition with political muscle could force change, nothing would move forward. As a result, the Dome simply sat and aged, with annual maintenance costs frequently cited as a reason to bring it down.

At a minimum, pushing a final, scaled-down preservation plan into the hands of the voters might serve as a last-ditch effort to save the structure before subjecting it to demolition. With no action proposed or anticipated, the once proud facility now served as a makeshift storage shed for nearby NRG Stadium while critics sniped at the futility of trying to save it. In frustration, a supportive *Houston Chronicle* editorial suggested that time was running out to do something significant before the 2017 Super Bowl, but the editors set the bar lower, suggesting that "a power wash, a coat of paint, landscaping, and maybe even hard hat tours, could make the Dome a sight worth seeing." They argued that, "with the right touches, the Dome could stand as an artistic installation for visiting crowds—or maybe just the world's largest lawn ornament. Either way, it would be an improvement on what we have now while preserving the building for any future ideas."[33]

The passage of time and years of political inactivity had rendered the Astrodome less relevant as a Houston landmark. Furthermore, it pushed many citizens who had been on the fence toward support of demolition, heightening chances for a future that involved the wrecking ball. As pieces of the Astrodome were sold off, the symbols and trappings of many people's childhoods would be gone. The ongoing neglect and slow gutting of the Dome's most prized content made it harder for Houstonians to maintain an emotional connection with the structure that best symbolized Houston's willingness to embrace modernity.

Just as "bond fatigue" diminished support for the bond initiative, "Dome fatigue" lessened support for renovation proposals that would require taxpayer funds. Unless they were emotionally involved in the issue, busy and struggling Houstonians pushed Dome revitalization to a low spot on their priority list and went on with their daily lives. As August approached, the Texans and rodeo officials briefed the Harris County commissioners about plans to work with the University of Houston's Hobby Center for Public Policy and Rice University's Baker Institute for Public Policy to determine the degree of public support for their plan to turn the Astrodome into a parkland that featured a miniature Astrodome replica. After years of inactivity and failure, the public was conditioned to support any idea that appeared to reflect progress. That, coupled with the popularity of Slattery's creative proposal and the success of the downtown park area called Discovery Green, increased the likelihood that the demolition and parkland conversion proposal could gain favorable public support.

Still, preservationists did gain a victory in January 2014, with

Cynthia Neely, a film company entrepreneur, and Ted Powell, a retired chemical engineer, successfully earning the Astrodome a spot on the National Register of Historic Places, an achievement that would allow a 20 percent federal tax credit to anyone investing in its preservation. Preservation consultant Ana Mod further suggested that this might open the door for a 25 percent state tax credit, too, although the achievement had little effect on blocking demolition. In making the case for preservation, Neely argued that the Astrodome was the first large domed structure not supported by internal columns. As a result, "it basically created a whole new style of architecture and made a lot of other famous buildings possible." With their victory in hand, preservationists had hoped to get the Texas Historical Commission to assign the Astrodome a protected status as a state landmark, which would establish a higher bar before demolition could unfold. Opponents of the designation expressed concern that it could tie the hands of developers, prompting the commission to delay a decision. Although demolition advocates appeared to be gaining headway, Neely and Powell had a strong record on the preservation front. The two had previously teamed up to successfully lead an effort to save a hurricane-damaged beach pavilion from demolition, obtaining $4.7 million in federal funds to do so. Their success offered tempered hope that creative measures might unfold to save the Astrodome.[34]

In December Judge Emmett sanctioned yet another proposal for Astrodome preservation. Espoused by the Urban Land Institute during a panel presentation on December 19, the proposal differed only slightly from Judge Emmett's August 2014 proposal to transform the Dome into the "world's largest indoor park," a kind of public green space for community usage for special events and other occasions. In contrast with Emmett's August proposal, the Urban Land Institute recommended raising the floor level of the Astrodome in order to create a parking garage that could accommodate fifteen hundred spaces. This garage would provide revenue streams to support the Dome, as well as for events held by the rodeo and the Texans. In an interview with the *Houston Business Journal*, Emmett pointed out that the Urban Land Institute unanimously recommended the Astrodome's preservation. Claiming that this latest proposal was the most robust call for preservation in recent years, Emmett also reported that a number of private firms had shown interest in managing the facility after its proposed transformation. While the Urban Land Institute's plan did not include a budget estimate, Emmett believe that it could be a turning point in the life of the Astrodome. "Whatever we do with the Dome right now," Emmett remarked, "it preserves it for future uses."[35]

Yet as 2014 came to a close, preservation advocates were considerably less optimistic about saving the Astrodome than they had been before the failed referendum. Powerful people and institutions had clear reasons to want the Astrodome eliminated from the Houston landscape. Years of debate and inaction had undermined public support for repurposing the Astrodome, and its future was in greater peril than ever before. In spite of his much publicized criticism of preservationist efforts, Hoffman movingly recalled his first visit to the Dome in the late 1980s, writing, "I thought it was terrific. It was air conditioned. The artificial turf was green. I could hear the crack of the bat crystal clear. They sold Dome Dogs and Dome Foam. It was big league baseball—beautiful." But the time had come, he asserted, to "demolish the Dome and replace it with a tasteful shrine and green space. Wouldn't it be better to have vivid memories of a shimmering 'Eighth Wonder of the World' and the incredible array of events that took place there?"[36]

In 2015 the Domers enjoyed a renewed sense of purpose as Judge Emmett—perhaps taking his cues from another fabled judge of Astrodome days gone by—continued to make progress on preserving the Eighth Wonder of the World. T-shirts emblazoned with an iconic Texas lone star above a drawing of the Astrodome and the words "Come and Take It!" became top sellers in the region, boldly connoting the fervor of Texas history by invoking the crude flag unveiled by Anglo settlers during the October 1835 battle of Gonzales. At one critical point, two competing vendors sparred via Twitter and other social media over the right to deploy the slogan, with its explicit references to the Texas Revolution, in the service of saving the Dome from the wrecking ball.[37]

In May 2015 Judge Emmett led a delegation that visited the Tropical Islands Resort, located some forty-five minutes south of Berlin. The delegates pointedly included leaders from the Urban Land Institute as well as former Houston Oilers defensive lineman and Houston Texans ambassador Carel Sith, who sat on the board of the Harris County Sports and Convention Corporation. A German theme park, Tropical Islands was built inside of a repurposed airship hangar. The resort features a beach, water slides, hotel rooms, and a simulated rain forest. Envisioning the repurposed Astrodome as a multiuse park, Emmett saw the German resort as a prime example of the many ways in which the Dome could enjoy a new lease on life in the shadows of the Texans' stadium. "The whole purpose really is to look at a building that is twice the size of the Astrodome, that has been repurposed completely. They built an island resort in a Zeppelin hangar," Emmett remarked. "We're not trying to turn the Astrodome into a tropical island or anything like that, but we need to see what's involved in the public-private partnership, the engineering questions, what can be grown indoors."[38]

Not surprisingly, Judge Emmett has increasingly emerged as the standard-bearer for the Dome's preservation. He is quick to point out that the failed 2013 bond vote was not a referendum on demolishing the stadium but rather on the deployment of public money in support of repurposing the structure. "The polls that I've seen say people overwhelmingly support saving the Dome," he exclaims. "They just don't want to use their money to save it. The bond election in 2013 was poorly presented to voters. To this day, people still think they were voting for a convention center. That's what failed. People did not vote to tear it down, that wasn't on the ballot." He further notes that "we have an Astrodome that is fully paid for, and it would cost tens of millions of dollars to tear it down. So I'd rather spend that amount, or less, to turn it into something useful, and give it to the people who have already paid for it once." Moreover, the judge vows that any future bond votes will benefit from a more spirited public campaign. "When it's time to make a proposal, if there is a bond attached to it, I will be front and center, along with other people, to sell it," he remarks. "Were there lessons learned from the 2013 election? Absolutely. Whatever we present, we will present in a much more vigorous fashion."[39]

Indeed, even if those opposed to preserving the Astrodome were to succeed in bringing the landmark down, the elimination of this once grand structure could not erase the Astrodome's dramatic legacy. It is a structure that changed not only architecture, as Cynthia Neely successfully argued, but the nature of sports spectatorship throughout the world.

1

The Dome and Its Legacy

When the Dallas Cowboys unveiled their new stadium outside Dallas in Arlington, Texas, in 2009, some heralded it as the new standard in sports-related opulence. Jay Burress, CEO of the Arlington Convention and Visitors Bureau, was so proud of the cutting-edge, ultramodern structure that he boasted, "We're in the spotlight for the whole world."[1] Initially it was named Cowboys Stadium. As a sign of the times, the facility received a lucrative sponsorship and was subsequently rechristened AT&T Stadium in 2013.

Jerry Jones, the Cowboys owner, inked a naming rights deal with the telecommunications giant AT&T that reportedly would bring the team $17 to $19 million per year for an undisclosed period, although typically deals of this nature are at least twenty years in duration. The deal was about more than money, though, with a joint statement asserting the Cowboys and AT&T "will work together to deliver an interactive game day experience for fans like no other."[2]

Walter P. Moore and Associates, the same firm responsible for supervising the structural engineering of the Astrodome, offered their expertise for this new stadium. The engineering challenges had shifted from concerns about structural integrity to a more intense focus on material science and aesthetics. Since the Astrodome had proved that large-scale indoor construction was achievable, the Cowboys were building a more expansive monument to sport.

The structure was designed with beams a quarter mile long. Such ambitious design required custom molds and high-strength steel imported from Luxembourg. The specialized metal had to be pretested for tensile strength using ultrasonic technology. The roof archways were designed with assembly pins able to withstand nineteen million pounds of force, the equivalent of fifty-nine Boeing 777 airplanes. To ensure an impressive aesthetic outcome, sixty-five hundred square feet of ultra-clear glass was specially formulated using low-iron technology that was initially developed in England for museum display use.[3]

Instead of a fixed roof, as the Astrodome had, a sophisticated and complex retractable roof was installed. The roof structure was designed with chemically welded pvc panels and a retractable roof fabric that was engineered to withstand 115 MPH winds.[4]

The giant facility included marble floors and sumptuous skyboxes. Jones ordered three thousand television screens for the new facility, including what was for a brief time the world's largest stadium-based television screen. For those who preferred viewing the game on their smaller personal devices, dramatic steps were taken to ensure that wireless access was widely available.[5] As the stadium opened, team officials consistently referred to the facility as "the world's most technologically advanced entertainment venue."[6]

The overabundance of technology allowed fans to watch on-field action while waiting for concession food, buying souvenirs, or even when wandering into the restrooms. The massive structure, with a capacity that could exceed one hundred thousand, was constructed at a cost of $1.3 billion dollars, more than four times the cost of the Astrodome when adjusted to reflect present-day values.

The construction of the Dallas Cowboys' new venue, as impressive as it was, reflected an opulent trend that was unfolding elsewhere in North America. In New York, the Steinbrenner family pushed to construct a new Yankee Stadium at a cost of $1.5 billion. It was publicly unveiled in 2009, slightly over a month before Cowboys Stadium was put into service. It, too, was equipped with a giant screen, along with approximately fourteen hundred smaller television screens placed throughout the ballpark. As with the Texas facility, it included luxurious skyboxes and abundant retailing space as well, though it was an open-air venue. Not to be outdone, the Giants and Jets unveiled MetLife Stadium in nearby East Rutherford, New Jersey, as Yankee Stadium was being introduced. Despite not having a protective roof, its cost was $1.6 billion, the most expensive sports facility ever built in the United States. It featured luxuries galore, including more than twenty-one hundred high-definition television screens.

As the twenty-first century unfolded, cities such as Indianapolis, Milwaukee, Minneapolis, and Phoenix put plans forward to build new and luxurious indoor stadiums, too. Whether it had a fixed roof or a retractable roof, a climate-controlled indoor sports facility was no longer a novelty.

What Roy Hofheinz envisioned as he agreed to step up to supervise Astrodome construction changed the face of sports spectatorship. No stadium in North America has had a more profound and far-reaching influence on the design and overall operation of today's modern sports facility than Houston's famed Astrodome. Built-in restaurants—some opulent, some casual—were unique to the Astrodome but are commonplace in today's Major League sports venues. High-end food is now woven into ballpark offerings as a matter of routine, with regional favorites included on concession stand menus. Although hot dogs, beer, and soft drinks are still popular stadium options, the food selection has expanded immensely to more closely resemble what was initially offered to those attending early Astrodome events—even if, over time, Astrodome food evolved into less appetizing fare after Hofheinz was no longer in charge.

The giant scoreboard that was pioneered by Hofheinz is another feature that is built into every major stadium in the United States today. Even Minor League ballparks and midlevel university venues have invested in large screens, validating Hofheinz's pioneering impulse to feature in-house video entertainment long before others perceived it as an essential part of the sporting experience.

Whether they are attending a Minor League game in Altoona, Pennsylvania, or an NFL game in the shadows of Manhattan, carefully planned on-screen entertainment has become the norm for sports fans, with a commercial edge as a driving force behind the professionally produced content. Although Hofheinz was visionary in so many ways, rapid changes in technology may have reshaped the game day experience in ways even he might not have envisioned.

In addition to installing giant screens and television monitors throughout new sports facilities, team owners now work with corporate sponsors and vendors to integrate wireless technologies for smaller personal devices such as smart phones so that fans can pull up statistics, communicate with friends, and otherwise customize their entertainment experience before, during, and after each game. Nevertheless, both Hofheinz and Roone Arledge, ABC's visionary sports guru, had the foresight to understand that video-based entertainment was a powerful force that would recalibrate much of American culture long before others involved with sports management had any sense of the immense power that evolving communication technologies might hold.

As impressive as the Astrodome was in its opening decades, its construction was part of a broader architectural history that featured an evolutionary increase in luxury. As the twentieth century unfolded, other grand edifices were built, gradually paving the way for a facility like the Astrodome to be constructed.

In the 1920s and 1930s gleaming new stadiums were built in Chicago, Cleveland, and Los Angeles. As with the Astrodome, these facilities were publicly funded. However, Soldier Field, Cleveland Municipal Stadium, and the Los Angeles Memorial Coliseum were more like the massive edifices built for major universities than the futuristic Astrodome. The scope and variety of consumer-oriented amenities offered within these giant venues were not unlike what could be found in less impressive structures. Even Yankee Stadium, a remarkably advanced facility for its time, was limited in its high-end amenities.

These sports venues were not built with an emphasis on integration of cutting-edge technology, nor were they designed with a meticulous focus on catering to a newly emerging consumer-driven fan experience. Moreover, the municipally funded venues were constructed as civic monuments, with the hosting of professional team sports as an afterthought.

After World War II, Milwaukee's County Stadium set the stage for more lavish construction to unfold, even though this ballpark was somewhat austere. Unlike most prewar sports structures, the Milwaukee ballpark was built with taxpayer funds as a foundation, and, in keeping with the rise of automobile culture, it was surrounded by wide expanses of parking, much as later occurred with the Astrodome, Shea Stadium, and other major facilities.

County Stadium was still a relatively spartan facility, with very few bells and whistles. However, the opening of that new ballpark launched the process of postwar franchise relocation, enticing the Boston Braves to move their operations to Milwaukee in 1953, the stadium's inaugural year of operation. A year later the St. Louis Browns moved to Baltimore, to be renamed the Orioles, and in 1955 the Athletics moved from Philadelphia to Kansas City. Such team movement led some community leaders to ante up greater sums for stadium construction as a way to impress, lure, and retain team owners.

In that vein, the shift of two New York teams to the West Coast more profoundly recalibrated the modern stadium construction landscape. San Francisco's Candlestick Park and Dodgers Stadium in Los Angeles were more impressive edifices than the norm when they were unveiled in 1959 and 1962, respectively, but they were largely ballparks, not all-purpose entertainment venues. In between this construction, the U.S. Department of the Interior spearheaded construction of a large multipurpose facility in Washington, DC. What was later renamed Robert F. Kennedy Stadium as a tribute to the slain New York senator was unveiled in 1961. Though it was an American first in terms of adopting a circular design, its limited range of amenities was more in line with what was constructed on the West Coast than what was built in Houston.

New York City's Shea Stadium was philosophically similar to the all-purpose entertainment venues that the Astrodome would later inspire, despite its many shortcomings. It featured a 175-foot-wide scoreboard that could display photo slides, lead the crowd in sing-a-longs, and update scores from other games. It also integrated restaurant service, including the posh Diamond Club, and had the largest escalator system ever to be installed in a sports facility up to that time. Discussion was undertaken to install a dome on top of this facility, as also was proposed when the Dodgers were seeking to remain in Brooklyn, but high costs prevented that from ever occurring. Although Shea Stadium was touted as futuristic, the Gotham facility fell far short of the Astrodome in terms of its overall use of fan-friendly technologies and the general quality of its entertainment amenities.

When the Astrodome was built, other ballparks, with the possible exception of Shea Stadium, featured very basic concession stands, rudimentary scoreboards, and plainly clad ushers. By contrast, Hofheinz supplemented Astrodome concession stands with numerous restaurants while entertaining patrons with a massive, 474-foot-wide scoreboard unlike any other scoreboard before it. However, Hofheinz was not satisfied with those over-the-top touches, as forward thinking as they might have been.

He provided the extraordinarily wealthy with access to custom-designed, luxurious skyboxes, but he took steps to make certain that the less affluent enjoyed the game day experience, too. Every seat was well engineered and padded, theater-style, meaning that even the cheapest seats would be much more comfortable than the old wooden and metal seats or benches in other sports facilities.

Hofheinz and his colleagues at the Houston Sports Association took pride in bringing the fans a sense of luxury not seen in other stadiums. In a Houston Sports Association publication touting the Astrodome's inaugural season, the cover read, "The Astrodome is more than a stadium—it is a way of treating people." Yet another headline from the publication exclaimed, "Every fan's a king!" and further bragged that "the Emperors of the mighty, ancient Roman Empire would turn chartreuse with envy if they could return to earth and see the luxurious seating enjoyed by every sports fan who enters the Astrodome." The HSA publication went on to assert that "the patrons of the Astrodome [are] the world's most pampered customers."[7]

To make the experience truly special for all visitors, Hofheinz tried to introduce a game day showcase beyond what others had considered at the time. He hired Evelyn Norton Anderson, a Houston fashion designer with credits in Hollywood and New York, to create unique uniforms that would make attending events at the Astrodome much more memorable. Norton Anderson custom-tailored specialized uniforms to be worn by the entire stadium staff, not just selected workers. This seemingly minor touch created an ambiance not found in sports venues anywhere else.

The futuristic outfits, tweaked and approved by Hofheinz, improved the entertainment environment while offering all patrons a unique customer experience. The uniforms established a dramatic, show-like atmosphere, more like that of a theme park than a sporting event, as fans went to an Astrodome restaurant, headed to seats, or requested assistance or information during events. The stylish outfits brought a futuristic aura that Hofheinz deemed important for setting the right tone as this groundbreaking edifice was unveiled. Validating the wisdom of his decision, *Houston Chronicle* fashion editor Beverly Maurice excitedly asserted that "every one of those new uniforms is out of this world!"[8]

The groundskeepers were outfitted with space suits and the food service staff wore clothing that fit the theme of the restaurant to which they were assigned. Instead of plainly dressed ushers, young, attractive female ushers wore outfits with short skirts that brazenly served to heighten their sex appeal. Specialized uniforms were even designed for the cashiers. ESPN writer Paul Lukas observed in 2010, more than a decade after the team left the Astrodome, that under Hofheinz's watch the Astros "were arguably the most uniform-obsessed organization in sports history."[9]

The uniforms were such a success that Evelyn Norton Anderson provided fashion guidance for other sports organizations, too, including several NFL teams. Although Houston did not feature cheerleaders with specially tailored costumes, as unfolded in Dallas during the 1970s, Hofheinz's focus on uniforms as part of the overall Astrodome experience prompted other team owners to consider strategies that framed sporting events as part of a broader entertainment experience. Prior to the Astrodome, team owners and leagues were content to market their on-field product and offer little else. After the Astrodome, a more global marketing strategy that addressed the broader entertainment landscape began to unfold.

Although some may believe that modern retro stadiums marked a move away from the Astrodome's innovative, high-tech, and modern trajectory, more careful analysis would suggest that the Astrodome's influences could be seen there, too. As an example, within Baltimore's Camden Yards, the first retro ballpark, is the luxurious Camden Club, an upscale facility where season ticket holders and guests can munch on gourmet crab cakes and other high-end fare while seated in an area that overlooks the field. The club affords well-heeled fans an ideal view of a giant, high-definition monitor in the outfield, while numerous screens inside the club allow patrons to experience on-field action without even having to look in the direction of the playing field. Even ancient Wrigley Field and Fenway Park, both over one hundred years old, feature large-screen entertainment and sophisticated audio equipment that brings digital clarity to an old-style experience.

The technology that Hofheinz integrated into the Astrodome, although now obsolete, created a new standard that shaped modern football stadiums and retro ballparks alike. Before other stadiums had monitors installed throughout the ballpark, the Astrodome put television screens in skyboxes, then installed them in and around concession areas. Some patrons and team officials probably thought this touch was bizarre and unnecessary, but today it has become the standard in venues new or old.

What has changed, however, are the ground rules and decision making that drive the fan experience as it relates to new stadium construction. When Hofheinz envisioned the Astrodome, he saw it as a modern public square, a place where people of all income levels could come together to share a relatively common experience, not unlike the festive environment he created at the dance parties that he organized as a young teen. The admission charge may have introduced a crass commercial dimension to what Hofheinz envisioned as a larger-than-life, entertainment-based public square.

The town square of previous generations had been undermined by America's transition to an automotive culture and structural changes to inner cities in the 1960s. With more citizens residing in suburban homes, bringing an entire community together became increasingly problematic and interactions became more frequently tied to commerce. For many Americans, shopping malls became de facto public meeting spaces as inconvenient parking and fears about potential crime made inner city locations less attractive.

Sensing such change, Hofheinz initially considered putting his energies into shopping mall construction. The development of postwar malls was largely punctuated by a movement to urban outskirts and the suburbs. In that regard, when his proposed mall plan was scuttled by Frank Sharp's ability to entice anchor retailers to his Sharpstown Mall project, Hofheinz may have lost an opportunity, but he was better positioned to focus on the type of project that might unify a population that was either moving outward to the suburbs or balkanizing along class lines within the urban core.

When he chose to invest his time and energy in the Astrodome and Astroworld, the sizeable entertainment complex that surrounded the legendary sporting venue, he supervised construction that served to unify metropolitan Houston with a highly unique complex of entertainment options. The Astrodome catered to a wide swath of the general public despite its overtly commercial underpinnings.

The public record of Houstonians describing a highly diverse array of Astrodome moments, emanating from people of all income levels, not just the elite and wealthy, was one reason, among many, that Houston's citizens were so reluctant to tear down the old facility when many other communities had unemotionally dismantled their aging ballparks, quickly replacing them after perhaps a brief nostalgic pause. In community after community, an earlier generation of sports facilities were dismantled, with land converted to less glamorous alternative purposes, typically without dramatic fanfare or emotional tension.

Although some patrons admittedly basked in greater luxury than others after the Astrodome was unveiled, for Hofheinz that strategy of tiered extravagance was a way to raise construction and operational revenues in a manner that would minimize the cost for Harris County taxpayers and visiting sports fans. In short, his goals were predicated on making a luxurious sporting experience viable for as many income levels as was possible, not just the most affluent, even if the luxury afforded to the most affluent patrons was much more over-the-top and lavish than anything that others had tried before.

The Astrodome was a venue that middle-class patrons could visit regularly, while still being sufficiently reasonable in cost for lower-class patrons to visit less frequently. When the Astrodome opened in 1965, Astros tickets were available for $1, the equivalent of about $7.50 today. A more coveted ground-level seat sold for $7.50, a sum that would be approximately $55 in 2015. By comparison, when the new Yankee Stadium opened in 2009, a single ground-level seat behind home plate was sold for a whopping $2,500; lower-tier seats cost less but were still well beyond the capacity of many typical sports fans. Even if more affordable seats could be had in places far away from prime locations, lower-income fans were not afforded the sort of regal experience that Hofheinz tried to deliver to all patrons.

Low-income fans have been squeezed out of a luxurious stadium experience in other ways, too—and perhaps as a negative consequence of more recent efforts to provide increasingly opulent stadium-based luxuries that were initially introduced in Houston. As an example, several new ballparks have placed simple bench-type seating in lower-priced locations far removed from the field of play, a throwback to prewar ballpark planning.

In addition, to raise substantial new revenues, many teams have introduced personal seat licenses (PSLS), fees that fans are required to pay simply to be eligible to buy season tickets. These fees range from $500 to in excess of $20,000 per seat. Team owners have often allocated funds collected from PSLS to the amount they claimed to pay when constructing a new stadium, taking full credit for those funds as part of their contribution to the total cost of stadium construction. Typically taxpayers pick up what remains, often subsidizing land acquisition costs and surrounding infrastructure expenses while funding hundreds of millions of dollars of stadium-related construction costs.

Scholarship suggests that the taxpayer role in stadium construction has been understated, and a more recent trend to build a different venue for each sports team has intensified the level of taxpayer subsidy. In a 2005 study of ninety-nine stadium and arena projects, urban scholar Judith Grant Long isolated the Hubert H. Humphrey Metrodome in Minneapolis as the most taxpayer friendly of all facilities used by major professional sports teams analyzed, while asserting that stadium projects tend to vastly underestimate their costs to the public. Tangible data suggests that underreporting is in the 40 percent range.[10]

Although the Astrodome was no longer in service when Long's study was released, its findings validated the public policy benefits that Hofheinz hoped to provide with a heavily used multi-purpose venue. The Metrodome, a fully enclosed domed facility like the Astrodome, employed a multiuse model similar to the strategy that Hofheinz implemented. Its use by a professional football team, a Major League Baseball team, and a major college football team, in addition to the scheduling of various other events, allowed the taxpayers of Minnesota to have a venue that required less taxpayer subsidy even if the facility itself had clear shortcomings.

Paradoxically, this Minneapolis venue is no longer in service; as with the Astrodome, it has fallen victim to the quirky dynamics of modern stadium subsidy trends. A new generation of team owners understand that their sports teams are coveted community assets, sometimes using veiled threats to relocate. As a result, many owners have been able to extract much higher levels of taxpayer support for their newer sports palaces. Over the decades the burden of stadium financing has gradually shifted from team owners and those who might profit handsomely from stadium-related entertainment to the general public, be they taxpayers or ticket holders. In addition, single-use stadiums that might host other events intermittently but are more tightly controlled by a single team for the benefit of that team's owner have emerged as the model that guides today's professional sports landscape.

These venues are less taxpayer and fan friendly, in part because they are built to maximize profits for a single team owner. The goal of return on taxpayer investment is more often an afterthought. One might criticize Hofheinz because public dollars that could not be fully repaid were used to construct the Astrodome. However, this was a trend that unfolded and took root in the 1950s, before Hofheinz began working on the Astrodome project. Team owner funding of sports venues was the standard before World War II. Nevertheless, unlike many present-day team owners, Hofheinz worked tirelessly to minimize the amount of public dollars required for construction, turning to taxpayer subsidies only when it became clear that the Astrodome project could not be completed as envisioned without some form of taxpayer support.

Though the PSL concept had not yet gained traction when the Astrodome was built, Hofheinz creatively employed other means to minimize taxpayer subsidies. As an example, Hofheinz began to offer guided tours at a cost of one dollar, a strategy that was immensely popular and innovative and helped to bring in more than four hundred thousand new visitors in the first year. Although some were initially critical of such tours, arguing that charging patrons to see what taxpayers helped to build was not appropriate, tours are now a common feature of the modern stadium experience.

Such tours have evolved into more profitable ventures than even Hofheinz might have envisioned. As an example, the New York Yankees charge $25 for a "classic tour," one that is forty-five minutes to an hour in duration, with a "gold" tour available on game days for $35. Not to be outdone, Jerry Jones and the Dallas Cowboys charge $27.50 for a forty-five-minute "VIP" tour and $17.50 for a self-guided tour, with the option of birthday party tour packages that range from $600 to $1,000 for a party of twenty.

Unlike present-day owners, Hofheinz creatively used skybox rentals to offset the high cost of building and maintaining a state-of-the-art facility. Doing so allowed him to charge less affluent sports fans more modest amounts. What has unfolded since the Astrodome's construction runs counter to the spirit of what Hofheinz tried to achieve.

The White Hutchinson Leisure and Learning Group, culling U.S. Bureau of Labor sources for 2011, reveals that "the [highest-income] 20% of . . . households now spend more on location-based entertainment and admissions to sporting events than . . . the other 80% of . . . households combined." Attendance at live events, sporting or otherwise, is far from inclusive. A large segment of the population does not attend such entertainment, whether by choice or as a result of economic factors. Those in the lowest rungs of income are particularly vulnerable, according to the report, which revealed that over a sixteen-year period "lower-income households generally showed the greatest percentage declines in venue-based spending." To counter the increased cost of venue-based live entertainment, middle- and lower-class Americans have increasingly invested in electronic entertainment, more often choosing to watch such events at home.[11] In short, the luxury experience at a premium venue that Hofheinz worked so diligently to bring to a broad swath of Houston's population is presently primarily enjoyed by an upper-income elite, with the lower classes marginally represented.

Hofheinz succeeded in part because a diverse constituency of people who benefited from what he built. The minority community, although skeptical of many political leaders, was supportive of the Astrodome's initial construction because they trusted Hofheinz to protect their interests. Hofheinz's long history as someone who was supportive of civil rights aided him in that regard. As mayor, he quietly and without fanfare phased out segregated water fountains and restroom facilities for minorities, and when challenged on integration issues, he did not hesitate to publicly support minority rights. For example, when a prominent white woman indicated that she would not let her children sit near black children at the Houston Public Library because she did not know "what they'd catch," Hofheinz, without a moment of hesitation, suggested, "maybe tolerance."[12]

In the Astrodome he similarly employed what he called the "green policy," in essence indicating that minority citizens would have all of the same rights and privileges as those with more power, including access to exclusive areas, as long as those individuals paid the same amount for a desired amenity. Although this policy has been embedded into the fabric of twenty-first-century America, at the time it was a departure from what leaders in some American cities had done. The civil rights movement had created an uneasy tension in southern cities, including Houston, but Hofheinz did not allow entertainment to become a site of cultural conflict, with race and class presenting as barriers to inclusion. Again, Hofheinz's vision proved to be a model that was acceptable and sustainable for the long term, even if some leaders struggled to accept that reality.

The Astrodome's construction also reflected a broader shift in American culture, one that saw a Sun Belt state taking the lead in innovation. It was a harbinger of the shift of many other forms of influence from the traditional northeastern power centers to a rising population base in the south and the west. As the Astrodome was unveiled, it served as a sign that fast-growing southern cities such as Houston no longer had to look to eastern cities such as New York for leadership in fashion, style, and architecture.

Nevertheless, Hofheinz and his colleagues were very much cognizant of the sociocultural sway of the northeastern power brokers. It is likely why they brought New York–based Praeger, Kavanagh, and Waterbury on board as engineering consultants and perhaps why the New York Yankees were invited to play the first exhibition game in the Dome. But Hofheinz's willingness to innovate with dramatic flair made Houston a clear leader in the area of sports-related architecture. Hofheinz's biographer, Edgar Ray, asserts that the Astrodome boasted "more 'world's firsts' than any other sports and entertainment structure ever built."[13]

The ambitious design achieved Hofheinz's goal of putting Houston on the map, while influencing stadium design in numerous and profound ways. David McCombs, an expert on Texas leisure, asserts that "the Astrodome was a stunning structure [that] brought world attention to Houston as a place of high technology and daring." McCombs further argues that "it was the first stadium since the Colosseum to draw people just to see the architecture."[14]

When the Astrodome opened, it was the most futuristic sports structure in the world. Over time, the unique luster that the Astrodome achieved diminished. Yet, as other cutting-edge indoor entertainment facilities were built, periodic upgrades allowed the modern features of the Astrodome to keep it in the conversation.

It is likely that no human being alive today knows more about the Astrodome's overall design and engineering than Narendra K. Gosain, a retired structural engineer now serving as a senior consultant for Walter P. Moore and Associates. Gosain was welcomed to Walter P. Moore in 1972 by Kenneth Zimmerman after the Astrodome was fully completed, yet Zimmerman and Gosain collaborated on Astrodome-related work often, and as Zimmerman readied for retirement in the early 1980s, he passed the torch to Gosain.

When Bud Adams insisted that design changes were necessary to make the Astrodome more profitable for the Houston Oilers, Gosain led the engineering team that added seating, expanded concourse space, made entry and exit more efficient and accessible, while phasing out Hofheinz's giant scoreboard. It was a bittersweet project for Gosain, but while executing it, he learned much about the structural nuances of this unique sports landmark.

Although now retired, Gosain returns to his engineering offices in downtown Houston as an engineering consultant, and when the Astrodome is involved, one can sense sincere enthusiasm in his voice. Nevertheless, the enthusiasm is tinged with a stoic recognition that the future of this grand edifice is precarious.

Gosain often leafs through what he calls the "layer cake," a giant, canvas book of complex and intricate, floor-by-floor architectural drawings that chronicles every possible design element of this amazing structure. He can identify things that no other human would notice in these plans and is rightfully proud of the work undertaken by Walter P. Moore and Associates, the company to which he has dedicated a lifetime of professional expertise.

On site at the Astrodome, Gosain enthusiastically points to features that he helped design to improve access for visitors with disabilities, while identifying unique design elements inside the building that will ensure that the structure remains useful and sound for many generations to come, but only if demolition is somehow avoided. He is a tall, elegant man who takes immense pride in the achievement that was the Astrodome, but he is realistic about the Dome's future. As he showed us the facility, it was clear that he would be immensely saddened if the Astrodome faced the wrecking ball. Gosain holds out hope that some plan to save the Astrodome might emerge, but the rejected referendum means that the Astrodome, despite its historic significance, is on extremely shaky terrain.

The Astrodome changed the way Houstonians perceived their city, but its impact was considerably more profound than that. The Astrodome exposed team owners and league officials to a new model for sports spectatorship, particularly as it relates to the most affluent patrons. To attract their dollars, Hofheinz designed uniquely appointed skyboxes and a private, club-based, upscale restaurant experience. Two private restaurants allowed the wealthiest patrons to dine in exclusivity, comfortably segregated from other fans. The introduction of luxury skyboxes allowed the affluent a fully segregated experience, one that is built into every modern stadium and arena in professional sports today.

When Hofheinz planned out his luxury skyboxes, stadium construction experts did not consider the upper levels of the stadium to be valuable and coveted real estate. In fact, they did not envision this as a space that would attract a high-end clientele. Instead, engineers, general contractors, and architects looked at these areas as places to insert electrical wiring, pipes, ductwork, and other utilitarian items. As plans for the facility were underway, architect Hermon Lloyd admitted that installing luxury skyboxes was "an afterthought as far as we were concerned [but] when Roy saw that space he felt he could sell private boxes for what back then were fabulous amounts. We didn't see how he could do it, but we put in the boxes. Ever since then, there hasn't been a big stadium built without boxes."[15]

As significant a change as that was, Hofheinz altered the dynamic for average spectators, too. Instead of settling for barely warm, foil-wrapped hot dogs, beer, and soft drinks, spectators could dine in three on-site restaurants that were open and available to the general public, while having full access to theater-style cushioned seats.

Within a nation that values modernity, particularly in a city that has elevated it to a supreme ideal, the likelihood that the Astrodome will survive the wrecking ball is not high. Architectural scholar Steven Strom compellingly asserts that "Houston's unfaltering adherence to modernity went hand in hand with a boundless faith in the future, along with the certainty that modernity cloaked its city with an aura of progressivism. The consequence of that crusade for modernity has been the destruction of the city's past, both distant and more recent."[16] In such a culture, preservation becomes increasingly difficult.

As with the Astrodome, highly ornate railroad stations were once the focal point for major metropolitan areas, not to mention an intense source of civic pride. Railroad historians Ed Breslin and Hugh Van Dusen describe these community assets as places that "personified and reflected America's secular spirituality fueled by the belief that life could endlessly be enhanced by aesthetic beauty, industrial might, technological know-how, and creature comforts."[17] However, in city after city, these once coveted transportation landmarks have been dismantled and replaced with less impressive and more utilitarian facilities that have become inconspicuous—or worse yet, eyesores.

Sports stadiums have a somewhat different trajectory than railroad stations. Instead of regressing to lower cost, utilitarian designs, these facilities have become increasingly luxurious. Stadium construction has become decidedly modern and much more intensely focused on adding unique and ornate touches that set new standards for entertainment. In Jacksonville, Florida, and Phoenix, Arizona, to name but two examples, football and baseball facilities include swimming pools, so that patrons can watch sporting events while swimming, in addition to dining and pursuing other forms of relaxation. Facilities throughout the nation have woven in other over-the-top luxuries that reflect the inspiration Hofheinz initially provided.

New ballparks, whether infused with old-time charm or predicated on unabashed modernity, have pushed beyond the boundaries of Hofheinz's vision. Nevertheless, his pioneering ideas served to pave the way for the unique designs that we see today and a level of conspicuous consumption no one could have envisioned a mere generation ago.

Although some made fun of the Astrodome's over-the-top opulence, its success as a venue set the stage for sports-related construction that was to follow in other cities. Television news icon David Brinkley moved to Houston upon retirement from ABC News, and when pondering the Astrodome's legacy, he stated, "I've heard the jokes, but I like the idea of a town that is not afraid to be comfortable, that is not afraid to spend its money, that is not afraid of excessive luxury, and that has learned how to enjoy it."[18] The standard of luxury established by the Astrodome set the bar higher for all other sports organizations. Even Boston's century-old Fenway Park, controlled by the tradition-laden Red Sox, has undergone a major facelift and now features luxurious appointments, including an exclusive club facility for high-end season ticket holders and luxury-oriented, terrace-style seating above its massive outfield wall.

For better or worse, the opulence of modern sports stadiums was pioneered by Hofheinz. His incredible energy, talent, and creativity allowed Houston to limit the degree of taxpayer support necessary to achieve an extraordinary level of luxury at a time when other sports facilities were relatively pedestrian in nature. Since then, a new opulence may be responsible for pricing some fans out of a luxurious game-day experience, but from all evidence currently available, such an outcome was not one that Hofheinz ever intended. Instead, his focus on opulence was not far removed philosophically from the high-energy events that he had organized many decades earlier as a teen growing up during the Great Depression. His objective in the late 1950s and early 1960s was to construct an impressive and unique venue, one that would entertain all Houstonians with style and flair, while impressing a much more global audience with a luxurious facility that showcased the city's "can-do" spirit.

When Hofheinz took on the Astrodome project, he was regarded as a serious candidate for Texas governor, although he never sought the position. He had numerous sufficiently powerful friends who could have helped him achieve such a goal. However, Hofheinz was propelled to pursue a path that focused on entertainment, perhaps the result of a Depression-era upbringing that made special moments such as his brief visit to the circus as a young man such a memorable time in his life.

After spearheading the Astrodome and Astroworld, a colossal entertainment venue, he bought a majority interest in the Ringling Bros. Circus, the company that had entertained him so successfully as a youngster. He later invested heavily in Mattel, a major toy manufacturer. After suffering a stroke, Hofheinz saw his investment portfolio derailed by a combination of recessionary times, a high-inflation economy, and managerial missteps at Mattel. Hofheinz was forced to liquidate his Astrodome holdings and all else that he had worked so hard to build. Although he changed the nature of sports spectatorship with a dramatic flair and had accomplished remarkable civic and professional feats throughout his life, he fell victim to the same unforgiving market forces that buffeted many Americans with lesser skills and abilities.

Hofheinz's investment in leisure was not a complete miscalculation. The U.S. Bureau of Labor Statistics indicates that leisure spending in American households rose from $211 in 1950 to $269 in 1960, but by the 1972–73 fiscal year the amount rose to $455 and by 1986 was a whopping $1,172.[19] Hofheinz could see this trend unfolding, even if he ultimately miscalculated in terms of the companies that were best positioned to benefit from such trends, perhaps letting the passions of early youth cloud his judgment. Hofheinz was right, however, in determining that people were ready to be entertained in vast, enclosed stadiums that offered a broad range of amenities and luxuries.

Civic leaders may dismantle the Astrodome and perhaps repurpose the land on which it was built, but the Dome will always be remembered as a unique structure that changed the trajectory of sports and entertainment architecture in a nation that prides itself on its leadership in both sports and entertainment. In looking at the sports landscape with a more global perspective, British historian James Walvin remarks that when it came to sports, Americans "invariably made it bigger, more spectacular, and often as not, more lucrative."[20] The Astrodome's construction and what has followed in sports-related architecture provide powerful and compelling evidence that Walvin's assertion is on target.

American cities are quick to dispose of massive sports landmarks as they age, but Europeans have chosen to retain and preserve the ancient entertainment venues of Greek and Roman antiquity. It is a difference that speaks volumes about the cultural priorities of the old world and the new. That millions of citizens continue to visit and are awed by these ancient European landmarks is impressive, but the remarkable, can-do mindset that inspires innovative American construction is commendable in its own right. Yet the acclaimed Houston sportswriter Mickey Herskowitz astutely reminds us that the fate of the Astrodome as the Eighth Wonder of the World was never certain, that even the great landmarks of antiquity were vanquished by the vicissitudes of time. "Of the original Seven Wonders of the World," he writes, "only the Pyramids still exist. The statue of Zeus, erected in 432 BC, was melted down for religious medals. The Temple of Diana was destroyed by the Goths in 262 AD. The Colossus of Rhodes was shattered by an earthquake in 224 BC."[21]

Whether as an artifact in the pages of the history books or as a repurposed civic project, the Astrodome will always occupy a special place in the evolution of Houston as a truly international city. When an energetic and enthusiastic Roy Hofheinz decided that a massive, air-conditioned entertainment complex could revolutionize how Houstonians experienced baseball, football, music, rodeos, and a variety of other entertainment endeavors, the world of sports-related architecture was changed forever. The legacy of Hofheinz and the many people who worked tirelessly to build the Astrodome is secure regardless of whether the grand facility remains standing or, having been dismantled, is rightly celebrated for its many and lasting innovations in engineering and entertainment, and the history to which it played host.

Acknowledgments

This book would not have been possible without the support and encouragement of a wide range of friends and colleagues. Our research efforts in Texas benefited from the energy and expertise of a host of different people, including Chief Mark Bricker of the Clute Police Department, Chris Day, Logan Goodson, Dene Hofheinz Mann, Richard Moore, and Paul Orseck. Special thanks are also due to the Houston Astros' Mike Acosta, Mick Dell'Orco, and Larry Dierker. Our project was further improved by the firsthand knowledge of Mickey Herskowitz. His frequent contact with many of the key individuals involved with the Astrodome's birth and subsequent history helped us to enhance our analysis in ways that otherwise would not have been possible.

We are grateful for the insights shared by Lynn Edmundson, who serves as executive director for Historic Houston, and James Glassman from *Houstonian* magazine. We are especially thankful for direction provided by the *Houston Chronicle*'s highly capable reporters Craig Hlavaty and Ken Hoffman. Greg Yerke, who serves in the Special Collections Department of the University of Houston Libraries, provided generous guidance, as did Walter P. Moore and Associates' Narendra Gosain, Rick Craft, and Molly Harris. Dr. Gosain deserves a special shout-out for providing us with a wealth of insider information about the Astrodome's engineering innovations, as well as for a guided tour of the Dome itself in July 2013.

Our work would simply not have been possible without the support of our friends and colleagues at Penn State Altoona, including Lori Bechtel-Wherry, Brian Black, Kira Condee-Padunova, Todd Davis, Michele Kennedy, Drew McGhee, Nick Mohammed, Kevin Moist, Peter Moran, Mary Lou Nemanic, Kay Tate, and Nancy

Vogel. We are also indebted to Monmouth University's Lynne Clay, Nancy Mezey, Laura Moriarty, Judy Ramos, and Michael Thomas. Similarly, we are thankful for the scholars who unfailingly shared their time and expertise, including Jason Bruce Chrystal, Neil deMause, Craig and Katherine Doherty, Marie Hardin, Benjamin Lisle, Mark Ludak, Edgar Ray, Robert Reed, Scott Reinardy, Steven Riess, Fred Schiff, Campbell Titchener, and Gregory Wolf. We are grateful to our many colleagues in the Association for Education in Journalism and Mass Communication, the North American Society for Sport History, and the Society for American Baseball Research. This book benefited at every turn from our access to the resources housed in the Houston Public Library, the Pennsylvania State University Libraries, the University of Houston Library, and the University of Texas at Austin's Perry-Castañeda Library. We are especially thankful for the enthusiasm and advice of the librarians and curators who work in the special collections of these world-class facilities.

We are appreciative of the many efforts—not to mention the incredible patience—exhibited on our behalf by the good folks at the University of Nebraska Press, including Senior Editor Robert Taylor and Associate Acquisitions Editor Courtney Ochsner. We are also thankful for Sabrina Stellrecht, Joy Margheim, and many others in Lincoln whose behind-the-scenes work helped to improve the quality of our project. Finally, our work has been supported in innumerable ways by such well-meaning friends and family members as Denis Corrigan, Melanie Hancock, Mark Lockenmeyer, Tatyana Moraczewski, Patrick Murphy, Jim Nantz, Neil Rudel, Joe Studlick, Andy Womack, and Fred Womack, who generously shared his memories of the Dome's heady early days in the 1960s. The great gifts of love and encouragement provided by the Harshbarger, Lumadue, Trumpbour, Womack, and Zary families—particularly from our wives, Jill Trumpbour and Jeanine Womack—make everything possible.

Notes

Prologue

1. Edgar Ray, *The Grand Huckster: Houston's Judge Roy Hofheinz, Genius of the Astrodome* (Memphis TN: Memphis State University Press, 1980), 257.

2. Robert C. Trumpbour, "The Brooklyn Dodgers, the Move to Los Angeles, and the Search for Villains: Was Walter O'Malley a Bum, a Victim, or Something Else?," in *Mysteries from Baseball's Past: Investigation of Nine Unsettled Questions*, ed. Angelo Louisa and David Cicotello (Jefferson NC: McFarland, 2010), 149–83.

3. Robert Lipsyte, "Astrodome Opulent, Even for Texas," *New York Times*, April 8, 1965, 50.

4. "Colt .45's Start Park with a Bang," *New York Times*, January 4, 1962, 52.

5. Leonard Koppett, "Big League Baseball Opens on Nine Fronts Tomorrow," *New York Times*, April 11, 1965, S1.

6. Arthur Daley, "Ball Park, Texas Style," *New York Times*, April 9, 1965, 24.

7. Robert Lipsyte, "Johnson Attends Opening of Houston's Astrodome," *New York Times*, April 10, 1965, 1.

8. Robert Lipsyte, "Houston Is Hardly Wild About Its Astrodome," *New York Times*, April 11, 1965, S3.

9. Philip Lowrey, *Green Cathedrals: The Ultimate Celebration of All 271 Major League and Negro League Ballparks Past and Present* (Reading MA: Addison Wesley, 1992), 47.

10. Larry Dierker, "Dome Deserved Better Than Sharing," *Houston Chronicle*, February 2, 2014, B1.

11. Houston Sports Association, "World's Largest Air Conditioner Gives Astrodome Perfect Weather," in *Inside the Astrodome: The Eighth Wonder of the World* (Houston: Houston Sports Association, 1965), 49–55.

12. Ray, *Grand Huckster*, 341.

13. "1960–1969 Attendance," Ballparks of Baseball: The Fields of Major League Baseball, http://www.ballparksofbaseball.com/1960–69attendance.htm. The attendance figures offered at this site are more precise than the estimates offered in Ray, *Grand Huckster*, 341.

1. Ray, *Grand Huckster*, 8.

2. Ray, *Grand Huckster*, 11.

3. U.S. Census Bureau, *Census of Population: 1960*, vol. 1, part 45 (Washington DC: U.S. Government Printing Office, 1962), 55.

4. Ray, *Grand Huckster*, 18.

5. Ray, *Grand Huckster*, 28.

6. Ray, *Grand Huckster*, 40.

7. Ray, *Grand Huckster*, 42.

8. Ray, *Grand Huckster*, 111.

9. Ray, *Grand Huckster*, 133.

10. Ray, *Grand Huckster*, 128.

11. Jenny Meeden Bailey, "Matrimony and the Mayors: Three First Ladies of Houston," *Houston History Monthly* 5.1 (Fall 2007): 32.

12. Robert Caro, *The Years of Lyndon Johnson: Means of Ascent* (New York: Alfred A. Knopf, 1990), 192.

13. Ray, *Grand Huckster*, 231.

14. Ray, *Grand Huckster*, 236.

15. Ray, *Grand Huckster*, 241.

16. Alden Hatch, *Buckminster Fuller: At Home in the Universe* (New York: Crown, 1974), 3.

17. "Rome Visit Gave Idea for Stadium," *Houston Tribune*, April 8, 1965, section II, 11.

18. Jason Bruce Chrystal, "The Taj Mahal of Sport: The Creation of the Houston Astrodome" (PhD diss., Iowa State University, 2004), 20–27.

19. Clark Nealon, Robert Nottebart, Stanley Siegel, and James Tinsley, "The Campaign for Major League Baseball in Houston," *Houston Review* 7.1 (1985): 27.

20. Trumpbour, "Brooklyn Dodgers."

21. Houston Sports Association, "The Man and the Idea," in *Astrodome: Eighth Wonder of the World* (Houston: Houston Sports Association, 1966), 5.

22. Roger Kahn, *A Season in the Sun* (New York: Diversion Books, 2012), 53.

23. Ray, *Grand Huckster*, 261.

24. Bob Rule, "Tax Bonds Will Save on Interest," *Houston Press*, January 10, 1961, 1.

25. Dick Peebles, "Ballots, Baskets, and Challenges," *Houston Chronicle*, January 16, 1961, section 5, 1–2.

26. Bob Rule, "Sidelights," *Houston Press*, January 16, 1961, 16.

27. George W. Eddy, Sound-Off, *Houston Post*, January 21, 1961, section 2, 3.

28. Phillip M. Blair, Sound-Off, *Houston Post*, January 21, 1961, section 2, 3.

29. Kenneth E. Zimmerman and Narendra K. Gosain, "Astrodome: An Engineering Marvel of the 1960s" (paper presented in the Texas Section of the annual meeting of the American Society of Civil Engineers, Houston, September 29–October 2, 2004), 2.

30. Ray, *Grand Huckster*, 270.

31. "Suit Filed Challenging Legality of Sports Bonds for Stadium," *Houston Chronicle*, February 6, 1961, 1.

32. "Stadium Bond Contest Dropped," *Houston Chronicle*, April 7, 1961, 1.

33. Marshall Verniaud, "Hopes for Stadium by 1962 Dim," *Houston Post*, April 29, 1961, 1.

34. Ray, *Grand Huckster*, 271–72.

35. Frank Finch, "Gaily Decorated Colt Stadium Puts Most Ballparks to Shame," *Los Angeles Times*, May 8, 1962, B2.

36. Ray, *Grand Huckster*, 283.

37. Ray, *Grand Huckster*, 305.

38. Ray, *Grand Huckster*, 274.

39. "Stadium Fund Not Enough Says Architect," *Houston Chronicle*, May 25, 1962, 1.

40. "County Rejects Quonset Stadium," *Houston Chronicle*, June 4, 1962, 1.

41. "County, HSA Sign Stadium Agreement," *Houston Chronicle*, November 15, 1962, 1.

42. "Oilers Owner, HSA Feud over Stadium," *Houston Chronicle*, August 22, 1962, 1.

43. Ray, *Grand Huckster*, 287.

44. "Stadium Low Bid $19.4 Million," *Houston Chronicle*, November 29, 1962, 1.

45. Ernest Bailey, "Stadium Bond Foes Charge Subsidy—Predict Higher Taxes," *Houston Press*, December 14, 1962, 1.

46. Ernest Bailey, "Stadium Can't Hike Taxes, Officials Say," *Houston Press*, December 21, 1962, 1.

47. Chrystal, "Taj Mahal of Sport," 200–212.

48. "Ours? Tops, Bar None," *Houston Chronicle*, December 18, 1962, section 4, 6.

49. "National League Eying Stadium Vote Says Giles," *Houston Chronicle*, December 21, 1962, section 6, 2.

50. Chrystal, "Taj Mahal of Sport," 218–21.

51. Ray, *Grand Huckster*, 289.

52. Ray, *Grand Huckster*, 304–5.

53. Ray, *Grand Huckster*, 305.

54. Chrystal, "Taj Mahal of Sport," 248–51.

55. "Smith and Hofheinz Oppose Civic Center," *Houston Chronicle*, June 23, 1964, 9.

56. "Hofheinz Says He'll Take Loss Gracefully," *Houston Chronicle*, June 28, 1964, 18.

57. Chrystal, "Taj Mahal of Sport," 262–63.

58. Dick Peebles, "LBJ: Everybody Will Visit Dome," *Houston Chronicle*, April 10, 1965, section 1, 1.

59. Sandra Bybee, "Opening Night: A Society Tableau," *Houston Post*, April 10, 1965, section 1, 12.

60. Dierker, "Dome Deserved Better," B1.

61. Andy O'Brien, "The Stadium That Could Revolutionize Sport," *Montreal Star*, May 15, 1965, weekend magazine, 32.

62. Howard Taubman, "Show Biz: The Big Dome," *New York Times*, June 6, 1965, section 5, 3.

63. Roy Terrell, "Fast Man with a .45," *Sports Illustrated*, March 26, 1962, 32.

64. Roone Arledge, *Roone: A Memoir* (New York: Harper Collins, 2003), 31.

65. *Newsweek*, April 26, 1965, 66.

66. Joe Jares, "The Big Screen Is Watching," *Sports Illustrated*, May 31, 1965, 30.

67. Houston Sports Association, *Inside the Astrodome*, 1, 3.

2. Of Cows and Construction

1. Ray, *Grand Huckster*, 265.

2. Joe R. Feagin, "The Global Context of Metropolitan Growth: Houston and the Oil Industry," *American Journal of Sociology* 90.6 (May 1985): 1214.

3. John O. King, *Joseph Stephen Cullinan: A Study of Leadership in the Texas Petroleum Industry, 1897–1937* (Nashville TN: Vanderbilt University Press, 1970), 213.

4. Chrystal, "Taj Mahal of Sport," 37.

5. Kendra Santos, "Where Big Is Better: The Houston Livestock Show and Rodeo Is a Texas-Sized Treat," *American Cowboy*, January/February 1997, 62–63.

6. Kate Morris, "Rodeo Closes with Mark for Boots on the Ground," *Houston Chronicle*, March 24, 2014, section 1, 1.

7. Sarah Rufka, "Houston Gives: Houston Heroes," *Houston Chronicle*, March 30, 2014, special section, 15.

8. Jayme Fraser, "Houston Livestock Show and Rodeo: A Day of Rain and Records," *Houston Chronicle*, March 17, 2014, B1.

9. Joy Sewing, "Houston Gives: Education: Rodeo Focuses on Scholarship and Education," *Houston Chronicle*, February 26, 2012, special section, 23.

10. Jim Saye, "The Houston Livestock Show and Rodeo: A Historical Perspective," *Houston History* 7.1 (Fall 2009): 4.

11. Lisa Teachey, "On the Trail Again: Salt Grass Riders' Publicity Stunt Saved Rodeo," *Houston Chronicle*, February 12, 1998, A29.

12. *Go Texan Monthly Newsletter* 5.2 (February 25, 2011): 1.

13. Saye, "Houston Livestock Show," 11.

14. Dick Peebles, "Commission to Seek Information on Feasibility of Stadium Here," *Houston Chronicle*, February 19, 1958, F1.

15. "Archer Romero and Company, California State Fair Exhibition," August 1958, and "Cow Palace, San Francisco," n.d., Astrodome Project, Planning, box 94-274-1, Robert Minchew Collection, University of Texas, Austin.

16. Dick Peebles, "Stadium Group Mulls over Unique Plans," *Houston Chronicle*, May 5, 1958, B2.

17. Report of the Harris County Board of Parks Commissioners to Harris County Commissioners Court, June 20, 1958, 25 pages, Astrodome Collection, 1958–68 files, folder 18, Houston Public Library.

18. "County Stadium Bond Issue Gets July Ballot Spot," *Houston Post*, June 24, 1958, section 4, 1.

19. Clark Nealon, "Post Time," *Houston Post*, July 25, 1958, section 4, 1.

20. Neil Addington, "Fat Stock Show Offers County Site for New Project," *Houston Post*, June 25, 1958, 1.

21. "Fine Leadership for Bond Drive," *Houston Post*, July 3, 1958, section 2, 4.

22. "Bond Issue Gets Boost from C of C," *Houston Post*, July 10, 1958, section 6, 2; "25 Ex-pros on Stadium Committee," *Houston Post*, July 14, 1958, section 4, 1.

23. Mickey Herskowitz, "Perini, Says Weisbrod, Rates Houston as 10 Club Possibility," *Houston Chronicle*, July 17, 1958, section 4, 1.

24. "North Side Fans Seek New Athletic Stadium," *Houston Chronicle*, July 31, 1958, section 6, 3.

25. Chrystal, "Taj Mahal of Sport," 49.

26. "Board Drops Plan for Stadium Site in Memorial Park," *Houston Chronicle*, November 12, 1958, A1.

27. "City Officials Pledge Neutral Stand on Stadium Policy," *Houston Chronicle*, November 13, 1958, B1.

28. Clark Nealon, "Marion Offers Rent Guarantee in New Stadium," *Sporting News*, February 25, 1959, 20.

29. Chrystal, "Taj Mahal of Sport," 66–73.

30. "Federal Aid Enters Debate on Coliseum," *Houston Post*, March 1, 1960, 1.

31. Tom Omstead, "Harris Officials to Back Park Board Stadium Site," *Houston Post*, February 24, 1960, 1.

32. Tom Omstead, "Stock Show's Decision May Swing Stadium," *Houston Post*, February 28, 1960, 1.

33. "North Side Petition Added to Coliseum Fight," *Houston Post*, March 3, 1960, 3.

34. Tom Omstead, "North Side Offers Free Arena Site," *Houston Post*, March 13, 1960, 1.

35. Chrystal, "Taj Mahal of Sport," 75; Berry Garvin, "2 New Angles on Stadium," *Houston Press*, March 25, 1960, 1.

36. "Stock Show Swings to South Main Site," *Houston Post*, June 10, 1960, 1.

37. Roy Graham, "Dallas and Fort Worth Architects Propose Air-Conditioned Arena with 'Supper Club,'" *Sporting News*, August 31, 1960, 13.

38. Clark Nealon, "Ultra-Modern Stadium Called 'Last Link' in Houston's Pitch for a Big-Time Club," *Sporting News*, August 31, 1960, 13.

39. Ray, *Grand Huckster*, 260.

40. Report of the Harris County Board of Parks Commissioners, 17.

41. Terrell, "Fast Man with a .45," 32.

3. Going Pro

1. Robert Reed, *Colt .45s: A Six-Gun Salute* (Houston: Lone Star Books, 1999), 12.

2. Adam Liptak, "The Supreme Court, Throwing Curveballs," *New York Times*, March 29, 2013, C21.

3. Campbell Titchener, *The George Kirksey Story: Bringing Major League Baseball to Houston* (Austin TX: Eakin Press, 1989), 52.

4. Benjamin Rader, *In Its Own Image: How Television Has Transformed Sports* (New York: Free Press, 1984), 16.

5. Titchener, *George Kirksey Story*, 37.

6. King, *Joseph Stephen Cullinan*.

7. Reed, *Colt .45s*, 19.

8. Reed, *Colt .45s*, 18.

9. John Wilson, "Kirksey, First Astro Backer, Sells His Stock," *Sporting News*, May 21, 1966, 13.

10. "Texas Group Wanted Busch to Buy Cards' Radio Rights," *Sporting News*, March 4, 1953, 10.

11. "Prexy Giles Spends 36 Hours in St. Louis Overseeing Cards' Sale," *Sporting News*, March 4, 1953, 10.

12. Reed, *Colt .45s*, 18.

13. Terrell, "Fast Man with a .45," 32.

14. Jack Gallagher, "$20,000,000 Bond Issue Vote on July 26 on Houston Stadium," *Sporting News*, July 2, 1958, 20.

15. *Toolson v. New York Yankees, Inc.*, 346 U.S. 356 (1953).

16. J. Gordon Hylton, "Why Baseball's Antitrust Exemption Still Survives," *Marquette Sports Law Review* 9.2 (1999), 391–402.

17. Jack Walsh, "Sports Bill Wins in House, but Faces Hurdle in Senate," *Sporting News*, July 2, 1958, 20.

18. "Frick, Trautman Praise Action on Sports Measure," *Sporting News*, July 2, 1958, 20.

19. Michael Lomax, "Stadiums, Boosters, Politicians, and Major League Baseball's Reluctance to Expand," in *The Rise of Stadiums in the Modern United States: Cathedrals of Sport*, ed. Mark Dyreson and Robert C. Trumpbour (New York: Routledge, 2010), 92–109.

20. Hal Lebovitz, "Cleveland Is Joyful; Tribe Directors Vote to Stay Indefinitely," *Sporting News*, October 22, 1958, 18.

21. For detailed insight on this issue, see Russell D. Buhite, *The Continental League: A Personal History* (Lincoln: University of Nebraska Press, 2014).

22. Buhite, *Continental League*, 71–72.

23. Rob Edelman, "*What's My Line?* and Baseball," *Baseball Research Journal* 43.2 (Fall 2014): 39.

24. Buhite, *Continental League*, 94.

25. Hylton, "Why Baseball's Antitrust Exemption Still Survives," 401.

26. Reed, *Colt .45s*, 31.

27. Reed, *Colt .45s*, 32.

28. Reed, *Colt .45s*, 32–33.

29. Reed, *Colt .45s*, 36–38.

30. Ray, *Grand Huckster*, 264.

31. Clark Nealon, "N.L. Group in Houston Buys Buffs," *Sporting News*, January 25, 1961, 9.

32. Titchener, *George Kirksey Story*, 97.

33. "Colts Add .45's to Name: We're Pistols, Not Horses," *Sporting News*, December 6, 1961, 33.

34. J. G. Taylor Spink, "Colts Shooting the Works in Apache Junction Plant," *Sporting News*, November 15, 1961, 2.

35. Clark Nealon, "Colts Will Lasso Gal Fans: Hire Woman Publicist," *Sporting News*, April 4, 1962, 13.

36. Reed, *Colt .45s*, 74.

37. See Jerry Izenberg, *The Greatest Game Ever Played: The Incredible Battle between the New York Mets and the Houston Astros for the '86 National League Pennant* (New York: Henry Holt, 1988).

38. Michael Gershman, *Diamonds: The Evolution of the Ballpark* (New York: Houghton Mifflin, 1993), 194.

39. Houston Sports Association, *Astrodome*, 1.

40. Benjamin Dylan Lisle, "'You've Got to Have Tangibles to Sell Intangibles': Ideologies of the Modern American Stadium, 1948–1982" (PhD diss., University of Texas, Austin, 2010), 199.

41. Reed, *Colt .45s*, 207.

42. Reed, *Colt .45s*, 203.

4. Zimmerman and the Grand Plan

1. Lynwood Abram, "Kenneth E. Zimmerman, Helped Create Astrodome: Worked on Many Notable Projects during Long Career," *Houston Chronicle*, December 24, 2008, B7.

2. See Vincent C. Jones, *Manhattan: The Army and the Atomic Bomb* (Washington DC: Center of Military History, 1985).

3. See Charles Johnson and Charles Jackson, *City behind a Fence: Oak Ridge, Tennessee, 1942–1946* (Knoxville: University of Tennessee Press, 1981); and Russell Olwell, *At Work in the Atomic City: A Labor and Social History of Oak Ridge, Tennessee* (Knoxville: University of Tennessee Press, 2004).

4. Abram, "Kenneth E. Zimmerman," B7.

5. Abram, "Kenneth E. Zimmerman," B7.

6. "Dragline Rips into S. Main Stadium Site," *Houston Chronicle*, February 2, 1961, section 1, 1, 2.

7. Chrystal, "Taj Mahal of Sport," 226.

8. Narendra K. Gosain, interview by the authors, July 22, 2013, at Walter P. Moore and Associates, Houston.

9. Zimmerman and Gosain, "Astrodome," 4.

10. Gosain interview, Moore and Associates.

11. Gosain interview, Moore and Associates.

12. Gosain interview, Moore and Associates.

13. Gosain interview, Moore and Associates.

14. Gosain interview, Moore and Associates.

15. Zimmerman and Gosain, "Astrodome," 4–5.

16. Gosain interview, Moore and Associates.

17. Zimmerman and Gosain, "Astrodome," 7.

18. Narendra K. Gosain, interview by the authors, July 22, 2013, at NRG Astrodome, Houston.

19. Zimmerman and Gosain, "Astrodome," 7.

20. Zimmerman and Gosain, "Astrodome," 8–9.

21. Gosain interview, Moore and Associates.

22. Chrystal, "Taj Mahal of Sport," 231–32.

23. Chrystal, "Taj Mahal of Sport," 233–35.

24. Chrystal, "Taj Mahal of Sport," 233–35.

25. Chrystal, "Taj Mahal of Sport," 236.

26. Chrystal, "Taj Mahal of Sport," 239–40.

27. Zimmerman and Gosain, "Astrodome," 6.

28. Chrystal, "Taj Mahal of Sport," 242.

29. Fred Womack, correspondence with authors, April 30, 2015.

30. Chrystal, "Taj Mahal of Sport," 243.

31. Zimmerman and Gosain, "Astrodome," 6.

32. Zimmerman and Gosain, "Astrodome," 6.

33. Gosain interview, Moore and Associates.

34. Zimmerman and Gosain, "Astrodome," 6–7.

35. Chrystal, "Taj Mahal of Sport," 243–44.

36. Chrystal, "Taj Mahal of Sport," 276.

37. Gosain interview, Moore and Associates.

38. Fred Womack, correspondence with authors, May 25, 2015.

39. Chrystal, "Taj Mahal of Sport," 304.

40. Chrystal, "Taj Mahal of Sport," 305–6.

41. Chrystal, "Taj Mahal of Sport," 306–7.

42. Zimmerman and Gosain, "Astrodome," 1, 3.

43. The Astrodome's 2014 construction cost was estimated by using Consumer Price Index data, as furnished by "The Inflation Calculator" at http://westegg.com.

44. Chrystal, "Taj Mahal of Sport," 335.

45. Terry Blount, "Oilers Have Never Been Happy Campers Indoors," *Houston Chronicle*, March 26, 1995, B29.

46. Dale Robertson, "City Sports Owners Try Something New," *Houston Chronicle*, October 6, 2000, B1.

47. Blount, "Oilers Have Never Been Happy," B29.

48. Ed Fowler, *Loser Takes All: Bud Adams, Bad Football, and Big Business* (Atlanta: Longstreet Press, 1997), 32.

49. Raymond J. Keating, "The NFL Oilers: A Case Study in Corporate Welfare," *Freeman* (Foundation for Economic Education), April 1, 1998, http://fee.org/freeman/detail/the-nfl-oilers-a-case-study-in-corporate-welfare.

50. Keating, "NFL Oilers."

51. Dierker, "Dome Deserved Better," B1.

52. Keating, "NFL Oilers."

53. Gosain interview, Moore and Associates.

54. Gosain interview, Moore and Associates.

55. Michael L. Graczyk, "Astrodome Scoreboard Headed for Scrap Heap," *Los Angeles Times*, September 4, 1988, http://articles.latimes.com/1988-09-04/sports/sp-2073_1_astrodome-scoreboard.

56. Gosain interview, Moore and Associates.

57. Gosain interview, Moore and Associates.

58. Gosain interview, Moore and Associates.

59. Gosain interview, Moore and Associates.

60. Gosain interview, Moore and Associates.

61. Abram, "Kenneth E. Zimmerman," B7.

5. The Grass Isn't Always Greener

1. John Pastier, "Shaggy Rug Story: The Greening of the Astrodome," *Cite: The Architecture and Design Review of Houston* (Rice Design Alliance) 24

(Spring 1990), 10, http://offcite.org/wp-content/uploads/sites/3/2010/03/Shaggy RugStory_Pastier_Cite24.pdf.

2. Chrystal, "Taj Mahal of Sport," 281–82.

3. Chrystal, "Taj Mahal of Sport," 282.

4. Barbara Moran, "Artificial Turf and How It Grew," *American Heritage of Invention and Technology* 20.4 (Spring 2005), 8–16, http://www.innovationgateway .org/content/artificial-turf-and-how-it-grew-0.

5. Chrystal, "Taj Mahal of Sport," 283.

6. Chrystal, "Taj Mahal of Sport," 283–84; Lowrey, *Green Cathedrals*, 46.

7. Chrystal, "Taj Mahal of Sport," 290.

8. Chrystal, "Taj Mahal of Sport," 300.

9. Chrystal, "Taj Mahal of Sport," 301.

10. Chrystal, "Taj Mahal of Sport," 302–3.

11. Moran, "Artificial Turf."

12. Murry R. Nelson, *American Sports: A History of Icons, Idols, and Ideas* (Santa Barbara CA: Greenwood, 2013), 73.

13. Phillip Jennings Turf Farms, "Tifway 419 Bermuda," 2009, http://www. sodfather.com/turf-grass/tifway-419-bermuda.asp.

14. Moran, "Artificial Turf."

15. Chrystal, "Taj Mahal of Sport," 317.

16. Chrystal, "Taj Mahal of Sport," 235–36.

17. Moran, "Artificial Turf."

18. Chrystal, "Taj Mahal of Sport," 318.

19. Moran, "Artificial Turf."

20. Moran, "Artificial Turf."

21. Moran, "Artificial Turf."

22. Chrystal, "Taj Mahal of Sport," 319.

23. Pastier, "Shaggy Rug Story," 10.

24. Moran, "Artificial Turf."

25. Chrystal, "Taj Mahal of Sport," 319–20.

26. Chrystal, "Taj Mahal of Sport," 320–21.

27. Chrystal, "Taj Mahal of Sport," 322.

28. Houston Sports Association, *Astrodome*, 25.

29. Jan Reid, "The Real Mean Green," *Texas Monthly*, December 1979, 152–54, 259–66.

30. Pastier, "Shaggy Rug Story," 10.

31. Paul Levy, "Take Us Out to the Ball Game," *Minneapolis Star-Tribune*, May 3, 1987, Sunday Magazine, 26.

6. Fractious Dome Futures

1. "Superbly Done—Houston Will Have Much to Show Off for the Super Bowl, but What Becomes of the Dome?" (editorial), *Houston Chronicle*, May 22, 2013, B6.

2. Jeff Duncan, "Ready for Kickoff: Just One Year after Its Near Demise, the Superdome Emerges in Better Shape Than Before the Storm," *Times-Picayune*, September 24, 2006, national section, 1.

3. Anna Mod, *Building Modern Houston* (Charleston SC: Arcadia, 2011), 7.

4. Mike Snyder, "Writer Larry McMurtry Casts a Sardonic Eye on the Dome in 1965," *Houston Chronicle*, July 28, 2014, D1.

5. Jennifer Latson, "Dome Hit with Fire Code Violations," *Houston Chronicle*, July 18, 2008, B1.

6. Wood, *Dodger Dogs to Fenway Franks*, 101–10, quote on 101.

7. Larry Dierker, "Opening of Dome Was Peek into the Future," *Houston Chronicle*, April 8, 1990, 12G.

8. Lowell Cohn, "A New Look at Candlestick," *San Francisco Chronicle*, April 2, 1993, E1.

9. Ken Hoffman, "Astrodome Dining: Here's the Scoop on Why It's Bland," *Houston Post*, May 12, 1991, B13.

10. John Williams, "Stadium Vote Defied Projections," *Houston Chronicle*, November 10, 1996, A1.

11. David Barron, "Raising the Roof: Outdoor Baseball in Houston Is a Hit," *Houston Chronicle*, March 31, 2000, A1.

12. Michael McKenzie, *Arrowhead: Home of the Chiefs* (Lexena KS: Addax, 1997), 30–31.

13. Bill Murphy, "Opposition to Dome Project Eases a Bit: Rodeo, Texans Are Negotiating to Make Sure Their Rights Are Guarded," *Houston Chronicle*, August 6, 2008, B2.

14. Bill Murphy, "Financial Crunch May Stall Effort on Astrodome Hotel: Project Also Still Waiting for Texans, Rodeo to OK Lease," *Houston Chronicle*, December 8, 2008, B2.

15. Renee Lee, "Poverty Up, but So Is Income Increase across City," *Houston Chronicle*, September 20, 2012, A1.

16. Elizabeth Kneebone, *Growth and Spread of Concentrated Poverty, 2000 to 2008–2012* (Washington DC: Brookings Institution, July 31, 2014).

17. Lori Kriel, "View of Immigration More Positive: Majority in Area Appreciate Diversity, Economic Impact, Annual Rice Survey Finds," *Houston Chronicle*, April 25, 2014, A1.

18. Ericka Mellon, "Bonds: City, HISD, HCC See $2.7 Billion in Measures Pass," *Houston Chronicle*, November 7, 2012, B1.

19. Kiah Collier, "Poor Pitch, 'Bond Fatigue' Likely Did in Astrodome," *Houston Chronicle*, November 7, 2013, A1.

20. Kiah Collier, "Work on Astrodome to Start Soon: Cleanup Project Worth $8 Million Precedes Vote on Facility's Fate," *Houston Chronicle*, October 4, 2013, B1.

21. Kiah Collier, "A Second Chance to Score Dome Seat? Success of First Sale Has Officials Looking to Again Cash in on Memorabilia," *Houston Chronicle*, August 18, 2014, A1.

22. Craig Hlavaty, "Houston Getting Super Bowl 51 Means Goodbye to the Astrodome, Right?," *The Texican* (blog), *Houston Chronicle*, May 21, 2013, http://blog.chron.com/thetexican/2013/05/houston-getting-super-bowl-51-means -goodbye-to-the-astrodome-right/#10732101=0.

23. Craig Hlavaty, "Love Houston? There's a T-Shirt For That!," *The Texican* (blog), *Houston Chronicle*, July 24, 2014, http://blog.chron.com /thetexican/2014/07/love-houston-theres-a-t-shirt-for-that/#25368101=0.

24. Ken Hoffman, "What to Do with the Astrodome? It's Simple—Dismantle the Dome and Sell It Off Piece by Piece," *Houston Chronicle*, August 19, 2010, Star section, 1.

25. Ken Hoffman, "Sunday Mail Delivery: Dome Naysayers Might Not Be from around Here," *Houston Chronicle*, November 10, 2013, Star section, 2.

26. Kiah Collier, "Harris County: Ditching Dome May Cost Less," *Houston Chronicle*, March 20, 2013, A1.

27. Kiah Collier, "County: Dome Demo Figures Full of Holes," *Houston Chronicle*, March 22, 2013, B1.

28. Jayme Fraser, "Super Bowl LI: Is It Doomsday for the Dome?—Successful Bid for NFL's Big Game May Hasten Demise of Iconic Stadium," *Houston Chronicle*, May 23, 2013, A1.

29. Kiah Collier, "Harris County: 'Family Chat' on Dome Planned," *Houston Chronicle*, May 7, 2014, B1.

30. Kiah Collier, "Plan: Raze Dome, Build Park: County to Study $66 Million Idea Suggested by Rodeo, Texans," *Houston Chronicle*, July 11, 2014, A1.

31. "Behind the Rodeo and Texans' Scheme to Get Rid of the Astrodome in Their Midst," Swamplot (blog), July 11, 2014, http://swamplot.com/behind -the-rodeo-and-texans-latest-scheme-to-get-rid-of-the-astrodome-in-their -midst/2014-07-11/.

32. "A Silly Plan—Dome Proposal by the Rodeo and Texans Reveals a Boomtown Short-Term Mentality" (editorial), *Houston Chronicle*, July 20, 2014, B17.

33. "Dome Plans—With Plan A Defeated and NO Plan B, Harris County Has until 2017 to at Least Get a C Plan" (editorial), *Houston Chronicle*, February 2, 2014, B11.

34. Allen Turner, "Despite National Listing Dome Could Still Be Razed," *Houston Chronicle*, February 1, 2014, A1.

35. Joe Martin, "New Plan Would Preserve Astrodome, Judge Emmett Says," *Houston Biz* (blog), *Houston Business Journal*, December 23, 2014, http://www .bizjournals.com/houston/blog/2014/12/new-plan-would-preserve-astrodome -judge-emmett.html.

36. Ken Hoffman, "Doomed Dome? Not in This Filmmaker's Documentary," *Houston Chronicle*, March 11, 2015, http://www.houstonchronicle.com/life

/columnists/hoffman/article/Doomed-Dome-Not-in-this-documentary-6127732.php.

37. David Barron, "The Case of the Dueling 'Come and Take It' T-Shirts," *Sports Update* (blog), *Houston Chronicle*, November 15, 2013, http://blog.chron.com/sportsupdate/2013/11/the-case-of-the-dueling-come-and-take-it-shirts/.

38. Robert Arnold, "County Judge Arrives in Berlin in Search of Astrodome Solutions," Click2Houston.com, May 1, 2015, http://www.click2houston.com/news/county-judge-arrives-in-berlin-in-search-of-astrodome-solutions/32721896.

39. Ken Hoffman, "What Works: The Man Who Would Save the Astrodome," *Politico*, May 21, 2015, http://www.politico.com/magazine/story/2015/05/ed-emmett-houston-astrodom-117958.html#.VWNX3GA4JiY.

7. The Dome and Its Legacy

1. Michael Young, "Pride in Dallas May Be Stadium in Arlington: Thumbs Up All Around for Building, Not Just Its Location to the West," *Dallas Morning News*, June 6, 2009, A16.

2. Gary Jacobson, Karen Robinson-Jacobs, and David Moore, "No Place Like Renamed Home," *Dallas Morning News*, July 26, 2013, A1.

3. Jeff Mosier, "Cowboys Stadium—Going the Extra Yard—New Stadium Requires More Than Ordinary Material Methods," *Dallas Morning News*, August 2, 2008, 1A.

4. Jeff Mosier, "Cowboys New Home-Stadium Designed to Take Whatever Blows Through," *Dallas Morning News*, September 22, 2008, 1A.

5. Victor Godinez, "Carriers Work for Smooth Reception," *Dallas Morning News*, January 31, 2011, A1.

6. Jeff Mosier, "Cowboys, Cisco Tout Technology," *Dallas Morning News*, June 18, 2009, B2.

7. Houston Sports Association, *Astrodome*.

8. Ray, *Grand Huckster*, 311.

9. Paul Lukas, "Astros History Is Out of This World," ESPN: Page 2, April 15, 2010, http://sports.espn.go.com/espn/page2/story?page=lukas/100415.

10. Judith Grant Long, "Full Count: The Real Cost of Funding Major League Sports Facilities," *Journal of Sports Economics* 6.2 (May 2005): 119–43.

11. White Hutchinson Leisure and Learning Group, "Household Entertainment Spending Up 58% since 1995," *Leisure eNewsletter* 12.7 (October–November 2012), https://www.whitehutchinson.com/news/lenews/2012_november/article102.shtml.

12. Ray, *Grand Huckster*, 219.

13. Ray, *Grand Huckster*, 295. While the Astrodome was certainly the first domed stadium in American sports, scholars point to the field under the Queensboro Fifty-Ninth Street Bridge in New York City, operated by the Negro National League New York Cubans in the 1930s, as the first covered stadium in the Major Leagues. See Lowrey, *Green Cathedrals*, 47.

14. David McCombs, *Spare Time in Texas: Recreation and History in the Lone Star State* (Austin: University of Texas Press, 2009), 93.

15. Ray, *Grand Huckster*, 305.

16. Steven Strom, *Houston: Lost and Unbuilt* (Austin: University of Texas Press, 2010), 5.

17. Ed Breslin and Hugh Van Dusen, *America's Great Railroad Stations* (New York: Viking Studio, 2011), x.

18. McCombs, *Spare Time in Texas*, 94.

19. Eva Jacobs and Stephanie Shipp, "How Family Spending Has Changed in the U.S.," *Monthly Labor Review*, March 1990, 20–27.

20. James Walvin, *Leisure and Society, 1830–1950* (London: Longman, 1978), 114.

21. Mickey Herskowitz, "Dome's Status as Wonder Disappearing with Oilers," *Houston Chronicle*, February 17, 1997, B3.

Bibliography

Abram, Lynwood. "Kenneth E. Zimmerman, Helped Create Astrodome: Worked on Many Notable Projects during Long Career." *Houston Chronicle*, December 24, 2008, B7.

Addington, Neil. "Fat Stock Show Offers County Site for New Project." *Houston Post*, June 25, 1958, 1.

"Archer Romero and Company, California State Fair Exhibition." August 1958. Astrodome Project, Planning, box 94-274-1, Robert Minchew Collection, University of Texas, Austin.

Arledge, Roone. *Roone: A Memoir*. New York: Harper Collins, 2003.

Arnold, Robert. "County Judge Arrives in Berlin in Search of Astrodome Solutions." Click2Houston.com, May 1, 2015. http://www.click2houston.com/news /county-judge-arrives-in-berlin-in-search-of-astrodome-solutions/32721896.

Bailey, Ernest. "Stadium Bond Foes Charge Subsidy—Predict Higher Taxes." *Houston Press*, December 14, 1962, 1.

———. "Stadium Can't Hike Taxes, Officials Say." *Houston Press*, December 21, 1962, 1.

Bailey, Jenny Meeden. "Matrimony and the Mayors: Three First Ladies of Houston." *Houston History Monthly* 5.1 (2007): 29–35.

Barron, David. "The Case of the Dueling 'Come and Take It' Shirts." *Sports Update* (blog), *Houston Chronicle*, November 15, 2013. http://blog.chron .com/sportsupdate/2013/11/the-case-of-the-dueling-come-and-take-it-shirts/.

———. "Raising the Roof: Outdoor Baseball in Houston Is a Hit." *Houston Chronicle*, March 31, 2000, A1.

"Behind the Rodeo and Texans' Scheme to Get Rid of the Astrodome in Their Midst." *Swamplot* (blog), July 11, 2014. http://swamplot.com/behind-the -rodeo-and-texans-latest-scheme-to-get-rid-of-the-astrodome-in-their -midst/2014-07-11/.

Blair, Phillip M. Sound-Off. *Houston Post*, January 21, 1961, section 2, 3.

Blount, Terry. "Oilers Have Never Been Happy Campers Indoors." *Houston Chronicle*, March 26, 1995, B29.

"Board Drops Plan for Stadium Site in Memorial Park." *Houston Chronicle*, November 12, 1958, A1.

"Bond Issue Gets Boost from C of C." *Houston Post*, July 10, 1958, section 6, 2.

Breslin, Ed, and Hugh Van Dusen. *America's Great Railroad Stations*. New York: Viking Studio, 2011.

Buhite, Russell D. *The Continental League: A Personal History*. Lincoln: University of Nebraska Press, 2014.

Bybee, Sandra. "Opening Night: A Society Tableau." *Houston Post*, April 10, 1965, section 1, 12.

Caro, Robert. *The Years of Lyndon Johnson: Means of Ascent*. New York: Alfred A. Knopf, 1990.

Chrystal, Jason Bruce. "The Taj Mahal of Sport: The Creation of the Houston Astrodome." PhD diss., Iowa State University, 2004.

"City Officials Pledge Neutral Stand on Stadium Policy." *Houston Chronicle*, November 13, 1958, B1.

Cohn, Lowell. "A New Look at Candlestick." *San Francisco Chronicle*, April 2, 1993, E1.

Collier, Kiah. "County: Dome Demo Figures Full of Holes." *Houston Chronicle*, March 22, 2013, B1.

———. "Harris County: Ditching Dome May Cost Less." *Houston Chronicle*, March 20, 2013, A1.

———. "Harris County: 'Family Chat' on Dome Planned." *Houston Chronicle*, May 7, 2014, B1.

———. "Plan: Raze Dome, Build Park: County to Study $66 Million Idea Suggested by Rodeo, Texans." *Houston Chronicle*, July 11, 2014, A1.

———. "Poor Pitch, 'Bond Fatigue' Likely Did in Astrodome." *Houston Chronicle*, November 7, 2013, A1.

———. "A Second Chance to Score Dome Seat? Success of First Sale Has Officials Looking to Again Cash in on Memorabilia." *Houston Chronicle*, August 18, 2014, A1.

———. "Work on Astrodome to Start Soon: Cleanup Project Worth $8 Million Precedes Vote on Facility's Fate." *Houston Chronicle*, October 4, 2013, B1.

"Colt .45's Start Park with a Bang." *New York Times*, January 4, 1962, 52.

"Colts Add .45's to Name: We're Pistols, Not Horses." *Sporting News*, December 6, 1961, 33.

"County, HSA Sign Stadium Agreement." *Houston Chronicle*, November 15, 1962, 1.

"County Rejects Quonset Stadium." *Houston Chronicle*, June 4, 1962, 1.

"County Stadium Bond Issue Gets July Ballot Spot." *Houston Post*, June 24, 1958, section 4, 1.

"Cow Palace, San Francisco." N.d. Astrodome Project, Planning, box 94-274-1, Robert Minchew Collection, University of Texas, Austin.

Daley, Arthur. "Ball Park, Texas Style." *New York Times*, April 9, 1965, 24.

"Dick Allen Quotes." *Baseball Almanac*. 2015. http://www.baseball-almanac.com/quotes/quoalln.shtml.

Dierker, Larry. "Dome Deserved Better Than Sharing." *Houston Chronicle*, February 2, 2014, B1.

———. "Opening of Dome Was Peek into the Future." *Houston Chronicle*, April 8, 1990, 12G.

"Dome Plans—With Plan A Defeated and NO Plan B, Harris County Has until 2017 to at Least Get a C Plan" (editorial). *Houston Chronicle*, February 2, 2014, B11.

"Dragline Rips into S. Main Stadium Site." *Houston Chronicle*, February 2, 1961, section 1, 1, 2.

Duncan, Jeff. "Ready for Kickoff: Just One Year after Its Near Demise, the Superdome Emerges in Better Shape Than Before the Storm." *Times-Picayune*, September 24, 2006, national section, 1.

Dyreson, Mark, and Robert C. Trumpbour, eds. *The Rise of Stadiums in the Modern United States: Cathedrals of Sport.* New York: Routledge, 2010.

Eddy, George W. Sound-Off. *Houston Post*, January 21, 1961, section 2, 3.

Edelman, Rob. "*What's My Line?* and Baseball." *Baseball Research Journal* 43.2 (Fall 2014): 36–41.

Feagin, Joe R. "The Global Context of Metropolitan Growth: Houston and the Oil Industry." *American Journal of Sociology* 90.6 (May 1985): 1204–30.

"Federal Aid Enters Debate on Coliseum." *Houston Post*, March 1, 1960, 1.

Finch, Frank. "Gaily Decorated Colt Stadium Puts Most Ballparks to Shame." *Los Angeles Times*, May 8, 1962, B2.

"Fine Leadership for Bond Drive." *Houston Post*, July 3, 1958, section 2, 4.

Fowler, Ed. *Loser Takes All: Bud Adams, Bad Football, and Big Business.* Atlanta: Longstreet Press, 1997.

Fraser, Jayme. "Houston Livestock Show and Rodeo: A Day of Rain and Records." *Houston Chronicle*, March 17, 2014, B1.

———. "Super Bowl LI: Is It Doomsday for the Dome?—Successful Bid for NFL's Big Game May Hasten Demise of Iconic Stadium." *Houston Chronicle*, May 23, 2013, A1.

"Frick, Trautman Praise Action on Sports Measure." *Sporting News*, July 2, 1958, 20.

Gallagher, Jack. "$20,000,000 Bond Issue Vote on July 26 on Houston Stadium." *Sporting News*, July 2, 1958, 20.

Garvin, Berry. "2 New Angles on Stadium." *Houston Press*, March 25, 1960, 1.

Gershman, Michael. *Diamonds: The Evolution of the Ballpark.* New York: Houghton Mifflin, 1993.

Godinez, Victor. "Carriers Work for Smooth Reception." *Dallas Morning News*, January 31, 2011, A1.

Gosain, Narendra K. Interviews by the authors. July 22, 2013, at Walter P. Moore and Associates, Houston, and July 22, 2013, at NRG Astrodome, Houston.

Go Texan Monthly Newsletter 5.2 (February 25, 2011): 1.

Graczyk, Michael L. "Astrodome Scoreboard Headed for Scrap Heap." *Los Angeles Times*, September 4, 1988. http://articles.latimes.com/1988-09-04/sports /sp-2073_1_astrodome-scoreboard.

Graham, Roy. "Dallas and Fort Worth Architects Propose Air-Conditioned Arena with 'Supper Club.'" *Sporting News*, August 31, 1960, 13.

Hatch, Alden. *Buckminster Fuller: At Home in the Universe*. New York: Crown, 1974.

Herskowitz, Mickey. "Dome's Status as Wonder Disappearing with Oilers." *Houston Chronicle*, February 17, 1997, B3.

———. "Perini, Says Weisbrod, Rates Houston as 10 Club Possibility." *Houston Chronicle*, July 17, 1958, section 4, 1.

Hlavaty, Craig. "Houston Getting Super Bowl 51 Means Goodbye to the Astrodome, Right?" *The Texican* (blog), *Houston Chronicle*, May 21, 2013. http:// blog.chron.com/thetexican/2013/05/houston-getting-super-bowl-51-means -goodbye-to-the-astrodome-right/#10732101=0.

———. "Love Houston? There's a T-shirt for That!" *The Texican* (blog), *Houston Chronicle*, July 24, 2014. http://blog.chron.com/thetexican/2014/07 /love-houston-theres-a-t-shirt-for-that/#25368101=0.

Hoffman, Ken. "Astrodome Dining: Here's the Scoop on Why It's Bland." *Houston Post*, May 12, 1991, B13.

———. "Doomed Dome? Not in This Filmmaker's Documentary." *Houston Chronicle*, March 11, 2015. http://www.houstonchronicle.com/life/columnists /hoffman/article/Doomed-Dome-Not-in-this-documentary-6127732.php.

———. "Sunday Mail Delivery: Dome Naysayers Might Not Be from around Here." *Houston Chronicle*, November 10, 2013, Star section, 2.

———. "What to Do with the Astrodome? It's Simple—Dismantle the Dome and Sell It Off Piece by Piece." *Houston Chronicle*, August 19, 2010, Star section, 1.

———. "What Works: The Man Who Would Save the Astrodome." *Politico*, May 21, 2015. http://www.politico.com/magazine/story/2015/05/ed-emmett -houston-astrodom-117958.html#.VWNX3GA4JiY.

"Hofheinz Says He'll Take Loss Gracefully." *Houston Chronicle*, June 28, 1964, 18.

Houston Sports Association. *Astrodome: Eighth Wonder of the World*. Houston: Houston Sports Association, 1966.

———. *Inside the Astrodome: Eighth Wonder of the World*. Houston: Houston Sports Association, 1965.

Hylton, J. Gordon. "Why Baseball's Antitrust Exemption Still Survives." *Marquette Sports Law Review* 9.2 (1999): 391–402.

Izenberg, Jerry. *The Greatest Game Ever Played: The Incredible Battle between the New York Mets and the Houston Astros for the '86 National League Pennant*. New York: Henry Holt, 1988.

Jacobs, Eva, and Stephanie Shipp. "How Family Spending Has Changed in the U.S." *Monthly Labor Review*, March 1990, 20–27.

Jacobson, Gary, Karen Robinson-Jacobs, and David Moore. "No Place Like Renamed Home." *Dallas Morning News*, July 26, 2013, A1.

Jares, Joe. "The Big Screen Is Watching." *Sports Illustrated*, May 31, 1965, 30.

Johnson, Charles, and Charles Jackson. *City behind a Fence: Oak Ridge, Tennessee, 1942–1946*. Knoxville: University of Tennessee Press, 1981.

Jones, Vincent C. *Manhattan: The Army and the Atomic Bomb*. Washington DC: Center of Military History, 1985.

Kahn, Roger. *A Season in the Sun*. New York: Diversion Books, 2012.

Keating, Raymond J. "The NFL Oilers: A Case Study in Corporate Welfare." *Freeman* (Foundation for Economic Education), April 1, 1998. http://fee.org/freeman/detail/the-nfl-oilers-a-case-study-in-corporate-welfare.

King, John O. *Joseph Stephen Cullinan: A Study of Leadership in the Texas Petroleum Industry, 1897–1937*. Nashville TN: Vanderbilt University Press, 1970.

Kneebone, Elizabeth. *Growth and Spread of Concentrated Poverty, 2000 to 2008–2012*. Washington DC: Brookings Institution, July 31, 2014.

Koppett, Leonard. "Big League Baseball Opens on Nine Fronts Tomorrow." *New York Times*, April 11, 1965, S1.

Kriel, Lori. "View of Immigration More Positive: Majority in Area Appreciate Diversity, Economic Impact, Annual Rice Survey Finds." *Houston Chronicle*, April 25, 2014, A1.

Latson, Jennifer. "Dome Hit with Fire Code Violations." *Houston Chronicle*, July 18, 2008, B1.

Laymance, Reid. "Astros Top 50 Moments." *Houston Chronicle*, September 30, 2012, section 2, 4.

Lebovitz, Hal. "Cleveland Is Joyful; Tribe Directors Vote to Stay Indefinitely." *Sporting News*, October 22, 1958, 18.

Lee, Renee. "Poverty Up, but So Is Income Increase across City." *Houston Chronicle*, September 20, 2012, A1.

Levy, Paul. "Take Us Out to the Ball Game." *Minneapolis Star-Tribune*, May 3, 1987, Sunday Magazine, 26.

Lipsyte, Robert. "Astrodome Opulent, Even for Texas." *New York Times*, April 8, 1965, 50.

———. "Houston Is Hardly Wild About Its Astrodome." *New York Times*, April 11, 1965, S3.

———. "Johnson Attends Opening of Houston's Astrodome." *New York Times*, April 10, 1965, 1.

Liptak, Adam. "The Supreme Court, Throwing Curveballs." *New York Times*, March 29, 2013, C21.

Lisle, Benjamin Dylan. "'You've Got to Have Tangibles to Sell Intangibles': Ideologies of the Modern American Stadium, 1948–1982." PhD diss., University of Texas, Austin, 2010.

Lomax, Michael. "Stadiums, Boosters, Politicians, and Major League Baseball's Reluctance to Expand." In *The Rise of Stadiums in the Modern United*

States: Cathedrals of Sport, edited by Mark Dyreson and Robert C. Trump-bour, 92–109. New York: Routledge, 2010.

Long, Judith Grant. "Full Count: The Real Cost of Funding Major League Sports Facilities." *Journal of Sports Economics* 6.2 (May 2005): 119–43.

Lowrey, Philip. *Green Cathedrals: The Ultimate Celebration of All 271 Major League and Negro League Ballparks Past and Present.* Reading MA: Addison Wesley, 1992.

Lukas, Paul. "Astros History Is Out of This World." ESPN: Page 2, April 15, 2010. http://sports.espn.go.com/espn/page2/story?page=lukas/100415.

Martin, Joe. "New Plan Would Preserve Astrodome, Judge Emmett Says." *Houston Biz* (blog), *Houston Business Journal*, December 23, 2014. http://www.bizjournals.com/houston/blog/2014/12/new-plan-would-preserve-astrodome-judge-emmett.html.

McCombs, David. *Spare Time in Texas: Recreation and History in the Lone Star State.* Austin: University of Texas Press, 2009.

McKenzie, Michael. *Arrowhead: Home of the Chiefs.* Lexena KS: Addax, 1997.

Mellon, Ericka. "Bonds: City, HISD, HCC See $2.7 Billion in Measures Pass." *Houston Chronicle*, November 7, 2012, B1.

Mod, Anna. *Building Modern Houston.* Charleston SC: Arcadia, 2011.

Moran, Barbara. "Artificial Turf and How It Grew." *American Heritage of Invention and Technology* 20.4 (Spring 2005): 8–16. http://www.innovationgateway.org/content/artificial-turf-and-how-it-grew-0.

Morris, Kate. "Rodeo Closes with Mark for Boots on the Ground." *Houston Chronicle*, March 24, 2014, section 1, 1.

Mosier, Jeff. "Cowboys, Cisco Tout Technology." *Dallas Morning News*, June 18, 2009, 2B.

———. "Cowboys New Home-Stadium Designed to Take Whatever Blows Through." *Dallas Morning News*, September 22, 2008, 1A.

———. "Cowboys Stadium—Going the Extra Yard—New Stadium Requires More Than Ordinary Material Methods." *Dallas Morning News*, August 2, 2008, 1A.

Murphy, Bill. "Financial Crunch May Stall Effort on Astrodome Hotel: Project Also Still Waiting for Texans, Rodeo to OK Lease." *Houston Chronicle*, December 8, 2008, B2.

———. "Opposition to Dome Project Eases a Bit: Rodeo, Texans Are Negotiating to Make Sure Their Rights Are Guarded." *Houston Chronicle*, August 6, 2008, B2.

"National League Eying Stadium Vote Says Giles." *Houston Chronicle*, December 21, 1962, section 6, 2.

Nealon, Clark. "Colts Will Lasso Gal Fans: Hire Woman Publicist." *Sporting News*, April 4, 1962, 13.

———. "Marion Offers Rent Guarantee in New Stadium." *Sporting News*, February 25, 1959, 20.

———. "N.L. Group in Houston Buys Buffs." *Sporting News*, January 25, 1961, 9.

———. "Post Time." *Houston Post*, July 25, 1958, section 4, 1.

———. "Ultra-Modern Stadium Called 'Last Link' in Houston's Pitch for a Big-Time Club." *Sporting News*, August 31, 1960, 13.

Nealon, Clark, Robert Nottebart, Stanley Siegel, and James Tinsley. "The Campaign for Major League Baseball in Houston." *Houston Review* 7.1 (1985): 3–46.

Nelson, Murry R. *American Sports: A History of Icons, Idols, and Ideas*. Santa Barbara CA: Greenwood, 2013.

"1960–1969 Attendance." Ballparks of Baseball: The Fields of Major League Baseball. http://www.ballparksofbaseball.com/1960-69attendance.htm.

"North Side Fans Seek New Athletic Stadium." *Houston Chronicle*, July 31, 1958, section 6, 3.

"North Side Petition Added to Coliseum Fight." *Houston Post*, March 3, 1960, 3.

O'Brien, Andy. "The Stadium That Could Revolutionize Sport." *Montreal Star*, May 15, 1965, weekend magazine, 32.

"Oilers Owner, HSA Feud over Stadium." *Houston Chronicle*, August 22, 1962, 1.

Olwell, Russell. *At Work in the Atomic City: A Labor and Social History of Oak Ridge, Tennessee*. Knoxville: University of Tennessee Press, 2004.

Omstead, Tom. "Harris Officials to Back Park Board Stadium Site." *Houston Post*, February 24, 1960, 1.

———. "North Side Offers Free Arena Site." *Houston Post*, March 13, 1960, 1.

———. "Stock Show's Decision May Swing Stadium." *Houston Post*, February 28, 1960, 1.

"Ours?: Tops, Bar None." *Houston Chronicle*, December 18, 1962, section 4, 6.

Pastier, John. "Shaggy Rug Story: The Greening of the Astrodome." *Cite: The Architecture and Design Review of Houston* (Rice Design Alliance) 24 (Spring 1990): 10. http://offcite.org/wp-content/uploads/sites/3/2010/03/ShaggyRug Story_Pastier_Cite24.pdf.

Peebles, Dick. "Ballots, Baskets, and Challenges." *Houston Chronicle*, January 16, 1961, section 5, 1–2.

———. "Commission to Seek Information on Feasibility of Stadium Here." *Houston Chronicle*, February 19, 1958, F1.

———. "LBJ: Everybody Will Visit Dome." *Houston Chronicle*, April 10, 1965, A1.

———. "Stadium Group Mulls over Unique Plans." *Houston Chronicle*, May 5, 1958, B2.

Phillip Jennings Turf Farms. "Tifway 419 Bermuda." 2009. http://www.sodfather .com/turf-grass/tifway-419-bermuda.asp.

"Prexy Giles Spends 36 Hours in St. Louis Overseeing Cards' Sale." *Sporting News*, March 4, 1953, 10.

Rader, Benjamin. *In Its Own Image: How Television Has Transformed Sports*. New York: Free Press, 1984.

Ray, Edgar. *The Grand Huckster: Houston's Judge Roy Hofheinz, Genius of the Astrodome*. Memphis TN: Memphis State University Press, 1980.

Reed, Robert. *Colt .45s: A Six-Gun Salute*. Houston: Lone Star Books, 1999.

Reid, Jan. "The Real Mean Green." *Texas Monthly*, December 1979, 152–54, 259–66.

Report of the Harris County Board of Parks Commissioners to Harris County Commissioners Court. June 20, 1958. 25 pages. Astrodome Collection, 1958–68 files, folder 18, Houston Public Library.

Robertson, Dale. "City Sports Owners Try Something New." *Houston Chronicle*, October 6, 2000, B1.

"Rome Visit Gave Idea for Stadium." *Houston Tribune*, April 8, 1965, section II, 11.

Rufka, Sarah. "Houston Gives: Houston Heroes." *Houston Chronicle*, March 30, 2014, special section, 15.

Rule, Bob. "Sidelights." *Houston Press*, January 16, 1961, 16.

———. "Tax Bonds Will Save on Interest," *Houston Press*, January 10, 1961, 1.

Santos, Kendra. "Where Big Is Better: The Houston Livestock Show and Rodeo Is a Texas-Sized Treat." *American Cowboy*, January/February 1997, 62–63.

Saye, Jim. "The Houston Livestock Show and Rodeo: A Historical Perspective." *Houston History* 7.1 (Fall 2009): 2–15.

Sewing, Joy. "Houston Gives: Education: Rodeo Focuses on Scholarship and Education." *Houston Chronicle*, February 26, 2012, special section, 23.

"A Silly Plan—Dome Proposal by the Rodeo and Texans Reveals a Boomtown Short-Term Mentality" (editorial). *Houston Chronicle*, July 20, 2014, B17.

"Smith and Hofheinz Oppose Civic Center." *Houston Chronicle*, June 23, 1964, 9.

Snyder, Mike. "Writer Larry McMurtry Casts a Sardonic Eye on the Dome in 1965." *Houston Chronicle*, July 28, 2014, D1.

Spink, J. G. Taylor. "Colts Shooting the Works in Apache Junction Plant." *Sporting News*, November 15, 1961, 2.

"Stadium Bond Contest Dropped." *Houston Chronicle*, April 7, 1961, 1.

"Stadium Fund Not Enough Says Architect." *Houston Chronicle*, May 25, 1962, 1.

"Stadium Low Bid $19.4 Million." *Houston Chronicle*, November 29, 1962, 1.

"Stock Show Swings to South Main Site." *Houston Post*, June 10, 1960, 1.

Strom, Steven. *Houston: Lost and Unbuilt*. Austin: University of Texas Press, 2010.

"Suit Filed Challenging Legality of Sports Bonds for Stadium." *Houston Chronicle*, February 6, 1961, 1.

"Superbly Done—Houston Will Have Much to Show Off for the Super Bowl, but What Becomes of the Dome?" (editorial). *Houston Chronicle*, May 22, 2013, B6.

Taubman, Howard. "Show Biz: The Big Dome." *New York Times*, June 6, 1965, section 5, 3.

Teachey, Lisa. "On the Trail Again: Salt Grass Riders' Publicity Stunt Saved Rodeo." *Houston Chronicle*, February 12, 1998, A29.

Terrell, Roy. "Fast Man with a .45." *Sports Illustrated*, March 26, 1962, 32–42.

"Texas Group Wanted Busch to Buy Cards' Radio Rights." *Sporting News*, March 4, 1953, 10.

Titchener, Campbell. *The George Kirksey Story: Bringing Major League Baseball to Houston*. Austin TX: Eakin Press, 1989.

Toolson v. New York Yankees, Inc. 346 U.S. 356 (1953).

Trumpbour, Robert C. "The Brooklyn Dodgers, the Move to Los Angeles, and the Search for Villains: Was Walter O'Malley a Bum, a Victim, or Something Else?" In *Mysteries from Baseball's Past: Investigation of Nine Unsettled Questions*, edited by Angelo Louisa and David Cicotello, 149–83. Jefferson NC: McFarland, 2010.

———. *The New Cathedrals: Politics and Media in the History of Stadium Construction*. Syracuse NY: Syracuse University Press, 2006.

Turner, Allen. "Despite National Listing Dome Could Still Be Razed." *Houston Chronicle*, February 1, 2014, A1.

"25 Ex-pros on Stadium Committee." *Houston Post*, July 14, 1958, section 4, 1.

U.S. Census Bureau. *Census of Population: 1960*. Vol. 1, part 45. Washington DC: U.S. Government Printing Office, 1962.

Verniaud, Marshall. "Hopes for Stadium by 1962 Dim." *Houston Post*, April 29, 1961, 1.

Walsh, Jack. "Sports Bill Wins in House, but Faces Hurdle in Senate." *Sporting News*, July 2, 1958, 20.

Walvin, James. *Leisure and Society, 1830–1950*. London: Longman, 1978.

White Hutchinson Leisure and Learning Group. "Household Entertainment Spending Up 58% since 1995." *Leisure eNewsletter* 12.7 (October–November 2012). https://www.whitehutchinson.com/news/lenews/2012_november/article102.shtml.

Williams, John. "Stadium Vote Defied Projections." *Houston Chronicle*, November 10, 1996, A1.

Wilson, John. "Kirksey, First Astro Backer, Sells His Stock." *Sporting News*, May 21, 1966, 13.

Wood, Bob. *Dodger Dogs to Fenway Franks*. New York: McGraw-Hill, 1988.

Young, Michael. "Pride in Dallas May Be Stadium in Arlington: Thumbs Up All Around for Building, Not Just Its Location to the West." *Dallas Morning News*, June 6, 2009, 16A.

Zimmerman, Kenneth E., and Narendra K. Gosain. "Astrodome: An Engineering Marvel of the 1960s." Paper presented at the Texas Section of the annual meeting of the American Society of Civil Engineers, Houston, September 29–October 2, 2004.

Index

Minute Maid Park, 153–54
Mod, Anna, 146
Monsanto Chemical Corporation, 132, 134, 135
Monteith, Walter Embree, 8
Moore, Walter P., 102, 103
Moran, Barbara, 131
Morgan, Joe, ix, 88, 136
Morgan, W. B., 27
Morris, S. I., 27, 32, 128
Moses, Robert, xxii, 19, 27
Moss, Eric, 151
Mount Rushmore, 67
Muller, James P., 27
Murrow, Edward R., 64

NASA (National Aeronautics and Space Administration), xxiii, xxvi, 5, 34, 90
National Basketball Association, xiv, 93
National Football League, 21, 143
National Hockey League, 78
National League, 22, 23, 31, 33, 71, 74, 77
National Register of Historic Places, 167
NCAA (National Collegiate Athletics Association), xiii, 92, 93
Nealon, Clark, xviii, 47
Neely, Cynthia, 167, 170
Nelson, Lindsey, xii
Nelson, Murry R., 131
"New Dome Experience," 157
Newman, Frank, 28
New York Mets, xi, 90, 91
New York Yankees, ix, 34, 62, 70, 72, 76, 77, 78, 80, 90, 91, 92, 115, 127, 128, 129, 154, 182, 184
Nielsen, Jim, xiv
Nolan, Ed, 66, 67, 69
North Harris County Chamber of Commerce, 49
Norton Anderson, Evelyn, 176, 177
NRG Energy, 144, 149, 163, 164, 165

Oakland Athletics, 62, 92
Oakland Raiders, xvi
Oklahoma City 89ers, 127, 128
Oliver, Nate, 136
O'Malley, Walter, xxii, 19, 27–28, 74, 79, 84, 85

Oppenheimer, Robert, 102
Orioles Park, 152
Osborn, Tom, 92
Owens, Jim, x

Pace, Ginny, 89
Paisley, Brad, 40
Parker, Wes, 136
Pastier, John, 134, 138
Paul, Gabe, 39, 87, 88, 95
Peebles, Dick, 24, 34, 45
Perini, Lou, 73, 84
personal seat license (PSL), 180, 182
Petit, Bob, 93
Philadelphia Athletics, 70, 72, 73, 175
Phillip Jennings Turf Farms, 131
Phillips, Bum, xi, xvi
Polo Grounds, 6
Powell, Ted, 167
Praeger, Kavanagh, and Warterbury, 27, 105, 184
Presley, Elvis, 40, 94

Rader, Benjamin, 65
Ray, Edgar, 4, 10, 184
Rayburn, Sam, 10
Reed, Robert, 73
Reeves, W. Gail, 30
Reidenbaugh, Lowell, 127
Reliant Astrodome: AstroTurf, x, xxiv, xxv, 92, 120, 127–39; construction and engineering, 101–25; financing, 20–33; glare, 127–31; leaky roof, 116–18; natural grass, 127–32; preservation advocacy and demolition efforts, 149–70; renovation, 119–25
Reliant Stadium, 148–49
Republican National Convention, 94, 152
retractable roof design, xxi, 6, 27, 28, 148, 153, 172, 173
retractable upper-deck seating, 123–24
RFK Stadium, 27, 175
Rice, Grantland, 64
Rice Stadium, 104, 119, 138
Richards, Paul, 87, 89, 96, 127, 128
Rickey, Branch, 50, 55, 81, 83
Riggs, Bobby, xi, xv–xvi, 93
Ringling Bros. Circus, 3, 94, 147, 188